Register Your Book

at www.phptr.com/ibmregister/

Upon registration, we will send you electronic sample chapters from two of our popular IBM Press books. In addition, you will be automatically entered into a monthly drawing for a free IBM Press book.

Registration also entitles you to:

- Notices and reminders about author appearances, conferences, and online chats with special guests

- Access to supplemental material that may be available

- Advance notice of forthcoming editions

- Related book recommendations

- Information about special contests and promotions throughout the year

- Chapter excerpts and supplements of forthcoming books

Contact us

If you are interested in writing a book or reviewing manuscripts prior to publication, please write to us at:

Editorial Director, IBM Press
c/o Pearson Education
One Lake Street
Upper Saddle River, New Jersey 07458

e-mail: IBMPress@pearsoned.com

Visit us on the Web: www.phptr.com/ibmpress/

Praise for *Software Configuration Management Strategies and IBM® Rational® ClearCase®, Second Edition: A Practical Introduction*

"I wrote that the first edition of this book "communicates much of the experience, wisdom, and insight that was acquired along the way to discovering what [SCM] best practices are and how to implement/deploy them." The second edition is full of even more practical experience! It not only refines and expands upon earlier strategies and best practices, it also contains even more concrete "how-to" information about implementing and deploying them."

—Brad Appleton
co-author of *Software Configuration Management Patterns: Effective Teamwork, Practical Integration*

"Read this book when you're getting started with configuration management (CM); read it again in six months and once more two years later. *Software Configuration Management Strategies and IBM Rational ClearCase* goes beyond the basics to provide a coherent review of CM strategies for projects of all sizes and complexities."

—Jennie Brown, CM Specialist
IBM Corporation

"This book covers practical software configuration management (SCM), ClearCase UCM and ClearCase use for project teams. Every project lead and SCM specialist should (re)read this book before starting a project."

—Roger Jarrett, Senior Software Engineer
IBM Rational Software

"This second edition captures vital Unified Change Management (UCM) features and concepts. It brings the entire UCM feature set full circle and lays the ground work for a successful UCM implementation; Bellagio and Milligan continue where the first edition left off. The inclusion of composite baseline concepts, single stream development, performance tuning, and other features and concepts make this the core of any old or new Unified Change Management implementation.

It is rare that a second edition of a book can hold your interest like the first. This publication does just that...this continues to be the standard for users interested in Unified Change Management deployment."

—Adam Levensohn, Manager
IBM Rational Software

Software Configuration Management Strategies and IBM® Rational® ClearCase®

Second Edition

WebSphere® Books

IBM® WebSphere®
Barcia, Hines, Alcott, and Botzum

IBM® WebSphere® Application Server for Distributed Platforms and z/OS®
Black, Everett, Draeger, Miller, Iyer, McGuinnes, Patel, Herescu, Gissel, Betancourt, Casile, Tang, and Beaubien

Enterprise Java™ Programming with IBM® WebSphere®, Second Edition
Brown, Craig, Hester, Pitt, Stinehour, Weitzel, Amsden, Jakab, and Berg

IBM® WebSphere® and Lotus
Lamb, Laskey, and Indurkhya

IBM® WebSphere® System Administration
Williamson, Chan, Cundiff, Lauzon, and Mitchell

Enterprise Messaging Using JMS and IBM® WebSphere®
Yusuf

On Demand Computing Books

Business Intelligence for the Enterprise
Biere

On Demand Computing
Fellenstein

Grid Computing
Joseph and Fellenstein

Autonomic Computing
Murch

Rational® Software Books

Software Configuration Management Strategies and IBM Rational® ClearCase®, Second Edition
Bellagio and Milligan

Implementing IBM® Rational® ClearQuest®
Buckley, Pulsipher, and Scott

Project Management with the IBM Rational Unified Process
Gibbs

IBM Rational® ClearCase®, Ant, and CruiseControl
Lee

Visual Modeling with Rational Software Architect and UML
Quatrani and Palistrant

More Books from IBM Press

Irresistible! Markets, Models, and Meta-Value in Consumer Electronics
Bailey and Wenzek

Service-Oriented Architecture Compass
Bieberstein, Bose, Fiammante, Jones, and Shah

Developing Quality Technical Information, Second Edition
Hargis, Carey, Hernandez, Hughes, Longo, Rouiller, and Wilde

Performance Tuning for Linux® Servers
Johnson, Huizenga, and Pulavarty

RFID Sourcebook
Lahiri

Building Applications with the Linux Standard Base
Linux Standard Base Team

An Introduction to IMS™
Meltz, Long, Harrington, Hain, and Nicholls

Search Engine Marketing, Inc.
Moran and Hunt

Can Two Rights Make a Wrong? Insights from IBM's Tangible Culture Approach
Moulton Reger

Inescapable Data
Stakutis and Webster

DB2® Books

DB2® Universal Database V8 for Linux, UNIX, and Windows Database Administration Certification Guide, Fifth Edition
Baklarz and Wong

Understanding DB2®
Chong, Liu, Qi, and Snow

High Availability Guide for DB2®
Eaton and Cialini

DB2® Universal Database V8 Handbook for Windows, UNIX, and Linux
Gunning

DB2® SQL PL, Second Edition
Janmohamed, Liu, Bradstock, Chong, Gao, McArthur, and Yip

DB2® for z/OS® Version 8 DBA Certification Guide
Lawson

DB2® Universal Database V8.1 Certification Exam 700 Study Guide
Sanders

DB2® Universal Database V8.1 Certification Exam 703 Study Guide
Sanders

DB2® Universal Database V8.1 Certification Exams 701 and 706 Study Guide
Sanders

DB2® Universal Database for OS/390
Sloan and Hernandez

The Official Introduction to DB2® for z/OS®, Second Edition
Sloan

Advanced DBA Certification Guide and Reference for DB2® Universal Database v8 for Linux, UNIX, and Windows
Snow and Phan

DB2® Express
Yip, Cheung, Gartner, Liu, and O'Connell

Apache Derby—Off to the Races
Zikopoulos, Baklarz, and Scott

DB2® Version 8
Zikopoulos, Baklarz, deRoos, and Melnyk

Software Configuration Management Strategies and IBM® Rational® ClearCase®

Second Edition
A Practical Introduction

David E. Bellagio
Tom J. Milligan

IBM Press
Pearson plc

Upper Saddle River, NJ • Boston• Indianapolis • San Francisco

New York • Toronto • Montreal • London • Munich • Paris • Madrid

Capetown • Sydney • Tokyo • Singapore • Mexico City

IBM Press Program Manager: Tara Woodman, Ellice Uffer
IBM Press Consulting Editor: David West
Cover design: IBM Corporation
Published by Pearson plc
Publishing as IBM Press

Library of Congress Number: 200523397

IBM Press offers excellent discounts on this book when ordered in quantity for bulk purchases or special sales, which may include electronic versions and/or custom covers and content particular to your business, training goals, marketing focus, and branding interests. For more information, please contact:

U. S. Corporate and Government Sales
1-800-382-3419
corpsales@pearsontechgroup.com.

For sales outside the U. S., please contact:

International Sales
international@pearsoned.com.

This Book Is Safari Enabled

The Safari® Enabled icon on the cover of your favorite technology book means the book is available through Safari Bookshelf. When you buy this book, you get free access to the online edition for 45 days. Safari Bookshelf is an electronic reference library that lets you easily search thousands of technical books, find code samples, download chapters, and access technical information whenever and wherever you need it.

To gain 45-day Safari Enabled access to this book:
- Go to http://www.awprofessional.com/safarienabled
- Complete the brief registration form
- Enter the coupon code 0QGX-YOBF-DFIF-WOFU-IIER

If you have difficulty registering on Safari Bookshelf or accessing the online edition, please e-mail customer-service@safaribooksonline.com.

ISBN 0-321-20019-5
Text printed in the United States on recycled paper at R.R. Donnelley in Crawfordsville, Indiana.
Third Printing, July 2007

Dedications

To my wife, Laura

—Dave

To my wife, Maren

—Tom

Contents

Acknowledgments

The authors of this second edition would like to first thank Brian White, who did the heavy lifting involved with creating the first edition of this book and who was instrumental in providing the opportunity for us to contribute to this second edition. Thanks also go to the host of co-workers and customers who over the years have contributed to our greater understanding of the principles of SCM, the functioning of the products, and what SCM strategies work and which ones don't. Most notable among these are Ralph Capasso, Stef Schurman, Ryan Sappenfield, Rob Budas, Harry Abadi, Peter Hack, and George Moberly. Our long-suffering and ever-patient editors at Addison-Wesley, Mary O'Brien and Chris Zahn, deserve many thanks as well. We would also like to thank our families for their long sufferings during this process.

Those individuals who were instrumental in our first exposure and opportunities with ClearCase also deserve many thanks: Scott Elmenhurst, Denis LeBlanc, John Leary, David Crawford, Marsha Shehan, and Doug Fierro.

Much of the material new to this edition comes directly from the experience of the Rational field teams in engagement with customers using ClearCase and UCM. Some of those folks we would like to thank for their efforts in fleshing out strategies that work with many of our larger customer needs are Samit Mehta, Mike Nellis, Ana Giordano, Kartik Kanakasabesan, Daniel Diebolt, Jennie Brown, and Bryan Miller.

Special thanks to these people who put in the time to review this book and provide comments to help make the reading experience more enjoyable: Adam Levensohn, Brad Appleton, Darryl Hahn, Dennis Brown, Jennie Brown, Jim Tykal, and Roger Jarrett.

Finally, our thanks go out to everyone at IBM, Rational Software who keep ClearCase and UCM efforts moving forward. Keep up the good work.

About the Authors

David E. Bellagio

David has been involved in software development for the last 25 years, ever since he got addicted to it in high school. After realizing that he would not be a professional baseball player, he went on to receive his Bachelor of Science and Master of Science degrees in computer science, with honors, from Chico State University, California. David worked previously at CSC, Tandem Computers, ADP, and HP. He first began using ClearCase in 1994, and he spent the next four years deploying ClearCase to many developers while employed at ADP and HP. In 1998, he joined Rational Software as a technical field representative in the Pacific Northwest.

David currently is a Worldwide Community of Practice Leader for Enterprise Change Management at IBM, Rational Software. He works with customers and IBM teams to ensure successful deployment and adoption of Rational SCM solutions. David works with Rational field teams delivering workshops, seminars, and assessments to help improve software process and customer results. He also works onsite with customers around the world to define and manage successful deployment of Rational Software solutions.

David has presented these topics at Rational User Conferences:

1995: "Building Software with Clearmake on Non-ClearCase Hosts"

1996: "ClearAdmin—A Set of Scripts and Processes for Administrating ClearCase Sites"

2004: "UCM Stream Strategies and Best Practices"

David has also led the UCM Hands on Workshop sessions at the 2003 and 2004 Rational User Conferences.

David currently resides in Washington with his wonderful wife and three children. When time allows, he also enjoys brewing fine ales and mead. He can be reached via e-mail at *dbellagio@us.ibm.com.*

Tom Milligan

Tom Milligan is a Senior SCM Technical Marketing Engineer on IBM Rational Software's Worldwide Technical Marketing team. Prior to this assignment he worked in Rational Software's Western Region Consulting Organization.

Prior to joining Atria Software in 1995, Tom worked in Electronic Design Automation, Software QA, software tools acquisition and development as well as real-time embedded software development. Tom holds a B.A (Honors College) in Computer Science from the University of Oregon (1978).

Tom has spoken at the Rational User Conference several times:

1997:   "Integrating ClearCase NT with Third-Party Applications" (specifically, integrating ClearCase with Microsoft Word)

1999:   "Integrating Requisite Pro and DDTs"

2001:   "Using Perl with the ClearCase Automation Library (CAL)"

2003:   "ClearCase Performance Analysis, Monitoring and Tuning"

2004:   "Fundamentals of Good Software Configuration Management, ClearCase Performance Analysis, Monitoring and Tuning"

Tom has also published the following articles:

The Rational Edge

November 2001:   "Using Perl with Rational ClearCase Automation Library (CAL)"

September 2002:   "Using Perl with the Rational ClearQuest API"

July 2003:   "ClearCase Performance Analysis, Monitoring and Tuning (part 1)"

September 2003:   "ClearCase Performance Analysis, Monitoring and Tuning (part 2)"

Websphere Advisor

July/August 2003: "7 Attributes of Highly Effective SCM Systems"

Rational Developer Network

"ClearCase Cheat Sheet"

Tom was also keynote speaker at the 2003 Association of Configuration and Data Management (ACDM) Conference.

Tom resides on the central coast of California with his most excellent wife and three children. In his spare time Tom enjoys playing Ultimate (also known as Ultimate Frisbee), watching his kids play volleyball and soccer, and staying up late with his telescope. He can be reached via e-mail at *tmilligan@us.ibm.com.*

Preface to the Second Edition

Welcome to the second edition of *Software Configuration Management Strategies and IBM Rational ClearCase*! We have updated the first edition to enhance the strategies material and to reflect developments in the evolution of IBM Rational ClearCase.

What This Book Is About

This book is about the engineering discipline of software configuration management (SCM) and how the widely used SCM product ClearCase automates and supports SCM best practices through a model called Unified Change Management (UCM). This book covers basic SCM concepts, typical SCM problems encountered as projects and software systems grow in size and complexity, and how you can apply SCM tools and processes to solve these problems. Advanced SCM topics are also discussed, including managing large geographically distributed teams and combining the disciplines of SCM and change request management (or defect tracking).

Much material in the first edition of this book discussed the issues that arise in a software-development project and how an SCM tool should be able to address those issues. That first edition material has been left intact and, in some cases, expanded simply because it represents fundamental truths about software development that have not changed and that are unlikely to change as long as humans are involved in the process.

The second edition of this book expands on the first edition by adding those features introduced to ClearCase since the first edition—specifically, the ClearCase Remote Client, UCM-enforced single-stream projects, full support for unlimited parent/child stream hierarchies, composite baselines, and expanded and more flexible UCM policy configurations. Furthermore, we have added more discussion of ClearQuest and the new ClearQuest MultiSite product. UCM has evolved in many ways since the first edition was published, and many of the additions to this edition stem from our experiences in helping customers adopt and achieve success with ClearCase and UCM in their environment.

Beyond the functional enhancements to ClearCase and ClearQuest, we have included a discussion on monitoring and tuning ClearCase performance, as well as usage models for UCM that we have seen being successfully practiced since the first edition was published. We believe this expanded information will provide significant assistance in helping the reader get the most out of the UCM environment and understand the range of UCM development models that are supported and known to work.

This book is based on the experience gained by the authors working with some incredible people in the SCM field over the last 15 years. After reading it, you should have a better understanding of software configuration management, a better idea of the software development problems solved by using SCM tools and techniques, and a clear understanding of how you can use ClearCase to solve these problems and meet your SCM requirements. The authors sincerely hope you enjoy the book and find it valuable.

What You Need to Know Before Reading This Book

The key to your success is understanding SCM, the requirements for your software project, and how to apply an SCM tool to meet a project's requirements. This book will get you started if you are new to software configuration management. However, you will get the most out of this book if you already have some SCM experience and have used basic version control tools before. This book assumes that you are familiar with the software-development process. It will also be helpful if you have a specific development project in mind while you are reading.

Who You Are and Why You Should Read This Book

This book is not about the nitty-gritty details of writing ClearCase triggers and scripting home-grown integrations with legacy tools; instead, it will give you a high-level view of some common SCM scenarios and how ClearCase can be applied. If you are new to SCM or ClearCase, read this book cover to cover. If you have used ClearCase or have a strong foundation in SCM, look through the table of contents and pick chapters and sections that are of particular interest to you.

For a Software Engineer

The biggest thing an SCM tool can do for a software engineer is to stay out of the way. SCM should perform its function, yet be as transparent as possible. The SCM tool and how it is applied should maximize your ability to make changes to the software. Poor tools or poorly designed processes can add unnecessary time and effort to your work. This book can help you identify the areas in your SCM tools and processes to streamline. It discusses some new advances in the SCM area specifically designed for streamlining development. One of these is the notion of activity-based software configuration management. The idea here is to raise the level of abstraction from files to activities. This makes working with an SCM tool, tracking your changes, and sharing changes with other software engineers more intuitive.

If you're new to SCM, read Chapter 1, "What Is Software Configuration Management?" For an overview of the objects managed by ClearCase, see Chapter 4, "A Functional Overview of ClearCase Objects." To gain an understanding of how ClearCase is used on a daily basis from a development perspective, see Chapter 8, "Development Using the ClearCase UCM Model."

For a Software Project Manager or Technical Leader

As a leader for a software project, you are concerned with deciding what changes to make to a software system and then ensuring that those changes happen. Unplanned changes, made by well-meaning developers, introduce risk into the project schedule and can cause schedule delays and poor product quality. The capability to control and track change is essential to your project's success.

This book should help you gain a solid understanding of SCM, see why you need it, and learn how ClearCase can be used to solve problems you might encounter on projects. Specifically, see Chapter 6, "Project Management in ClearCase," and Chapter 7, "Managing and Organizing Your ClearCase Projects." If you are managing teams that are not all in one location, see Chapter 11, "Geographically Distributed Development," for a discussion of the issues and strategies involved.

For a Tools Engineer

The role of the tools engineer is often overlooked but is essential to success, particularly in large organizations. Your job is to figure out how to apply a given tool to the people, processes, and organization for which you work. This book gives you information about SCM and ClearCase that you can use to determine the best way to apply ClearCase to projects.

For Those Evaluating ClearCase

This book is a good starting point in evaluating ClearCase because it presents a number of common software-development scenarios, as well as more complex scenarios such as geographically distributed development. It discusses the requirements of SCM processes and tools in terms of a set of SCM best practices and shows how to apply ClearCase to support them. Included are overviews of the ClearCase out-of-the-box process Unified Change Management and ClearCase objects.

Use Chapters 1 and 2 to help determine the SCM tool requirements for your project. Look to the remaining chapters to determine whether ClearCase will meet your needs.

For Experienced ClearCase Users

If you are a long-time ClearCase user, this book is interesting from a general software configuration management perspective and might offer some insights into how to approach SCM solutions on your projects. It also offers some advice if you are being asked to support geographically distributed development teams (see Chapter 11).

The book contains an overview of the ClearCase out-of-the-box usage model, called Unified Change Management, which is a recent addition (see Chapter 3, "An Overview of the Unified Change Management Model"). If you are curious about integrating change request management with ClearCase, look at Chapter 12, "Change Request Management and ClearQuest." Look also through the table of contents and pick chapters and sections that are of particular interest to you.

How the Book Is Laid Out

Here is a brief summary of all the chapters.

- Chapter 1, "What Is Software Configuration Management?," provides a general introduction to software configuration management and the key best practices behind it. It answers these questions: What is software configuration management? What are SCM tools? What is the SCM process?

- Chapter 2, "Growing into Your SCM Solution," discusses the growing complexity of software-development projects and proposes that as projects grow in complexity, so does their need for richer SCM support. It covers the history of SCM tool evolution using five categories of software projects, ranging from software developed by a single individual to projects with many geographically distributed project teams.

- Chapter 3, "An Overview of the Unified Change Management Model," provides an overview of the ClearCase out-of-the-box usage model, Unified Change Management, which automates and supports a particular SCM process. The material is discussed in terms of the roles and responsibilities of the various team members, such as the architect, project manager, developer, and integrator.

- Chapter 4, "A Functional Overview of ClearCase Objects," provides a high-level description of ClearCase objects and concepts. This chapter serves as a bridge between general SCM terminology and ClearCase-specific terminology.

- Chapter 5, "Establishing the Initial SCM Environment," provides information on how to configure an initial SCM environment. It discusses the basics of ClearCase architecture and how to approach performance tuning and monitoring. The chapter also covers mapping the software architecture to the physical components in the SCM tool, and briefly discusses creating the SCM repositories and importing existing software.

- Chapter 6, "Project Management in ClearCase," focuses on the role of the project manager with respect to SCM. Particular attention is paid to automation and functionality in ClearCase that specifically support the project manager, including UCM-enforced configurable project policies. It also presents an example of creating a ClearCase project.

- Chapter 7, "Managing and Organizing Your ClearCase Projects," discusses the issues of coordinating parallel work. It also covers scenarios that involve multiple teams cooperating on a common release, development of multiple releases in parallel with multiple teams, coordination of IS/IT-style projects, and coordination of documentation-oriented projects.

- Chapter 8, "Development Using the ClearCase UCM Model," provides an introduction to using ClearCase, specifically focusing on the role of the developer. It shows you how to find and join an existing project, how to make changes to files to accomplish an activity, how to deliver the changes associated with the activity, and how to update the development workspace with changes made by other developers on the project.

- Chapter 9, "Integration," focuses on the role of the integrator and discusses several approaches to both intraproject and cross-project software integration using ClearCase and ClearQuest.

- Chapter 10, "Building, Baselining, and Release Deployment," covers baselining and how baselines and composite baselines are manipulated and used in defining and automating build and release systems.

- Chapter 11, "Geographically Distributed Development," discusses the organizational, communication, and technical challenges that need to be overcome to succeed in distributed development. It looks at three common scenarios of distributed development and the issues associated with each. Finally, this chapter discusses the technology provided by ClearCase MultiSite and ClearQuest MultiSite, and how to apply MultiSite to the three scenarios.

- Chapter 12, "Change Request Management and ClearQuest," covers the area of change request management (CRM), a subset of which is defect tracking. SCM and CRM are two closely related disciplines that together form comprehensive change management support. This chapter also provides a more detailed discussion of IBM Rational Clear-Quest and ClearQuest MultiSite, and how they work in concert with ClearCase to provide the foundation technology for the Unified Change Management model.

Conventions Used

The conventions used in this book fall into two categories: those having to do with presentation of the text and those dealing with UML diagrams in figures.

Commands and Notes, Warnings, and Tips

Command-line operations are called out with a monospaced font and prompt, as in this example:

```
prompt> command -flag1 -flag2
```

Long commands are written on multiple lines, for clarity (as shown here), but should be typed on one line. A code-continuation character (>>) is inserted in the line to indicate that it is all one line, as in this example:

```
prompt> longcommand longobject-identifier

>> -flag1 //machine/pathname

>> -flag
```

Notes, warnings, and tips appear in the text as follows:

Note
Particular points that need to be emphasized appear in the text in this font with an arrow to alert you.

Warning
The screened warning box is used to emphasize an issue or concern that might be encountered and should be avoided.

ClearCase Pro Tip
A screened box labeled with this denotes information that is specifically useful for people who are already using ClearCase. If you have not used ClearCase, you can skip the tips.

UML Diagram Format

This book includes diagrams that use a graphical modeling language called the Unified Modeling Language, or UML. For more information on UML, see *The Unified Modeling Language User Guide*, by Grady Booch, James Rumbaugh, and Ivar Jacobson [Booch, 1999].

Here is a description of the small subset of UML used in this book: An object is shown as a box, with text that describes the object. Lines represent associations between the objects, with text that describes the association. For example, "a house has a roof:"

The association can be annotated to provide additional information, such as how many objects can be connected. This is called the multiplicity of the association. For example, any given house has only one roof, and any given roof can be associated with only one house. Any given house can have many windows or no windows. Any given window can be associated with no house (before it is installed) or one house. These annotations would be represented as shown here:

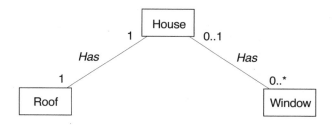

Is it really a house if there are no windows? If not, then you would use 1..n for the windows rather than 0..n.

A black diamond is another association annotation that is used to show composition. Composition means that one object is composed of another. Important semantics are implied by this type of association. One object "owns" the other. That is, owned objects can be created and removed, but once created, they live forever with the owning object. If the owning object is destroyed, its parts are also destroyed. For example, a database has database tables. When the database is destroyed, all the tables are also destroyed. This is represented in UML as shown here:

Finally, a UML relationship called generalization occurs between a general thing and a more specific kind of that thing. For example, the general thing could be a shoe; specific types of shoes are running shoes, hiking shoes, and tennis shoes. Generalization is represented by an open arrow pointing toward the general object, as shown here:

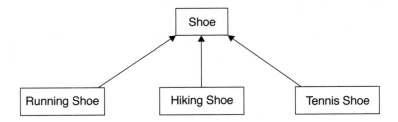

What Is Software Configuration Management?

The title of this chapter asks such a simple question, the answer to which, one would think, ought to be known by anyone with any kind of record in software development. In reality, it seems that few are able to actually articulate what is meant by that term *software configuration management*.

To be fair, those who have a record in software development recognize that there is a need to control what is happening in the development process, and, once controlled, there is a sense that the process can be measured and directed. From that recognized need, then, comes a good working definition of software configuration management:

> Software Configuration Management is how you control the evolution of a software project.

Slightly more formally, *software configuration management* (SCM) is a software-engineering discipline comprising the tools and techniques (processes or methodology) that a company uses to manage change to its software assets. The introduction to the IEEE "Standard for Software Configuration Management Plans" [IEEE 828-1998] says this about SCM:

> SCM constitutes good engineering practice for all software projects, whether phased development, rapid prototyping, or ongoing maintenance. It enhances the reliability and quality of software by:

- Providing structure for identifying and controlling documentation, code, interfaces, and databases to support all life-cycle phases

- Supporting a chosen development/maintenance methodology that fits the requirements, standards, policies, organization, and management philosophy

- Producing management and product information concerning the status of baselines, change control, tests, releases, audits, etc.

Clearly, software is easy to change—too easy. And not only is it easy to change, but it is unconstrained by the physical laws that serve as the guardrails of what is possible with hardware systems. Software is bounded only by the limits of the human imagination. Uncontrolled and undirected, imagination can quickly give rise to nightmare.

Today most software project teams understand the need for SCM to manage change to their software systems. However, even with the best of intentions, software projects continue to fail because of problems that could have been avoided through the use of an SCM tool and appropriate processes. These failures are reflected in poor quality, late delivery, cost overruns, and the incapability to meet customer demands.

To understand software configuration management, you might find it easier to look first at configuration management in a hardware-development environment. Hardware systems have physical characteristics that make the problems caused by the lack of sound configuration management easier to see.

For example, consider a personal computer. A computer has a processor, a mainboard, some memory, a hard drive, a monitor, and a keyboard. Each of these hardware items has an interface that connects it to other hardware items. Your mouse has a plug, and your computer has a port into which you plug your mouse, and, voilá, everything works.

If the plug on the mouse was not compatible with the port on the computer, there would be no way to connect the two pieces of hardware into a working system. Throughout the computer, there are many other similar interfaces. The processor and memory plug into the mainboard, the hard drive plugs into the computer, and the printer, monitor, and keyboard all have interfaces.

When the hardware is manufactured, the interfaces that are essential for the operation of the final system are easily seen. Therefore, they are well known and are carefully examined whenever changes are made to the hardware design.

For a hardware system, configuration management has the following aspects. Each system is numbered or identified and also has a version number. Each version number identifies different designs of the same part. For example, the model year for a car is a version number of that car. It is a 2003 Honda CRV, a 2004 Honda CRV, and so on. When the design of a hardware system is changed, the system gets a new version number.

A hardware system can be made up of hundreds, thousands, or tens of thousands of parts. The next thing that must be recorded is which versions of these parts go together. In manufacturing terms, this is often called a bill of materials. The bill of materials lists all the parts and specifies which version of each part should be used to build the system.

Parts are assembled into bigger parts, which simplifies the manufacturing process for large systems. In the personal computer example, you can say what version of the mouse, hard drive, processor, and monitor go together to make a complete system. Each of these parts, such as a hard drive, is made of many, many subparts, all of which must go together to have a working unit.

Software configuration management deals with all of the same problems as hardware configuration management (and more because of the lack of the guardrails that the laws of physics provide). Each software part has an interface, and software "parts" are plugged together to form a software system. These software "parts" are referred to by different names, such as subsystems, modules, or components. They must be identified and must have a version number. They also must have compatible interfaces, and different versions of parts can have different interfaces. Ultimately, you need a bill of materials to see which versions of which components make up the entire software system.

However, software configuration management is much harder to get right because software is much easier to change than hardware. A few keystrokes and a click of the Save button, and you've created a new version of the software. Unlike hardware, software manufacturing is very fast and can be performed hundreds of times a day by individuals on a software team. This is usually referred to as "performing a software build" or "building the software."

In this dynamic, changing environment, the discipline of SCM is brought to bear to ensure that when a final version of the entire software system is produced, all of the system's component parts can be brought together at the same time, in the same place, and can then be plugged together to work as required. Although most software project teams understand that they need SCM, many fail to get it right—not only because SCM is complex, but also because there isn't a clear understanding of specifically what a good SCM system should do. To begin to create that understanding for you, the rest of this chapter discusses key best practices of SCM in detail and introduces the concepts of the SCM tools and processes that are used to implement those best practices.

1.1   SCM Best Practices

When implementing SCM tools and processes, you must define what practices and policies to employ to avoid common configuration problems and maximize team productivity. Many years of practical experience have shown that the following best practices are essential to successful software development:

- Identify and store artifacts in a secure repository.
- Control and audit changes to artifacts.
- Organize versioned artifacts into versioned components.
- Organize versioned components and subsystems into versioned subsystems.
- Create baselines at project milestones.
- Record and track requests for change.
- Organize and integrate consistent sets of versions using activities.
- Maintain stable and consistent workspaces.
- Support concurrent changes to artifacts and components.
- Integrate early and often.
- Ensure reproducibility of software builds.

The rest of this section explains each of these best practices.

1.1.1   Identify and Store Artifacts in a Secure Repository

To do configuration management, you must identify which artifacts should be placed under version control. These artifacts should include both those used to manage and design a system (such as project plans and design models) and those that instantiate the system design itself (such as source files, libraries, and executables and the mechanisms used to build them). IEEE calls this *configuration identification:* "an element of configuration management, consisting of selecting the configuration items for a system and recording their functional and physical characteristics in technical documentation" [IEEE Glossary, 1990].

In terms of an SCM tool, identification means being able to find and identify any project or system artifact quickly and easily. Anyone who has managed a development project with no SCM or poor SCM can attest to the difficulty of finding the "right" version of the "right" file when copies are floating around all over the place. Ultimately, losing or misidentifying artifact versions can lead to the failure of a project, either by hindering delivery of the system because of missing parts or by lowering the quality of the system because of incorrect parts.

Organizing artifacts and being able to locate them are not enough. You also need fault-tolerant, scalable, distributable, and replicable repositories for these critical assets. The repository is a potential central point of failure for all your assets; therefore, it must be fault-tolerant and reliable. As your organization grows, you will add data and repositories, so scalability and distributability are required to maintain high system performance.

Another means of growth in today's software market is through acquisition, which affects many companies by resulting in the geographical distribution of development groups. The SCM tool, therefore, must be capable of supporting teams that collaborate across these geographically distributed sites.

Finally, the repositories should be backed up with appropriate backup and disaster-recovery procedures. Sadly, many companies overlook this last step, which can lead to severe problems.

1.1.2   Control and Audit Changes to Artifacts

After the artifacts have been identified and stored in a repository, you must be able to control who is allowed to modify them, as well as keep a record of what the modifications were, who made them, when they were made, and why they were made. We refer to this as the audit information. This best practice is related to the IEEE configuration management topics *configuration control* and *configuration status accounting,* defined, respectively, as "the evaluation, coordination, approval or disapproval, and implementation of changes to configuration items" and "the recording and reporting of information needed to manage a configuration effectively" [IEEE Glossary, 1990].

Using both control and audit best practices, an organization can determine how strictly to enforce change-control policies. Without control, anyone can change the system. Without audit, you never really know what went into the system. With audit information, even if you don't restrict changes, you can see at any time what was changed, by whom, and why. The audit information also enables you to more easily make corrections if errors are introduced. Using control and audit in balance enables you to tune your change control approach to best fit your organization. Ideally, you want to optimize for development productivity while eliminating known security risks.

1.1.3   Organize Versioned Artifacts into Versioned Components

When there are more than a few hundred files and directories in a system, it becomes necessary to group these files and directories into objects representing a larger granularity, to ease management and organization problems. These single objects, made up of sets of files and directories, have a number of different names in the software industry, including packages, modules, and development components. For the purposes of this book, an *SCM component* is a set of related files and directories that are versioned, shared, built, and baselined as a single unit.

To implement a component-based approach to SCM, you organize the files and directories into a single SCM component that physically implements a logical system design component. The Rational Unified Process (RUP) refers to the SCM component as a *component subsystem* [RUP 5.5, 1999] (RUP is a software-engineering process developed and marketed by Rational Software).

A component-based approach to SCM offers many benefits, as follows:

- *Components reduce complexity.*

  Use of a higher level of abstraction reduces complexity and makes any problem more manageable. Using components, you can discuss the 6 that make up a system instead of the 5,000 files subsumed under them. When producing a system, you need to select only 6 baselines, one from each component, instead of having to select the right 5,000 versions of 5,000 files. It is easier to assemble consistent systems from consistent component baselines than individual file versions. Inconsistencies result in unnecessary rebuilding and errors discovered late in the development cycle.

- *It is easier to identify the quality level of a particular component baseline than that of numerous individual files.*

  A component baseline identifies only one version of each file and directory that makes up that component. Because a component baseline contains a consistent set of versions, these can be integration-tested as a unit. It is then possible to mark the level of testing that has been performed on each component baseline.

  This method improves communication and reduces errors when two or more project teams share components. For example, a project team produces a database component, and another team uses it as part of an end-user application. If the application project team can easily determine the newest database component baseline that has passed integration testing, it will be less likely to use a defective set of files.

- *Instantiating a physical component object in a tool helps institutionalize component sharing and reuse.*

  After component baselines have been created and the quality level has been identified, project teams can look at the various component baselines and choose one that can be referenced or reused from one project to the next. Component sharing and reuse is practically impossible if you cannot determine which versions of which files make up a component. Component sharing between projects is not practical if you cannot determine the level of quality and stability for any given component baseline.

- *Mapping logical design components to physical SCM components helps preserve the integrity of software architectures.*

  In an iterative development process, pieces of the software architecture are built and tested early in the software life cycle to drive out risk. By mapping the logical architectural components to the physical SCM components, you gain the ability to build and test individual pieces of the architecture. This mapping between architecture and the implementation of the architecture leads to higher- quality code and cleaner interfaces between the components by preserving the integrity of the original architecture in the SCM tool.

1.1.4   Organize Versioned Components and Subsystems into New Versioned Subsystems

To allow management of highly complex software systems, you must be able to step beyond the management of individual components and group those components into subsystems. Beyond that, you must also be able to include other subsystems in the definition of a subsystem. This recursive definition of a subsystem as a collection of compatible components and subsystems allows incredibly complex systems to be hierarchically defined, controlled, and managed. Going back to the personal computer example, recall that the PC is composed of a processor, a mainboard, some memory, a hard drive, a monitor, and a keyboard. Each of these entities can be described as a subsystem—that is, a collection of components and other subsystems. Using this recursive method of describing the system, the structure of the entire PC can be specified and managed hierarchically, all the way down to the individual parts. Note that if you wanted, you could use this recursive method to specify the PC all the way down to its atoms. Furthermore, the subsystems defined in that hierarchy, such as the hard drive, can be reused in other PC designs. Figure 1-1 illustrates the hierarchical nature of subsystems.

The ability to use an SCM system to recursively define and manage the subsystems that make up a software system enables you to define and control very complex development efforts and to designate subsystems as projects that are independently controlled, managed, and released and that can become candidates for reuse in other projects.

1.1.5   Create Baselines at Project Milestones

At key milestones in a project, all the artifacts should be baselined together. In other words, you should record the versions of all the artifacts and components that make up a system or subsystem at specific times in the project. At a minimum, artifacts should be baselined at each major project milestone. In an iterative development process as prescribed by the Rational Unified Process [RUP 5.5], at a minimum, baselines should be created at the end of each project iteration.

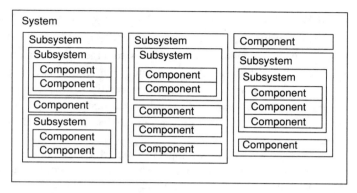

Figure 1-1 Decomposing larger systems into hierarchical subsystems makes it easier for complex entities such as this one to be defined and managed.

Typically, new baselines are created more frequently (sometimes daily) near the end of an iteration or release cycle. It can be useful to create baselines before each nightly build. This enables you to reproduce any project build, query what has changed between builds, and indicate the stability of a build using baseline quality attributes.

There are three main reasons to baseline: reproducibility, traceability, and reporting. Reproducibility is the ability to go back in time and reproduce a given release of a software system or a development environment that existed earlier. Traceability ties together the requirements, project plans, test cases, and software artifacts. To implement it, you should baseline not only the system artifacts, but also the project-management artifacts. Reporting enables you to query the content of any baseline and to compare baselines. Baseline comparison can assist in debugging errors and generating release notes.

Good traceability, reproducibility, and reporting are necessary for solving process problems. They enable you to fix defects in released products, facilitate ISO-9000 and SEI audits, and ultimately ensure that the design fulfills the requirements, the code implements the design, and the correct code is used to build the executables.

1.1.6   Record and Track Requests for Change

Change request management involves tracking requests for changes to a software system. These requests can result from defects found by a testing organization, defects reported by customers, enhancement requests from the field or customers, or new ideas produced internally.

Recording and tracking change requests supports configuration and change control as defined by IEEE (see the "Control and Audit Changes to Artifacts" section, earlier in this chapter). The critical points are that change requests are recorded and that the progress, whether through implementation or a decision never to implement, is tracked. Beyond simply tracking change requests, a good change-management process enables project management to prioritize and establish target dates for the inclusion of change requests in product releases. Chapter 12, "Change Request Management and ClearQuest," covers this best practice in more detail.

1.1.7   Organize and Integrate Consistent Sets of Versions Using Activities

Although all SCM systems provide version control at the file level, it is left to the software developer to keep track of which versions of which files go together to implement a logical, consistent change and to ensure that this change is integrated as a unit. This is a tedious, manual, and error-prone process. Mistakes are easy to make, especially if a developer is working on more than one change at a time. This can lead to build errors and lost development time. Mistakes also show up as runtime defects that can't be reproduced by the developer in his or her working environment.

Some SCM tools provide a way for developers to record which change request or defect they are working on. This information is used to track which file and directory changes make up a single logical change. Often this information is not used by the SCM tool, but is instead maintained only for reporting and auditing purposes. The key advantage of collecting this change information is streamlining the integration process and ensuring consistency of the configuration in any given working or build environment.

The grouping of file and directory versions is called a *change set*, or change package. (Some in the SCM industry distinguish between these two terms. The difference is subtle and has to do with the implementation. A change set is defined as the actual delta that comprises the change, even if it spans files. A change package is a grouping together of a set of file versions. In this book, I use the ClearCase term *change set* to refer to the grouping and manipulation of a change.) This grouping is mostly useful when the *change set* contains a single logical change. The change set approach has been around for a long time. In 1991, Peter Feiler wrote an excellent paper, "Configuration Management Models in Commercial Environments" [Feiler 1991], that describes the change set model.

Change sets are only the glue. There must be a link between the versions that are changed and the activity that is the "why" for the change. An *activity* represents a unit of work being performed. Activities can be of different types. For example, a defect, enhancement request, and issue are all activities. This unit of work ties directly into the change request management system and processes. An activity might also be a child of another activity that appears in the project-management system. The capability of the change set to tie together the disciplines of configuration management, change request management, and project management is where the power of the activity-based approach really becomes visible.

The key idea of activity-based SCM is to increase the level of abstraction from dealing with files and versions to dealing with activities. This is done first by collecting versions created during development into a change set and associating that change set with an activity. Activities are then presented throughout the user interface and used by SCM operations as the way to operate on a consistent set of versions.

The benefits of activity-based SCM are as follows:

- *Consistent changes cause fewer build and integration problems.*

    Integrating a consistent change set (single logical change) reduces build and integration errors caused by developers forgetting about files when delivering their changes. It also ensures that the testing was performed against the same versions being integrated, making integration errors less frequent.

- *Activities are logically how people group what they do.*

Generally, developers think about what feature, request for enhancement, or defect they are working on, which are all types of activities. By conforming to this activity-centric approach in the SCM tool and by using automation, developers are not required to know many details of the SCM implementation.

Activities are a level of abstraction that all project members can use in common, enabling project leaders, testers, developers, and customer support personnel to communicate more effectively.

- *Activities provide a natural link to change request management.*

Change request management (a subset of which is defect tracking) is an essential part of most software-development organizations, and tracking change requests is one of the key best practices of SCM. Instead of being a collection of versions in meaningless bundles, the change set should be tied to the change request stored in the change request management system. This combining of the change request and the change set allows accurate reporting of what defects were fixed and what files were changed between project baselines.

- *Activities provide a natural link to project management.*

Project managers are interested not only in what is being changed but also in the status of the change, who is assigned to it, and how much effort is estimated to be needed to implement the change. The change set links the project-management data for an activity to the files and versions that are changed. This link supports better automation, bringing advantages to the project leader without requiring extra effort on the part of the developer. For example, when a developer completes a change in the SCM tool, a change of status in the activity could be made automatically and would show up on a project report.

- *Activities facilitate reporting.*

Activity-based SCM allows all reports and tools to display information in terms of the changes made rather than the files and versions that went into making the change. This is more natural for everyone involved with a project.

- *Activities streamline code reviews.*

Traditionally, when performing code reviews, a reviewer receives a list of files and which versions of these files to review. The trick is determining which version to compare against when doing the review. Should you compare the latest version against the immediate predecessor, the last baseline, or some other version? It is unclear.

With the change set information, it is possible for the SCM tool to provide the developer with the predecessor version of the change set automatically. This makes performing code reviews easier and less error-prone.

- *Activities streamline testing efforts.*

  Testing organizations often work with software builds "thrown over the wall" by development organizations. They must determine what went into the build or what was different from the previous build to decide what needs to be tested and what level of testing is required.

  Most testing organizations do not have the resources to run the full test suite on every software build that development delivers. So, automatic reporting between two baselines that provides a list of the activities included in the new baseline is far easier to work with than a list of the hundreds of file versions that were modified from one baseline to the next.

1.1.8   Maintain Stable and Consistent Workspaces

The developer requires tools and automation to create and maintain a stable working environment. This maintenance involves periodically synchronizing changes with other team members in a way that results in a consistent set of shared changes that are of a known level of stability.

Consistency and stability in the developer's working environment maximize the developer's productivity. Without stable and consistent workspaces—private file areas where developers can implement and test code in relative isolation—developers spend significant time investigating erroneous build problems and are sometimes unable to build the software in their own workspaces. These problems can quietly sap time and available effort from any project.

A stable model allows developers to isolate themselves easily from disruptive changes going on in other parts of the project and for the developer to decide when it is appropriate to introduce change into the workspace. A stable model also allows a project to be isolated from disruptive changes occurring in a developer's workspace.

A consistent model means that when developers update their workspace, these updates will consist of a known, buildable, and tested set of versions.

1.1.9   Support Concurrent Changes to Artifacts and Components

Ideally, only one person would be making changes to any single file at a time, or only one team would be working on any single component at a time. Unfortunately, this is not always efficient or practical. The most obvious case is when maintaining a release in the field while developing the next release.

Early SCM tools forced users to serialize changes to files. This was inefficient, in that some developers were blocked waiting for other developers to complete their changes. It was also a problem from a quality standpoint. Blocked developers often worked around the system by getting a copy of the file without checking it out and modifying it outside SCM control. After the original developer checked in his or her changes, other developers would check out the file, copy their changes in place, and check the file back in, unknowingly removing the previous developer's

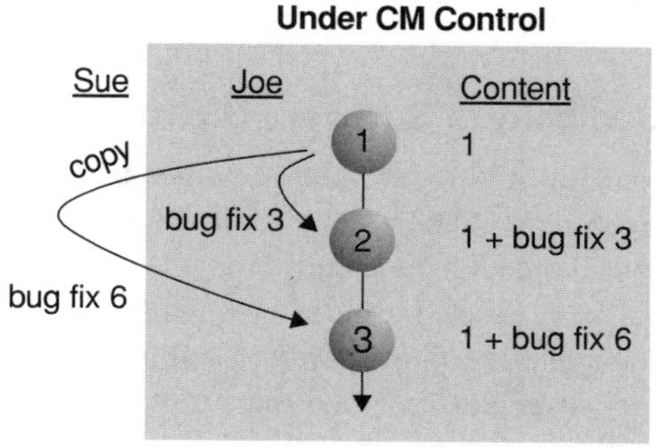

Figure 1-2 Serial development problems.

changes from the latest version of the file (see Figure 1-2). This problem is usually exposed when a bug reappears in the latest build of a system. Because the assumption is made that the bug has been fixed and already verified, full regression tests might not be run. If so, the reintroduced bug could make its way into released software.

One of the key things an SCM tool must support is the capability to modify the same files concurrently and to integrate or merge the changes made in parallel at the appropriate time. We see this requirement manifested in parallel development activities such as those just mentioned, as well as in a need to allow a single developer to work on two or more activities simultaneously, or allow multiple developers to work in isolation on a single feature before that feature is incorporated into the project. This might mean integrating at check-in time for two developers working on the same project, or it might mean scheduling an integration action when merging changes into the latest development work. By providing this support, developers aren't forced to work around the system or be blocked.

1.1.10 Integrate Early and Often

During integration, you will discover problems with interfaces and misunderstandings in the design. Both of these problems can have a major impact on the development schedule, so early discovery is essential. Plan integration points early in the development life cycle, and continue integrating often over the course of a software-development project.

If you do too good of a job at developer isolation (see the "Maintain Stable and Consistent Workspaces" section, earlier in this chapter), you might establish a model in which it is easy to remain too isolated. This problem can occur regardless of the tool you use because it is more often related to how you use a tool rather than the tool itself.

Development workspaces should be under the developer's control; however, project managers and integrators must have an automated and enforceable way to ensure that developers keep current with ongoing project changes. This is the classic dilemma of developer isolation versus project integration. The balance to be maintained here is to integrate as early and as often as possible without negatively impacting productivity (see the section "Isolation and Integration with ClearCase" in Chapter 9, "Integration").

1.1.11 Ensure Reproducibility of Software Builds

It is often necessary to find out how a software build was constructed and what went into its construction, to debug a problem or reproduce the same build. You must establish the proper procedures and provide sufficient automation to record who did the build, what went into each executable or library that was built, which machine it was built on, what OS version was running on that machine, and what command-line options were specified in the build step. When you have this build audit information, it is useful to have tools that enable you to do reporting. In particular, being able to compare two builds can often help debug problems. Sometimes bugs can be introduced simply by changing the optimization switches to the compiler.

Without being able to reproduce a software build, you will be unable to perform system maintenance and, therefore, to support a system distributed to your customers.

1.2　SCM Tools and SCM Process

SCM best practices are achieved by applying both processes and tools to a software-development project. This section briefly introduces both.

1.2.1　SCM Tools

SCM tools are software tools that automate and facilitate the application of the SCM best practices. As with a compiler, debugger, and editor, an SCM tool is an essential part of every software engineer's tool kit today.

It is unrealistic to try to maintain effective SCM without an SCM tool. In early SCM project environments, one or more individuals acted as the CM librarians. These librarians handed out pieces of software for people to work on, diligently recorded who had which pieces, and logged in new versions as people turned in changes. This approach is not competitive today because it is too slow, is too prone to error, and does not scale.

The goal of successful SCM is to allow as much change as possible while still maintaining control of the software. SCM tools help automate tedious, manual, and error-prone pieces of the SCM process, and can ensure that your project can support all of the SCM best practices.

1.2.2　SCM Process

A process defines the steps by which you perform a specific task or set of tasks. An SCM process is the way SCM is performed on your project—specifically, how an SCM tool is applied to accomplish a set of tasks.

A key mistake most people make is to assume that an SCM tool will, in and of itself, solve their SCM problems or support their SCM requirements. This is wrong! The picture will not hang itself if you buy a hammer and nails. It is not the tool itself that solves a problem, but rather the application of that tool. How you apply the SCM tool to your development environment is called the usage model, or SCM process. It is this model or process that will in part determine how successfully you address your SCM issues.

1.3 Summary

This chapter helped define software configuration management in simple terms as the mechanisms used to control the evolution of a software project. An understanding of what we mean by software configuration management is crucial because if we don't know what we want to do, we have no hope of converging on a good software-development environment. To enable this understanding, we specifically discussed software-development best practices and how they are enabled by a good SCM system. We also introduced the concepts of the SCM tools and processes that are used to implement those best practices. In Chapter 2, "Growing into Your SCM Solution," we begin to explain how to use those concepts and processes efficiently and effectively.

Growing into Your SCM Solution

When you understand the best practices behind software configuration management (SCM), you need to understand how to apply SCM processes and tools successfully. One of the biggest mistakes that people make is assuming that one size fits all or that one solution is the "right" solution. In reality, different software projects have different requirements and varying degrees of complexity. Thus, an SCM tool and process that works well for one project might be woefully inadequate for another. Requirements can also change over time. A software project that is just beginning likely has a very different set of requirements than those of a project that has been running for 18 months.

The key to successful SCM on any project is to allow as much change to occur to the software as possible without losing control over the software. Like a race car driver in a race, to win, you must speed up software development to the limit while still staying on the track. You must constantly tune the SCM process, as you would a race car engine or suspension, so that the overhead involved with the SCM tool meets the changing project requirements. In a nutshell, you must have an SCM tool that is highly customizable and flexible. You must be able to perform SCM tool customizations quickly and easily.

This chapter discusses the changes software projects undergo that influence the project's SCM process and tool requirements. It also discusses how SCM tools have evolved to solve SCM-related development problems in the context of five software project categories, and begins to discuss the specific characteristics in the ClearCase SCM tool that address those problems and categories.

2.1   Dealing with Changing Project Requirements

The tooling and process requirements for any software project change over time. For example, suppose you are a software developer for a small, integrated system vendor (ISV). You have developed a prototype of a new tool. A lunchtime demonstration of the prototype has caught the attention of one of the company's vice presidents, who decides that it is worth further development.

You form a team consisting of yourself, two more software developers, a technical writer, and a tester. As its first job, the team completes the first version of the product, which turns out to be very popular and a bestseller.

For the second release, you grow the team size to 12 members. The current requirements are to incorporate some complementary third-party components and expand the number of platforms on which the product will run. The team immediately begins work after finalizing the first release.

While the second release is being developed, a key customer reports some critical defects in the first release that must be fixed. A patch for the first release of the product is produced in parallel while the second release is being developed. This patch also must be incorporated into the second release.

At this point, the product catches the attention of a larger, well-established company. This company believes that the product will complement its existing product line, so it acquires the small ISV. The major development center for the new parent company is located in a different part of the country. The development team grows again to 25 members. The new team includes, among others, three more software developers located locally and five developers located remotely. Management decides to test the product using the parent company's testing group. Thus, your team needs to find a way to deliver software builds to the remote testing team.

Release 3 is full of new features and includes a number of integrations with the parent company's existing product line. As if this was not enough, a new project manager is assigned from the parent company. This manager has a different approach to change management and begins asking for more detailed reports on what changes are being made to the product and the status of those changes. And so it goes. Success breeds complexity.

Do you think that the SCM tools and processes used to implement Release 3 are the best choice to manage the development of the prototype? Do you think that the tools and processes used for Release 1 would readily support the development environment for Release 3? How do you think that your SCM tools and processes will scale as your projects and your company grow?

The changes that any software project will undergo over time fall roughly into four categories:

- Increasing complexity of the software system being developed
- Increasing complexity of the project environment needed to develop the software system
- Changing requirements based on the development life cycle phase
- Changes to an organization's management processes or personnel

The first two categories of change require scalability in tools and process. The second two change over time and are not easily predicted. Therefore, they require flexibility in both tools and process. The following subsections discuss these categories in detail.

2.1.1   Increasing Software System Complexity

As a software product evolves, it typically increases in complexity, usually with the addition of more features and functions after the initial design. Thus, more areas of the product must interact with each other, more things must be tested, and more possibilities for failure arise. This increase in complexity can be a big concern if steps are not taken to maintain the architectural integrity of the system while it evolves. (See the chapter "An Architecture-Centric Process" in *The Rational Unified Process: An Introduction, Third Edition,* for more information on the importance of software system architecture [Kruchten, 2003].)

From a configuration management standpoint, the increase in complexity takes several forms:

- Increase in the size of the software that is being managed
- Increase in the complexity of the problems that are to be solved
- Increase in the complexity of a maturing architecture
- Inclusion of third-party software components
- Increase in the number of platforms to support

Increasing Software Size and Architectural Complexity

Solving more complex problems with an existing software system requires more features. This increases the complexity of the system architecture and, thus, the size of the software system, in terms of both lines of code and the number of files being managed by the SCM tool. Thus, when considering an SCM tool, you need two primary capabilities. First, you need to be able to add new files to an SCM repository easily. If it is not easy to add new files, you might tend to add new functions to existing files, which might not make sense architecturally.

Second, you must be able to version-control directories. Version control is as important for directories as it is for files. As with files, directories have contents, which are files and other directories. These contents evolve over time (for example, a file can be added, renamed, or removed), and the tools used to manipulate or build the software will likely assume that the software directory structure is organized in a specific way. Versioning the directory structure enables you to easily rebuild previous releases of a software system or quickly roll back a Web site to a previous state. Without this capability, even though you might be able to reconstruct the specific file versions required to rebuild a previous release, you will not be able to reconstruct the corresponding directory structure, and the tools used to manipulate or build the software will not function.

Inclusion of Third-Party Components and Software Reuse

Component sharing, software reuse, and the use of third-party components all are essential elements of meeting the schedule demands of developing software systems today. This approach has been applied to hardware systems for a long time; the days when a company developed all of the pieces of a hardware system itself are no more. Software is experiencing a similar trend.

Use of third-party components and reuse of internally developed components among projects or organizations add complexity that SCM tools and processes must support. The key factor is ensuring that the components (regardless of their sources) are placed under SCM control. Ideally, this means that the components are accessed directly from their primary repositories. Less ideal is to put the delivered components under version control yourself. The first case usually requires some way to replicate or copy the repository and keep the data in the two copies in sync. The second case requires some way to import a set of files and directories, and then to import them again when an update or new release of a component is received.

Increasing Number of Platforms to Support

The capability to support more platforms brings with it some unique SCM challenges. As more platforms are supported, the load on the test organization increases. Often a separate porting group must be formed to optimize the release of new features on the main platforms while ensuring that the system will be available on all of the required platforms.

From an SCM perspective, new platform support usually involves two key concerns. First is access to the software on the new platform. This requires either that the SCM tool be directly supported on that platform or that some way exists to get the software out of the SCM repository and onto the desired platform.

The second concern relates to building the software. Software builds and SCM go hand in hand. If you cannot determine what versions of the files were used in a particular build, reproducing customer-reported problems will be difficult. Furthermore, providing patches to the release will be very difficult. SCM tools and processes must provide this information. This could be more difficult if the platform on which you need to build your system is not also supported by the SCM tool that you are using.

2.1.2   Increasing Project Environment Complexity

A project's development environment grows in complexity for the following reasons:

- An increase in the number of team members
- A need to support parallel development
- The location of development teams at different sites
- An increase in the number and frequency of product releases

Increasing Team Size and Parallel Development Support

The increasing complexity of an evolving software system usually requires changes in the complexity of the project-development team. Most often this is seen in an increase in team size or the number of teams. With only one developer, communication obviously is fast and efficient. With two, there is one line of communication. Four developers communicate in 6 lines, and 10 in 45. A team of 100 has 4,950 lines! With this many communication lines, disseminating information becomes more difficult and time consuming. Fast and accurate communication becomes essential to meeting project schedules and developing high-quality software systems.

From an SCM perspective, an increase in team size also increases contention for common software system files and resources. The SCM tool must support locking and concurrent changes to common files. *Concurrent changes* are changes made by two or more developers to the same files at the same time. The SCM tool must also support the capability for developers to work concurrently without destabilizing the other individual contributors or the project. Furthermore, the SCM tool must support merging or integration of the changes to recombine the work that was done in parallel. Concurrent changes made by two or more teams working on the same software system are referred to as *parallel development* (for example, a maintenance team working on Release 1.1 of a software system and a development team working on Release 2 of the same system). The issues of managing concurrent change and parallel development are core to SCM and are explored in more detail later in this chapter.

Geographically Distributed Development Teams

Another area of complexity introduced in the project environment is the need to support development teams located at different sites, or geographically distributed development. Geographically distributed development can involve two or more large teams, either at different sites in the same city or in different countries. It might also involve individuals working from home or while traveling.

Geographically distributed development severely increases the complexity of any software-development effort primarily because of communication issues. This topic is covered in detail in Chapter 11, "Geographically Distributed Development."

Increasing Number and Frequency of Product Releases

The number of releases supported in the field and the frequency of product releases can significantly affect the choice of tools and processes used for SCM. The number of releases is the number of different releases of a software system being supported at any given time. For example, a company might release Version 1 of a product, followed by Version 1.1, and then Version 2. When it releases Version 3, it must decide whether to continue to support Version 1 or to withdraw support for it, thereby forcing its customers to upgrade to a newer version. The more releases are supported, the more sophisticated and automated the patch, support, and testing processes must be. Some software systems are custom systems—that is, every system at every customer site has been modified explicitly for that customer. In that case, the number of supported product releases directly relates to the number of customers. Each one of those releases is often called a variant of the software system. For example, there might be a major release, such as Release 1, but 10 variants of that release for each of 10 customers.

Customer variants are one of the most complex configurations that an SCM tool must support. If you must work with this constraint, you need to build in process support and automation for moving bug fixes between variants. Otherwise, bug fixes will not be efficiently propagated to other variants and might even be lost or overlooked. (New and smaller companies with only one product should be careful not to fall into the trap of developing variants unless this is explicitly part of their business model because this increase in complexity comes at a cost and does not scale well.)

Also contributing to complexity is the frequency of product releases. More frequent releases mean more automation to make the release process less error-prone and more efficient. (I have seen anything from releases every two years to daily releases.)

2.1.3   Changing Life Cycle Phase

As a project moves through development life cycle phases, the project's requirements for SCM tools and processes will change. Life cycle phase changes differ from the previous two change categories, system complexity and project environment complexity, which typically increase over time. Life cycle phase requirements increase and decrease as the project progresses. This is seen particularly in a project that is practicing an iterative development approach. (See the chapter "Dynamic Structure: Iterative Development" in [Kruchten, 2003] for more information on the iterative development approach.)

Good SCM tools and processes maximize your ability to make changes while still maintaining effective control over the software. For example, early in the life cycle, you want to encourage as much change as possible, so you should relax controls. As a software system approaches time to release, you want to make explicit decisions about what changes can and cannot be made, usually based on assessing risk. At this point, you want strict controls and accurate tracking of the changes being made. Therefore, to maximize the rate of change, you must be able to modify the SCM tool controls from life cycle phase to life cycle phase.

A process-oriented example of changing project requirements based on life cycle phase is the level of approval required for accepting changes into the project build. In early phases of development, you might require only a peer-level code review. Late in the development cycle, the approval of a change-control board might be required before changes are accepted into the project build.

The balance at each life cycle phase should be between auditing and enforcement. Auditing is the recording of who made a change, what change was made, when the change was made, and why a change was made. By auditing, you can loosen controls, thus allowing changes to be made more rapidly while ensuring your ability to back out of a change or determine why a change was made. Auditing must be automated and must be as transparent to the end user as possible, to involve a minimal amount of overhead. That is, the SCM tool automatically should record as much information as possible.

Enforcement is proactive control that disallows changes unless certain conditions are met. This can hinder the speed at which change occurs because approvals or additional steps are required before changes can be made. Enforcement is essential, however, when applied at the right time during the development life cycle.

2.1.4   Changing Processes and Personnel

The fourth category of change in project requirements results from changes to an organization's processes or personnel (particularly management). Of the four categories of change, process and personnel changes are the most unpredictable and often the most severe in their impact. The two changes usually go hand in hand. The most extreme example is an acquisition, in which new management is brought in to run the project using the acquiring company's processes, procedures, and tools.

Process Changes

Process changes usually result from a desire to fix existing problems or perceived problems in the software-development process. Often the project team itself suggests changes in existing tools and processes. This internal effort is often the most effective. Sometimes process change results from an organization-wide effort to document and improve the organization's processes. The best examples of this are the Software Engineering Institute's Capability Maturity Model (SEI-CMM) assessments and ISO-9000 certifications. (For more information on the SEI-CMM, refer to [Humphrey, 1989] and the SEI Web site, *http://www.sei.cmu.edu/*. For more information on ISO standards, see the ISO Web site, *http://www.iso.ch/*.) Most often, the organization makes these efforts to show customers or prospects that it develops quality software by meeting industry standards on software development. (Organization-wide process change can often be ineffective, or even destructive, unless the project teams themselves are engaged and feel some ownership in the process improvement efforts.)

Process-related efforts often result in changes to the SCM tool, changes to the way the tool is used, or the development of additional automation layers on top of an existing SCM tool. Process change should be made explicitly to fulfill the SCM requirements of a project. This is an important point. Some process changes are requested to have an SCM tool mimic a function available in a different tool. The question to ask before implementing such a change is "What requirement is being satisfied by this function?" There might, in fact, be a better way to fulfill the requirement in the existing SCM tool than by simply mimicking a feature available in a different SCM tool. There should be an understanding of how the process changes will improve either productivity or quality. Ideally, a means will exist to measure the effect of a process change. Process change simply for the sake of change is not a good idea.

Personnel Changes

Personnel changes are equally hard to predict and plan for. These happen in any number of ways. A common example is a change in project manager. Every project manager brings experience from previous projects that influences management and development style. Changes to management often cause a change in process and tools, particularly when a project manager is being replaced because of project problems.

Another personnel issue that can affect the SCM tools and process is the mix of experience on a software team over time. A project at its start might have a high degree of experienced personnel who have used SCM tools for many years and understand the product they are developing, as well as all aspects of the system architecture. As the team size increases, not all team members can have a detailed understanding of all areas of the system architecture. Many team members might be fairly new to software development, and some might have limited exposure to SCM and development in a team environment. A project team with less experience might require any or all of the following:

- Additional controls on who can change which pieces of the software system
- Control of SCM functions based on the role of a user

- Improved ease of use of the SCM tool
- Additional user training in tools and processes

2.2   Evolution of SCM Tools

Not so many years ago, a software product typically was developed by one person, and there was little need for SCM. As software products grew in size and complexity, their development required more than a single individual. Projects remained relatively easy to manage when project teams consisted of two or three individuals all sitting close to each other. However, it was not long before project teams grew to tens and even hundreds of developers, who might not be located at the same site.

Early on, SCM processes were developed to manage change. Typically, these processes were performed manually. One or more librarians were tasked with controlling who could access the source code. To modify a file, the developer filled out a form (paper-based) and submitted it to the librarian. This form recorded which files needed to be modified and why. The librarian ensured that none of the files was being modified by someone else at the same time. If the file was free, the librarian gave a copy of it to the developer and recorded when and to whom it was checked out. The developer, when done, provided the modified copy of the file to the librarian, who recorded the new file and placed it in the appropriate archive.

Soon SCM tools were developed to help automate and assist librarians with their jobs. Usually one tool dominated on any given operating system. The basic version-control features of these tools were as follows:

- To maintain a library or repository of files
- To create and store multiple versions of files
- To provide a mechanism for locking (to enforce serialized change to any given file)
- To identify collections of file versions
- To extract/retrieve versions of files from the repository

Early SCM tools provided these basic version-control capabilities and automated the manual-librarian approach to SCM. A developer could check out a file without the intervention of a librarian. While the file was checked out, others could not modify it. When the developer was done, the file was checked in and a new version of the file was created automatically. Today the check-out/check-in model remains fundamentally unchanged.

One widely used SCM tool was the source code control system (SCCS), developed by Bell Laboratories in the early 1970s. An alternative to SCCS was the revision control system (RCS), developed by Walter Tichy at Purdue University. Both RCS and SCCS became the predominant SCM tools on the UNIX platform. Most mainframe machines at the time also had their own primary SCM tool. For example, the configuration management system (CMS) was part of the Digital Equipment Corporation (DEC) VAX/VMS operating system. (In terms of SCM tool evolution, this chapter uses UNIX as an example. Similar tool evolution was occurring in the mainframe environment. In fact, there were even some SCM features built into a few punch card systems.)

These early version-control tools usually offered a way to label or mark a particular version of each file for a set of files. This is called a *configuration* and was used to identify a specific version of the overall product (such as Release 1).

These tools greatly improved efficiency over the manual approach. They offered the classic SCM capabilities of being able to identify pieces of the system, control change to those pieces, and have an audit trail of who modified which files and when.

Of course, software-development projects continued to increase in complexity and size, thereby requiring larger teams and more coordination. The individuals supporting these version-control tools began developing layers of abstraction, using scripts, on top of the underlying functionality to better handle the increase in complexity. At most companies, these layers on top of tools such as SCCS and RCS took on a life of their own, defining the usage model for how that company applied SCCS/RCS to its projects and providing more functionality than available in the basic tools.

These layers defined the first level of functionality that was to be incorporated into modern SCM tools. Modern tools extended the basic functionality of early tools by supporting improved parallel development, workspace management, and build and release management.

Today advanced capabilities are being added to many SCM tools. These advanced tools have objects and features that provide SCM support at a level of abstraction closely aligned with other aspects of software engineering, such as change request management and project management. These advanced SCM tools support versioning of all project artifacts (not just source code), software projects whose team members might not be located at the same site, component-based development, and activity-based configuration management.

The remainder of this chapter looks at SCM tool evolution by examining the kinds of problems software projects faced and the solutions employed to solve these problems. For smaller project teams, these problems could be solved using no SCM tool or early SCM tools. For larger project teams, old solutions would not adequately scale to solve new or larger problems, so improved processes and SCM tools were required.

2.2.1 Five Project Team Categories

To discuss SCM tool evolution in some meaningful way, the wide variety of software project types must be bounded. This section attempts to do this by defining five broad project categories. Some projects will not fit exactly into any one of them, and some might not fit into any. These categories are meant to provide a context in which to organize and discuss SCM problems and SCM tool solutions. The five categories are as follows:

- **Individual**—A team of 1 member, working on one product.
- **Small**—A team of 2 to 5 members, working on one product.
- **Modest**—A team of 6 to 15 members, working on one or more products in a family.

- **Major**—One to 10 cooperating teams of 2 to 30 members each, with fewer than 150 total members, working toward a common release of one or more products in a product family.

- **Extensive**—A large number of teams of various sizes cooperating on a release of one or more products, where the total number of team members is 150 or greater. (The term *extreme* was used in the first edition for the classification of team size and complexity we are referring to here as extensive. Given how strongly associated with programming that term has become [see (Beck 2000)], in this edition, we made the switch to *extensive*.)

Individual Projects

One person working on one software system (application) constitutes an individual project. This individual owns and controls all of the source code for the system. Example systems include tooling/scripting, Web-based personal home pages, small shareware systems, and systems developed for personal use. When only one person is working on one system, the SCM requirements are minimal. In general, the individual does not require an SCM tool to solve his or her problems. However, an SCM tool can offer such benefits as better organization, security, and recording of the flow of changes, thereby freeing the individual from doing version control via directory and file copies.

Small Project Teams

Small project teams consist of two to five developers working on a single software application. This team owns and controls all of the source code for its application. An organization might have any arbitrary number of these teams, but the teams do not share any source code or have any dependencies on other project teams. Example applications are small IS/IT applications, Visual Basic applications, small C/C++ applications, Web-based information-delivery applications, Web-based information-gathering applications, and small corporate intranet sites. Early SCM tool capabilities are typically adequate to support small project teams.

Modest Project Teams

A modest team is any number of smaller teams of 6 to 15 members that develop one or more software applications whose source they own and control. Minimal software sharing occurs between teams and is usually limited to a small number of well-defined core components. Few intercomponent dependencies exist. Examples include Java-based applications, complex Visual Basic applications, modest C/C++ applications, mission-critical IS/IT applications, modest Web-based e-commerce sites, and corporate intranet sites. Modest teams usually require the capabilities available in more modern SCM tools.

Major Project Teams

A major team consists of a small number (1 to 10) of cooperating teams of various sizes (2 to 30 members). Some interproduct code sharing and some intercomponent dependencies might occur. A major team might have some teams or team members located at different sites. The total number of members of all cooperating teams is less than 150 members. Product releases produced by major teams consist of changes contributed by the multiple teams, all collaborating on a common product release. Example applications include most software products produced by all but the largest ISVs, major mission-critical IS/IT applications, and major e-commerce Web sites. Major project teams almost always require the capabilities of a modern SCM tool. In some cases, they would benefit from some of the more advanced SCM tool capabilities.

Extensive Project Teams

An extensive project team consists of a large number of cooperating teams of various sizes (5 to 50 members), all working toward a common release of one or more products. The total number of members of all cooperating teams is 150 or greater. Significant code sharing and intercomponent dependencies occur. Extensive teams are highly likely to have teams and team members located at different sites. Product releases are usually longer (12 to 24 months). Example applications include large ISV applications, telecom/datacom systems, and military/government applications. Extensive project teams require the most flexible and advanced SCM capabilities they can find.

2.2.2 In the Absence of SCM Tools

Without an SCM tool, developers make different attempts to overcome the problem of managing multiple versions of files that make up an evolving software system. For individuals, this is often done using copies of system files. For smaller teams, an additional copy of the entire system directory structure can be created to store the latest versions of the software. This is called the shared copy approach. This section discusses both approaches to solving SCM problems without an SCM tool.

> **NOTE**
> The solutions presented here should be considered workarounds, given the availability of low-cost SCM tools. There is almost no reason not to employ some form of SCM tool on all your software-development projects.

Using File Copies to Support Early SCM

One of the first SCM-related problems was the storage of different versions of the software, specifically:

- Storing backup versions of the software system
- Storing intermediate working versions, of certain files or of all the files that make up the system, during the development process

Individuals developing their own software systems were the first to face these problems (see the "Individual Projects" section, earlier in this chapter). Let's consider an example. Suppose that you are writing a small personal-use application that reads in some data from an unformatted text file and outputs a formatted HTML file. You have written a lot of Perl and have a personal library of

Perl routines that you include in your application. The application consists of two files, genhtml and myfunctions.pl. You developed and tested this application and have been happy with it for a couple of months. Now you want to add some options to your genhtml script regarding how the HTML is formatted.

If you simply begin modifying the Perl script, you will lose the previous version of genhtml that worked. You need a way to store a copy of the previous version of your application as a backup before you begin making changes.

Without an SCM tool, the solution to these problems is rather simple and obvious: Store a complete backup copy of the entire system by copying the entire directory tree that contains the system—for example:

```
/mysystem_latest_version
/mysystem_release1
/mysystem_workstoday_jun3_1999
```

Make changes to the application under the directory mysystem_latest_version, and when it is stable or ready to be released, make a copy under a directory using a descriptive name such as mysystem_release1.

You can also use copies to store intermediate file versions. For example, you could save versions such as the following:

```
genhtml.bak
genhtml.bak2
genhtml.030699
genhtml.featureA_working
```

This solution works well for individuals; however, it becomes problematic for small projects and does not scale at all for modest- to extensive-size projects.

The Shared Copy Approach

With multiple uncontrolled copies of the software system residing on each developer's machine, the next SCM problem, which was first encountered by small teams, was keeping track of the location of the "good" software. The initial solution was to create a common system directory in which each team member could copy new versions of the files, a solution similar to that used by the individual. With the *shared copy approach,* each individual in a small team makes one or more copies of the software system in a private directory and works as if following the individual model, as described previously.

Here's an example. Suppose that you are part of a team of three, including Joe and Shirley, working on a small C-language application. The team has created one common system directory in which to store the finished code, so there are at least four copies of the system (see Figure 2-1). A team member who adds a new feature or makes a change copies the changed files into the common system directory (see Figure 2-2).

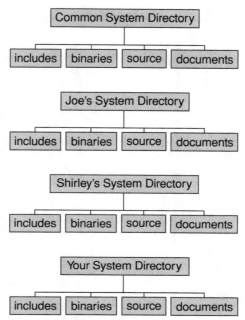

Figure 2-1   Copies of the system directory structure.

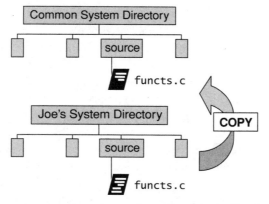

Figure 2-2   Using a copy to promote a change from directory to directory.

At first, the shared copy approach seems fine. But, in reality, it poses several new problems:

- The copy-over problem causes versions of files to be lost.
- Recovery from inappropriate changes made to the common code is difficult or impossible.
- The number of uncontrolled copies of files makes it difficult to determine where the latest version really exists.
- It is impossible to determine who made what change and when it was made.

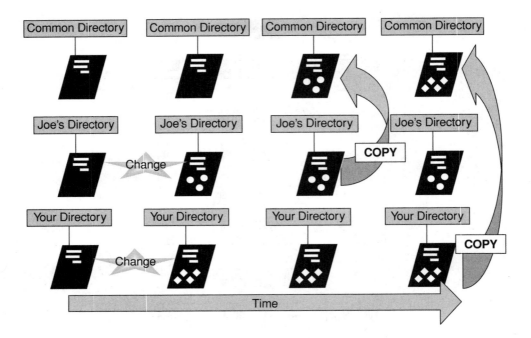

Figure 2-3   The copy-over problem.

The first problem, the copy-over problem, causes working versions to be lost. This happens when two developers work on the same file at the same time. They both take copies of the file from the common system directory and make changes. Then first one developer and then the other copies the new version to the common system directory, thus overwriting one of the new versions (see Figure 2-3). Using the shared copy approach, you have no way to know when parallel changes are occurring or to guard against them.

The second problem is that it is difficult or impossible to recover from inappropriate changes to the common source code. This is because there is no way to see what changes have occurred in the common project area and thus to determine who made those changes and when.

The third problem is that many copies of the application's files are stored in many places under many different names. It quickly becomes difficult to find out where the latest version of a file is located.

As described earlier, the initial solution to the problems introduced by using the shared copy approach was to assign a CM librarian to manage the system directory where shared, or common, artifacts were stored. This manual and error-prone approach to SCM was largely automated by early SCM tools.

The fourth problem, that of not being able to determine what changes have been introduced into a software system, and its corollary problem of being unable to determine who introduced a change, presents severe restrictions on the auditability of changes introduced into the software system and on project accountability. Auditability isn't just a concern for financial institutions or for projects concerned with regulatory compliance. Auditability, in this context, means the capability to determine that the desired features and fixes that should be in the software are actually there and the inverse: that the features and fixes that are in the software are there because they ought to be. Accountability simply means being able to discover who made a particular change to the software. This accountability is required, at a very basic level, to be able to ask a person about the specific changes they made to the software, but as the project grows, this capability allows an elaboration of the processes around project security to allow, for example, restrictions to be placed on who is permitted to make changes to the software system or to its parts.

2.2.3   Early SCM Tool Support

To manage multiple versions of system files, early SCM tools introduced the concept of an SCM repository that stored not only the latest copy of the system (as in the shared copy approach), but all versions of the files. How these tools automated the manual check-out/check-in model is described in the next section. Because every version of every file was being stored, disk space became the next problem these teams encountered. To combat this problem, early SCM tools introduced the notion of storing just the changes made between one file version and the next. This concept, called delta storage, is discussed in the "Delta Storage Mechanism" section, later in this chapter.

Early SCM tools, however, lacked the capabilities required to solve problems being encountered by modest and major project teams. These capabilities were typically implemented as scripts on top of early SCM tools. The problems encountered and the scripting solutions are described in the "Early Workspace Management," "Early Build Management," and "Early Release Management/Product Maintenance" sections in this chapter.

The SCM Repository and Check-Out/Check-In Model

Early SCM tools, many of which are still in use today, were based on the manual library system model. The tools created a repository in which to store the application files rather than storing them in the file system. A developer wanting to work on a file checked out the file. The check-out operation provided a copy of the file to work on, thereby ensuring that the developer worked on the latest version of the file. The check-out operation also recorded who performed the check-out and when it was performed, and often allowed the developer to record why the file was checked out.

The check-out also locked the file so that no one else could modify the file until it was checked back in. The developer would make changes to the checked-out file and then issue a check-in operation. This operation took a copy of the file from the developer and placed it in the repository. It also recorded who did the check-in and when, and usually asked the developer to record a brief description of what was changed. The check-in then released the lock on that file, thereby allowing other developers to make changes (see Figure 2-4).

The locking step was designed to avoid the problem encountered when two developers made changes to the same files at the same time (see "The Shared Copy Approach" section, earlier in this chapter). It had the effect of serializing changes to any file in the system. This introduced other problems, which are discussed in the "Concurrent Changes to the Same Project Files" section, later in this chapter.

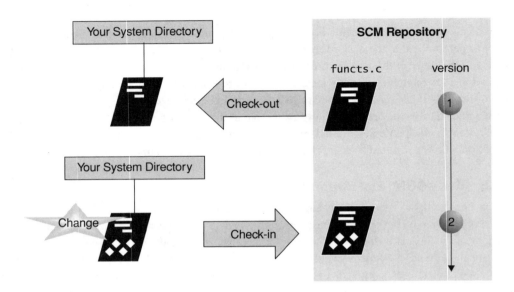

Figure 2-4   The check-out and check-in operations.

Delta Storage Mechanism

With the introduction of an SCM repository, every version of a file ever produced was stored. This caused a disk space problem at a time when disk space was not cheap. So, SCM tools introduced a new technique of storing only what had changed from one version to the next. What has changed is called a *delta*.

The delta storage mechanism conserved disk space at a cost, measured by the time it takes to construct any particular version of a file. Most SCM tools had an additional operation called Get or Fetch that was used to extract a specific version of a file from the repository.

Three basic approaches are taken to delta storage: forward, backward, and inline. The first, *forward delta* storage, stores the first version of a file in its entirety and then stores incremental deltas. The forward delta mechanism is very space-efficient because it does not require full contents of versions at every leaf node in the version tree. However, the more changes are made to a file, the longer the time it takes to construct versions of the file. Consequently, it takes the longest amount of time to construct the most-often-needed version, the latest one.

The second approach is called *backward delta* (or reverse delta) storage. This mechanism stores the latest version of the file in its entirety and keeps deltas of the previous versions. This greatly improves the time that it takes to construct the latest version, in comparison with forward delta storage. However, it is less inefficient in constructing earlier versions. Backward delta storage was used by RCS when it was first released. Since that time RCS' storage mechanism has been modified to use backward delta storage on the main trunk of development and forward delta storage on branches off of the main trunk.

The third mechanism, used by SCCS and ClearCase, is called *inline delta* storage. With this approach, no whole copy is stored. Instead, the deltas are stored in place in the file, with some special notation. In this way, constructing any version of the file takes a consistent amount of time.

ClearCase takes this approach even further: It caches a full copy of any version that is accessed often. These copies are stored in one or more managed caches called clear-text caches. In this way, all versions of a file that are being accessed on a regular basis are available immediately. A ClearCase utility, called the Scrubber, is used to remove versions from the cache that have not been recently accessed. The Scrubber can be configured to specify how often it runs and how long file versions remain in the cache. This allows the organization to optimize for both access speed and disk space use.

Early Workspace Management

Early SCM tools provided a means of getting only specific versions of files out of the repository. To construct a development environment, one needed to create a system directory structure and then populate it with the "right" versions of the "right" files. With many hundreds or thousands of files, this became difficult.

A new abstraction, not yet implemented in the early SCM tools, came into being, called the *workspace*. A workspace is a copy of all the "right" versions of all the "right" files in the "right" directories, which can then be used to perform a specific task. The process of creating and maintaining a workspace is called *workspace management*. For example, suppose that you are a developer and you need to fix a defect found in Release 1 of your application. You will need a copy of the Release 1 version of all the files organized in the Release 1 directory structure.

The lack of any workspace management in early SCM tools caused two problems:

- Errors and time lost because of inconsistent workspaces
- Longer integration times near the end of the development cycle

The first problem is caused by constructing a workspace by manually picking the wrong versions from the library. This is inefficient because these versions might not build together. Worse, they might build together, and you would end up fixing problems against the wrong source code. For example, suppose that you need to fix a bug in Release 1. You erroneously create a workspace using the latest versions of the files, not the Release 1 versions. You fix the bug. The integrator then tries to incorporate the files that you changed into the Release 1 versions of the files, causing everything to break.

The second problem, long integration times, results from developers being isolated with their own copies of the system files and having no means to easily update the files they are working on to include other team members' changes. Without additional tooling, you'll find it difficult and error-prone to update your workspace with changes that other developers are making, so you might continue to make changes against an ever older set of source versions. This situation might not be apparent until later in the development cycle. Essentially, the last period of useful development time is given up to getting everyone's changes to work with everyone else's changes.

To avoid these problems, much scripting work went into providing early workspace-management functionality. Scripts were written on top of the `Get` functionality provided by early SCM tools. These early tools did not do any version control on the product directory structure, so scripts also provided automation that re-created an empty directory tree and populated it with particular versions of the files. Which versions were used was another usage model decision that varied widely by project. Also needed were mechanisms to update these early workspaces with changes made by other project members. Scripting provided these as well.

As projects became more sophisticated and SCM tools caught up, workspace management became a key component of many modern SCM tools.

Early Build Management

Build management is the management of the build process both at the individual developer level and at the project level. This was another area in which SCM automation was required, to reduce errors and improve efficiency. The build management strategy for SCM should be to minimize build times, to conserve disk space, and to maintain an audit of the build itself. Early build management focused on the first two points. It incorporated aspects of workspace management. A development workspace was not populated with all of the source files and prebuild libraries required to perform a build. Instead, the build tools knew where to find the "right" versions of the files to be built/linked.

Suppose you were going to do a build. To find a file to compile or a library to link, the SCM-automated build would look first in your application directory, then in the common application directory, and finally in the latest production application directory (see Figure 2-5). (Many variants of the widely used UNIX build tool called make refer to this as viewpathing—see "VPATH Macro" in [Oram, 1991].) If the SCM system doesn't provide an audit facility that

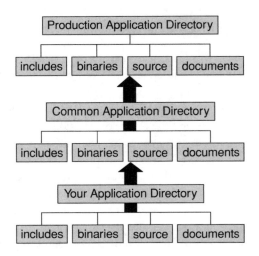

Figure 2-5   Build view path.

allows a comprehensive post-build review of exactly what went into a build, this automation brings with it new problems that in many ways are more insidious than the problems the automation was created to solve. Specifically, by using an implied search path to find a file, as described earlier, it became possible to have a workspace that was misconfigured in some way (for example, some crucial project-specific files or libraries were missing) but that would still yield a buildable system because a compatible, but wrong, version of the missing files would be found elsewhere in the search path. Without an audit facility provided by a robust SCM system, the fact that the system was built using the wrong configuration would often not be discovered until much later.

Early build management was established mainly to minimize the number of rebuilds, conserve disk space, and avoid having many uncontrolled copies of the software residing all over the network.

Early Release Management/Product Maintenance

Early release management focused on being able to rebuild a previous release so that it could be maintained (patched). An early solution was generally to copy the entire directory structure and the libraries being used from one major release to the next. This was a low-cost solution and required only more disk space. To fix a bug on Release 2, you went to the Release 2 area and used the Release 2 source libraries.

This worked, but it was an inefficient and error-prone process. Fixes to a release in the field also had to be made to the release being developed. Errors often were discovered when a known bug that had already been fixed reappeared in the latest release of the software. This was particularly problematic because often the bug showed up at the same customer site where it had originally been reported. That customer might have already been using a fixed version of the software when the new buggy release was installed (see Figure 2-6).

Release management incorporates aspects of workspace management and build management. The idea is that, starting from a clean slate, you create the right directory structure, extract the right files and their correct versions, and rebuild any important release of a software system from source.

The automation and scripting you do to support releasing and rebuilding are largely concerned with how file versions are labeled at release time. This is often trickier than you might expect. Files are in uncontrolled directory space, and a build can span multiple workspaces, so when you have a final build that successfully passes tests, it is crucial that you be able to determine what went into that build. This usually involves either scripting the labeling process with algorithms similar to those used to create the build environment or doing builds in a clean single workspace. The workspace script "extract these things from the library" becomes the script "label these things in the library." The "build the directory structure like this" piece of workspace management becomes the "remember how to build a directory structure like this" piece.

Typical problems at this stage included the following:

- Difficulties in developing the necessary scripting
- Differences in the algorithms used, causing the wrong versions to get labeled

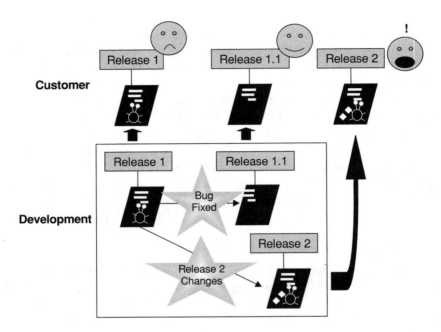

Figure 2-6   A bug reintroduced between releases.

- Failing to store the directory structure
- Failing to capture other aspects of the build environment, such as the version of the compiler that was used

See the "Modern Build and Release Management" section, later in this chapter, for details on how these problems are solved with modern SCM tools.

2.2.4 Modern SCM Tool Support

The amount of automation needed to support small teams early on was fairly significant. Very few modern SCM tools were available. Each company tended to build its own SCM tool layers and scripts. Worse, many projects in the same company built their own project-specific scripts. This meant that each project had to solve its own SCM problems and was plagued by issues in the SCM scripts that other projects in the same company had already solved or avoided. In the 1980s, the costs associated with maintaining these internal scripts became such that the decision to build versus buy took on a new slant. Modest-size project teams started looking for third-party solutions instead of trying to build their own.

A number of tools were developed, each approaching SCM from its own perspective. ClearCase was introduced to the market in the early 1990s. It provided out-of-the-box solutions to many of the problems that previously had required scripting. It was based on its own version-management technology and improved on a number of shortcomings of the predecessor tools of the time. It did not dictate any particular usage model, which further enhanced its success.

This section discusses some of the advances in modern SCM tools, including support for multiple individuals to modify the same file at the same time, support for multiple teams to modify the same software system at the same time, modern workspace management, and modern build and release management.

Concurrent Changes to the Same Project Files

When a developer checks out a file, typically the file is locked to that developer until he or she is done making changes. Locking via the SCM tool was used to solve the copy-over problem (see "The Shared Copy Approach" section, earlier in this chapter). However, locking also serializes changes to any one file, which can slow down development and, in some cases, may cause developers to work around the SCM tool by taking a copy of the source without checking out the file. One approach to reducing contention for files is to break up the system into more files. However, this does not adequately solve the problem because, no matter how small you break up a system, there will always be times when two or more developers need to access the same file. To remove the bottleneck, you need an SCM tool that supports the capability for two or more developers to change the same file at the same time. In addition, it must support a way to merge those changes at the right time.

ClearCase solves this problem by slightly modifying the check-out/check-in paradigm. Traditionally, when a file is checked out, nobody else can check it out until the original person either checks it in or cancels the check-out. With ClearCase, anyone can check out a file. Check-ins, however, are controlled by using different types of check-outs.

A check-out can be either of two different types: reserved or unreserved. In a *reserved check-out*, the person who has the file checked out is guaranteed to be the person who will check it in first. Thus, there may be only one reserved check-out for any given file. (For those of you familiar with SCM and ClearCase, you know that really this is one reserved check-out per element per branch, but we aren't there yet, so hang on.) If a file has a reserved check-out, attempts by other developers to perform a reserved check-out will fail. When the developer with the reserved check-out checks in the file, a new version is created for that file as usual. Figure 2-7 illustrates a reserved check-out and subsequent check-in.

An *unreserved check-out* differs from a reserved check-out only in that you cannot guarantee that you will be the next person to check in. There can be any number of unreserved check-outs on the same file. This means that even if a file has a reserved check-out, you can still check out the file using an unreserved check-out.

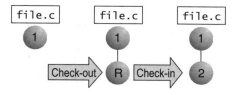

Figure 2-7   Normal reserved check-out.

In general, the first person (say, developer A) to check out a file acquires a reserved check-out. The second person (say, developer B) to check out the file will receive an error that indicates that the file is already on reserved check-out. Developer B can do one of three things:

1. Wait until developer A checks in

2. Go talk to developer A to see what changes are being made (a good idea) and how long they will take

3. Check out the file with an unreserved status

The unreserved check-out offers a way for any developer to get access to any file at any time. It avoids the problem of developers working around the SCM tool to gain access to a file that has been exclusively locked.

Figure 2-8 illustrates a file named file.c that has been checked out using both a reserved check-out made by developer A and an unreserved check-out made by developer B.

What happens during check-in? For developer A, who has a reserved check-out, check-in will proceed as usual. Developer B, who has an unreserved check-out, will receive an error when trying to check in until one of three things occurs:

- *Developer A, with the reserved check-out, checks in the file.*

   If developer A checks in the file, developer B, with the unreserved check-out, will not be able to immediately check in. ClearCase requires developer B first to merge B's changes with A's changes. This is done to avoid the copy-over problem described in "The Shared Copy Approach" section, earlier in this chapter. When this merge has been performed, then developer B can check in the file containing the combined changes. Figure 2-9 illustrates this scenario.

- *Developer A, with the reserved check-out, cancels the check-out.*

   Then developer B can check in without performing any merge operation because there are no changes to merge. Figure 2-10 illustrates this scenario.

- *Developer A, with the reserved check-out, changes the type of check-out from reserved to unreserved.*

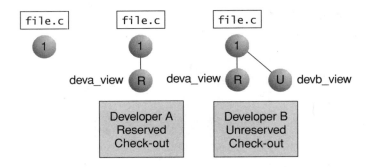

Figure 2-8   Reserved and unreserved check-outs.

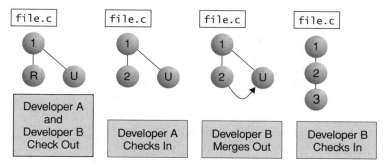

Figure 2-9   Reserved/unreserved check-out: normal resolution.

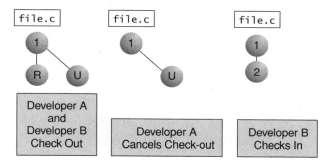

Figure 2-10   Reserved/unreserved check-out: resolution through cancellation.

With ClearCase, developer A can change the type of A's check-out from reserved to unreserved. In this case, the file now has multiple unreserved check-outs but no reserved check-outs. Developer B can now check in without performing any merge operation because there are no changes to merge. When this situation occurs, the first file to be checked in does not require any merge. Note, however, that developer A will now be required to merge developer B's changes before being able to check in, just as in the first case. Figure 2-11 illustrates this scenario.

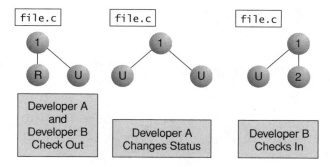

Figure 2-11   Reserved/unreserved check-out: resolution through change of reservation status.

By modifying the check-out/check-in paradigm using reserved and unreserved check-outs, and supporting a tool for merging file changes, ClearCase allows parallel changes to occur to the same files at the same time. Thus, you can avoid a common SCM bottleneck, as well as the errors and complexity introduced by the other workarounds.

Not only is it essential to be able to modify the same files at the same time, but you also must be able to work on parallel releases of the entire software system at the same time. This topic is covered next.

Parallel Development Support

Demand for more functionality available sooner in software development continues to increase. This leads to larger development teams and more complex software systems. Reducing time to market requires reducing or eliminating serialized change by supporting parallel development. Parallel development, or two or more individuals or teams making changes to individual files and/or an entire software system at the same time, also includes the capability to merge these changes after they have been made in parallel.

In the past, releases were developed serially: Release 1, followed by Release 2, and then Release 3, and so on. Ensuring that defect fixes made during maintenance were also made in later releases was sometimes problematic but manageable. To further reduce time to market, however, you must apply more resources so that you can develop Release 2 at the same time as Release 1, and sometimes Release 3 at the same time as well. This is parallel development occurring on the entire software system. Figure 2-12 illustrates the time savings associated with developing releases in parallel.

The introduction of parallel development not only decreases time to market, but also means that some functionality as well as defect fixes have to get into later releases. At this point, the shared copy approach to parallel releases truly breaks down. It requires too much overhead in merging work and maintenance time, and lacks traceability among the various copies of the files or the copies of the source libraries. However, doing parallel development is essential to surviving in the fast-growing, competitive software market. The next section explores the SCM tool

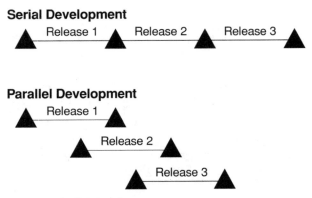

Figure 2-12   Serial versus parallel development.

approach used to support parallel development, which does not lose traceability between file versions and makes it easier to merge changes between parallel releases.

Branching is used to support parallel development across all files in a software system. A *branch* is a means of organizing file versions and showing their history. It is called a branch because the version organization looks like a tree. Early SCM tools used a built-in numbering convention that often became difficult to interpret. Modern SCM tools enable you to name branches, as can be seen in Figure 2-13, which has branches named main, fuji_rel1, fuji_rel2, and fuji_boston_rel2. The ability to use mnemonic names for branches provides an important capability that assists in making the development structure of a project self-describing. For example, if you see a branch with a name of 1.3.1, it is hard to determine what work might have been done on that branch. If, however, you see a branch with a name of release_1_bugfixes, it isn't a great leap to conclude that the branch likely contains work done to fix defects in Release 1 of the project.

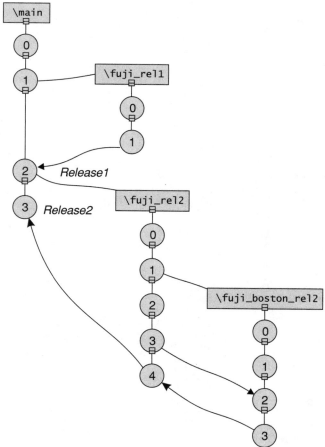

Figure 2-13 Version tree.

For any given file, a set of versions is produced over time. These are collected for any specific line of development, such as a release. When releases are developed in parallel, you must maintain multiple lines of development simultaneously. This is done by branching. A branch records the version from which it originated. This enables you to maintain parallel lines of development and see this record visually. Branching is similar to the unreserved check-outs used for individual files, except that branches are permanent.

Figure 2-14 shows an initial Release 1 that was produced on a branch called main. After the release was produced, development of Release 1.1 and Release 2 was executed in parallel.

Another key aspect to branching is the capability to merge (or integrate) changes from one release to the next. This is similar to the merge that occurs during an unreserved check-in, except that it occurs across the entire source code base. The record of the merge is important because it helps to determine what files require merging in the future and assists in auditing the flow of changes. Figure 2-15 shows a merge that has occurred from the final version of release 1.1 into both the main branch and into the Release 2 branch. Both merges are indicated by arrows from a version on one branch to a version on another.

In addition to developing parallel releases, there are other reasons for parallel work and branches:

- Prototype development
- Customer variants
- Platform variants or ports
- Serialized major releases
- Patches
- Patch bundles/service packs
- Emergency production fixes

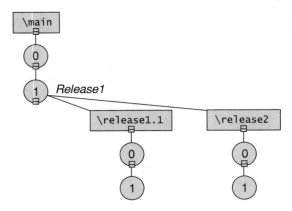

Figure 2-14   Version tree: Release 1.1 and Release 2 branching.

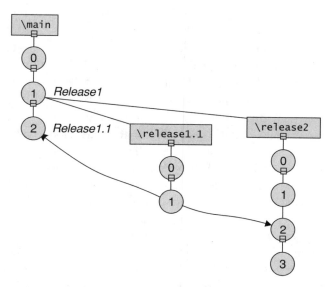

Figure 2-15   Version tree: Release 1.1 and Release 2 merging.

- Individual task isolation
- Promotion model support
- Individual workspace isolation

Regardless of the reasons, modern SCM tools must provide strong support for branching, to allow parallel development. They must also provide strong support for merging changes at the appropriate time. Merge support must be for both merging individual files and merging complete lines of development across the entire source code base.

Modern Workspace Management

As discussed in the "Early Workspace Management" section, earlier in this chapter, early tools such as SCCS did not provide any workspace management—only a means of pulling a particular version of a particular file from the library. Therefore, scripting was required. The key operations needing support were re-creating the product directory structure, populating the directory structure with the "right" file versions, and later updating a workspace to include newer versions.

The next generation of commercially available SCM tools, therefore, had to support these operations to support larger and more complex software-development efforts. Support for this in the SCM tools themselves reduced the amount of scripting required by each project team and reduced the number of errors that can result from manually creating, populating, and updating workspaces.

ClearCase provides workspace management out of the box. This is discussed in the section "Workspaces: Snapshot and Dynamic Views" of Chapter 4, "A Functional Overview of ClearCase Objects."

Modern Build and Release Management

Large teams usually face more complexity than smaller teams when building their software applications, making it more difficult to reproduce any given build. Modern build-and-release management techniques are aimed at ensuring that significant builds of the system are deterministic and can be reproduced and maintained. The build-and-release process involves the following steps:

1. **Identify the versions of the source to be built.** Modern tools provide a mechanism to identify and label specific versions of files. This labeling process identifies a consistent configuration. ClearCase provides both a mechanism to identify specific file versions (labeling) and a means to identify a set of file versions that make up a component. It also provides a means of creating versions of a component, called a baseline. Furthermore, ClearCase allows consistent configurations of baselines from different components to be organized into subsystems by using composite baselines. A composite baseline is a mechanism for grouping component baselines into a logical collection; this is discussed in more detail in subsequent chapters. Composite baselines, in turn, can themselves contain composite baselines. This capability to use composite baselines to recursively organize software systems into subsystems provides very complex projects with a powerful tool to define, control, and manage their work.

    An additional step that is often overlooked and not supported in early SCM tools is version control of the directory structure. Directories are versioned in ClearCase, so a particular version of a directory is identified when determining what sources to build. In this way, if you are building Release 1 of a system, you will see the directory structure as it was when Release 1 was built. If you are building Release 2, the directory structure will reflect the structure as it existed for Release 2.

2. **Create or populate a clean workspace that selects those versions (and is locked).** This step is the same as creating a workspace for doing development, except that no source files will be checked out and you want to ensure that versions of the files selected do not change or get updated while the build is in progress. So, there must be a means to lock the versions that are being selected. A clean workspace means that there are no unnecessary files or old build objects left around in the workspace prior to the build being performed.

3. **Perform and audit the build.** Building means turning the source into output files such as object files, libraries, and executables or downloadable images. Auditing is keeping track of how each output file was built. This includes recording who built it, when and on what platform it was built, which versions of any include files were referenced during the build, and which options were sent to the build tools (such as the compiler or linker). This audit trail can be used later to compare two different builds, assist in reproducing a build, serve as input to the labeling process, and so on. It is often necessary to be able to completely reproduce the build environment. This might mean storing the versions of

the build tools used, the operating system definitions files, and even the hardware machines used to perform the build.

4. **Stage the files produced by the build and the build audit.** Staging is the process of putting the built or derived objects under version control. This is another key step that is often overlooked. In particular, at least the derived object files and other files that are shipped to a customer or put onto the release media should be placed under version control, along with the audit information. This provides a secure copy of released media and supports component- based development because other teams can use specific versions of these runtime objects (such as libraries) instead of having to fully build the entire system.

5. **Identify the staged files.** When the files and their audit history have been placed under version control, the versions should also be identified by attaching a label or creating a new baseline.

6. **Produce the necessary media.** The final step is to produce the necessary media—for example, by burning a CD-ROM, downloading to an embedded processor, or pushing content to a Web site.

Chapter 10, "Building, Baselining, and Release Deployment," discusses how ClearCase supports build management and the release process.

2.2.5   Advanced SCM Tool Support

When projects reach extensive size, their primary difficulties concern communication and complexity. Managing change is imperative. Automation and more advanced administration capabilities are key to success.

Fundamental capabilities needed in an SCM tool for extensive-size teams include support for geographically distributed development, component-based development, and activity-based configuration management. These are discussed briefly here and in more detail later in the book.

Geographically Distributed Development

Geographically distributed development is the development of a software system by team members and/or teams located in different geographical regions. This could be teams or team members distributed at different sites in the same city or in different cities around the world. Such development is almost unavoidable in extensive-size projects and is becoming normal today because of the many acquisitions and mergers that are occurring. Chapter 11 covers this topic in detail.

Component-Based Development

Management of large, complex software systems being developed by extensive teams requires breaking down the software system into smaller building blocks. *Component-based development* is the development of a software system by decomposing it into smaller pieces called components, either during design or while rearchitecting an existing system. Components have well-defined interfaces and can have build-time or runtime dependencies on other components. (See the chapter "Components in Booch" in [Booch, 1999] for more general component information.) For configuration-management purposes, you need to be able to identify component versions and to assemble a consistent set of component versions, to create a version of the system as a whole.

The SCM best practice of component management is discussed in the section "Organize Versioned Artifacts into Versioned Components" in Chapter 1, "What Is Software Configuration Management?" ClearCase UCM support of component-based development is discussed in the ClearCase Components section in Chapter 3, "An Overview of the Unified Change Management Model."

Activity-Based Configuration Management

Activity-based configuration management is the management of changes to a software system that is based on higher-level activities (for example, task, defect, enhancement) rather than individual file versions. This requires an SCM tool to track which file versions implement the work required for a specific activity and then to present activities as a key object in the SCM tool. The idea is to reduce complexity and ensure that when the system says a fix for a defect is included in a specific build, all of the file-level changes required to implement that fix have, in fact, been included.

The best practice behind activity-based configuration management is discussed in the "Organize and Integrate Consistent Sets of Versions Using Activities" section in Chapter 1. ClearCase UCM support for activity-based configuration management is covered throughout the remainder of this book. Particular attention is given to the project manager role in Chapter 6, "Project Management in ClearCase," and to the developer role in Chapter 8, "Development Using the ClearCase UCM Model."

2.3   Summary

Software configuration management is an essential engineering discipline for the success of your software projects. A project's SCM requirements will change over time because of the increasing complexity of the software system being developed, the increasing complexity of the project environment needed to develop the software system, changing requirements based on the development life cycle phase, and changes to an organization's management processes or personnel.

The SCM tool that you use must be both flexible and scalable, so as to meet your changing project requirements. It is up to the project manager to take software configuration management seriously and to strike the right balance between process enforcement and configuration audit. The objective must be to maximize the rate of change (productivity) while still maintaining control, to produce a high-quality product on time with the required functionality.

ClearCase is a commercially available SCM tool that provides the capabilities described in this chapter. The remainder of this book focuses on how ClearCase supports SCM and the SCM best practices, and how it can be applied to a wide variety of software-development projects. Much of the discussion is oriented to the IBM Rational Software approach to managing change, called Unified Change Management (UCM).

CHAPTER 3

An Overview of the Unified Change Management Model

Although most software-development organizations recognize the value of and the need to use a software-configuration management tool to control software development, relatively few understand what effective software configuration management is. Even fewer have constructed a means for software configuration management that provides business value. This chapter explores exactly what Unified Change Management (UCM) is, along with the specific traits that allow it to provide value to a development organization. We discuss the underlying functionality of ClearCase and ClearQuest that serve as the foundations for UCM, and we explore the roles that exist in a software-development project, and how they intersect and interact with the UCM process.

3.1   What Is UCM?

Unified Change Management is a software-configuration management process for software development that spans the development life cycle, managing change to requirements, design models, documentation, components, test cases, and source code. The UCM model reflects the 20-plus years of experience Rational Software has providing software development and SCM solutions to a broad range of customers. Rational studied the companies using the general-purpose ClearCase solution and found that many of them followed similar usage model patterns. Rational studied these models and applied their best practices to define the UCM model, generalizing the implementation for easy configuration in diverse development environments.

Fundamental to UCM is the unification of the activities used to plan and track project progress with the artifacts being changed (see Figure 3-1). Implementation of the UCM model is realized by both process and tools:

- ClearCase manages all the artifacts produced by a software project, including system artifacts and project-management artifacts.

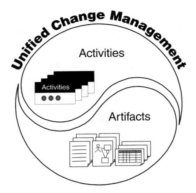

Figure 3-1   Unified Change Management, combining activities and artifacts.

- ClearQuest, while not required for UCM, provides enhanced management capabilities for the project's defects and requests for enhancements (referred to generically as activities), and provides the charting and reporting tools necessary to track project progress.

3.2   The Value of UCM

UCM was derived from observed best practices in thousands of development organizations that demonstrated a capability to develop software in a robust, scalable, and repeatable way. By automating these best practices, UCM provides value to a development organization in many ways, but four areas are key:

- Abstraction
- Stability
- Control
- Communication

These key areas are discussed next.

3.2.1   Abstraction

Through the unification of activities and artifacts, UCM raises the level of abstraction at which software development work is done. Humans naturally work at a high level of abstraction—that is, we work best on higher-level tasks, such as "Fix bug 22" or "Implement a search function for the Web page." We are less adept at keeping track of minute details of the things we do to accomplish those higher-level tasks. UCM lets practitioners work in the abstraction space at which humans are most efficient. While that work is underway, UCM uses the underlying functionality provided by ClearCase and ClearQuest to keep track of the details of what is done to individual artifacts and information about artifacts. This means that developers are able to do their tasks faster because they aren't encumbered by the burden of tracking the changes they make for each task; they are free to concentrate on the higher-level problems that make up their assigned tasks. This also means that integrating their tasks with the overall project will be faster and less error-prone because UCM will have kept track of the work they did and will guarantee that all of their work for an activity will be delivered to the project without the prospect of accidentally forgetting to include some work.

3.2.2 Stability

Stability is important to projects as a whole and to individual project team members. Stability in a project means that the project progresses in a known, controlled way with markers placed along the way to denote intermediate stable points. UCM provides project baselines as constructs that enable this type of project stability, as well as processes to manage these project baselines. UCM uses these baselines to implement a "baseline + change" approach to workspace configuration (see Section 3.3.2, "The UCM Baseline + Change Model").

To software developers, stability means that the work areas in which developers make their changes to project artifacts are private and isolated. Not sharing a workspace with multiple team members allows a developer to work without fear that an arbitrary, unplanned change to their workspace will impede their ability to work on their assigned activities. UCM makes it easy for developers to work in stable work areas. It allows this stability first by providing personal work-spaces, or "sandboxes," that are private. When a developer joins a UCM project, part of that process includes creating at least one individual, private workspace. This workspace is the area where developers modify and test their changes before committing them to the underlying repository. UCM automatically configures workspaces for the individual developer so that they conform to the development policies defined in the UCM project.

The second way UCM provides stability for developers is by providing automated facilities to allow developers to work individually or together in groups of their own choosing on their own isolated streams of development. By isolating development onto individual streams, developers can commit their code revisions to the repository at any time, whether the code is stable or not, without fear of destabilizing the project or other developers not sharing that stream. Conversely, developers know that they are protected from the changes that other developers might commit to the repository on their respective streams. The result is that developers can work on their tasks, checkpoint their changes as they determine appropriate, and then exercise the control that UCM provides to manage the flow of changes to and from other developers.

3.2.3 Control

A team of developers cannot work in isolation from one another and then expect a complex software system to materialize independently out of those isolated pieces. Along with the isolation that provides stability comes a need for some control to assist in managing, tracking, and controlling the flow of the changes that were made in isolation. UCM provides these mechanisms to automatically manage and track the changes a developer makes in a private work area and isolated stream. Then UCM provides the control mechanisms to assist in managing the flow of changes from a developer's isolated development stream to a project-integration area or to other developers; tracking, managing, and controlling the flow of changes from the project's integration area or from other developer's streams; and assisting in integrating those changes.

3.2.4 Communication

The same mechanisms that UCM uses to provide abstraction, stability, and control also yield information about individual activities, relieving developers of the burden of remembering the specific files and versions they created to fulfill activities on which they worked. Furthermore, the mechanisms that UCM provides for tracking and controlling the flow of changes in a project enables team leaders and also individual team members to quickly assess the status and progress of the project at any time with up-to-date information derived directly from UCM data.

ClearCase provides the foundation upon which the UCM process is built. ClearQuest is not required for the operation of UCM, but it can be used with UCM to provide significant advantages in communicating, tracking, and controlling the flow of activities through an organization's software-development process.

3.3   What Is ClearCase?

ClearCase is an SCM tool that provides automation and support for the SCM best practices (see the "SCM Best Practices" section in Chapter 1, "What Is Software Configuration Management?"). ClearCase provides an open architecture that is used to implement and automate a wide range of SCM solutions. ClearCase is employed in many different development environments on many types of applications, such as IS/IT systems, embedded systems, telecommunication systems, financial applications, Web site content, and other commercial and government software systems. Today companies in many diverse industries are successfully using ClearCase as the cornerstone of their SCM environments.

ClearCase solves a broad range of SCM-related problems and provides both general-purpose and specific solutions. The general-purpose solutions make very few assumptions about how ClearCase will be applied to a development environment. A certain amount of effort is required to determine how best to apply the general-purpose solution to specific SCM needs. This general-purpose SCM functionality is referred to in this book as base ClearCase. For those looking to apply SCM in the shortest period of time with the least effort, ClearCase also supports the UCM out-of-the-box usage model, which provides a specific solution. You must decide whether to invest in tailoring base ClearCase (the general solution) to your environment or to begin with the UCM model (the specific solution) and later extend it for your own requirements.

3.3.1 The ClearCase UCM Model

ClearCase UCM is based on two key concepts: activity-based SCM and component management. Both of these concepts are evident in the more advanced usage models built on top of ClearCase.

Activity-based SCM is a means of creating and manipulating a consistent change as a single named entity rather than a set of file versions. A set of versions is called a *change set* in ClearCase. The change set is an *attribute* of an activity. An *activity* is a named object that identifies the specific task, defect, feature, or requirement implemented or satisfied by the versions in the activity's change set.

Component management is a method of breaking a software system into smaller manageable pieces. Specifically, in ClearCase and SCM, component management is a means of collecting a set of files and directories into a larger entity that can be versioned and managed as a whole.

The UCM model focuses on minimizing the disruption to the software developer while maximizing the benefits gained from following sound SCM best practices. The project manager and integrator are provided with the tools necessary to manage the SCM aspects of the project in an intuitive fashion. Because the UCM model provides higher-level objects and a well-defined process, a significant number of manual steps have been automated. Therefore, for example, a developer does not need to understand the branching structure being used to manage parallel development.

Briefly, ClearCase UCM works as follows:

1. Software files and directories are organized into versioned components (ideally based on your system architecture).

2. Project managers create projects and assign project teams to work on these components.

3. Developers make changes to components, files, and directories based on assigned activities (tasks, defects, change requests).

4. New file and directory versions are collected during development and associated with activities (such as change sets).

5. When complete, activities and their associated change sets are delivered and integrated in a shared project-integration area.

6. New component baselines are created, tested, and promoted.

7. Component baselines are assembled into subsystems.

8. Subsystems are tested and released.

9. Subsystems are assembled into systems.

10. Systems are tested and released.

Next let's look more specifically at how the ClearCase UCM model works by attempting to understand its approach to workspace configuration.

3.3.2   The UCM Baseline + Change Model

ClearCase UCM provides support for the SCM best practices of organizing and integrating consistent sets of versions using activities and maintaining stable and consistent workspaces. This is done by implementing an approach to workspace configuration called a baseline + change model. A configuration consists of an identified set of files and directories in which there is only one version of each file and directory. You could define a configuration by specifying a list of files and the exact versions of each of those files, but that would be highly inefficient unless you are dealing with only a handful of files. This approach is also error-prone because you might pick an inconsistent set of file versions. Figure 3-2 shows an example of defining a configuration based on file versions. Each file, a through h, has a number of versions. A configuration picks a subset of the files and identifies one version of each file (for example, `filea` selects Version 1, `fileb` selects Version 3, and so on).

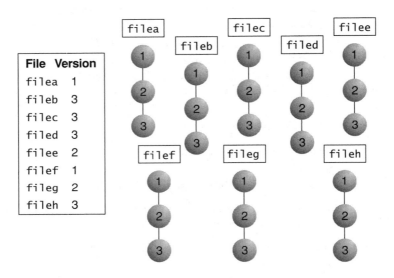

File	Version
filea	1
fileb	3
filec	3
filed	3
filee	2
filef	1
fileg	2
fileh	3

Figure 3-2   Example of file/version selection.

It is far easier to group files into a larger unit if the larger unit is versioned. In ClearCase UCM, that unit is a "component," and a version of a component is a "baseline." So, by picking a set of component baselines, ClearCase can automatically pick the right versions of the all files. In this way, you are more likely to get a consistent set of file versions. The set of component baselines defines the "foundation" for the stream's configuration. Because baselines cannot change content (they are immutable), you know that you have a stable point from which to begin your work. Figure 3-3 shows an example of picking component baselines. This is the "baseline" piece of the baseline + change model. Illustrated are two components, Alpha and Beta. Component Alpha contains five files, a through e, and has two baselines, BL1 and BL2, which select a particular version of each of the elements. Component Beta contains three files, f through h, and has three baselines, BL1, BL2, and BL3.

When you begin working in your development stream, you make changes to individual files and create new versions of files. You could list all the file versions you have created and select the component baselines and the file versions for your stream configuration. But this is an inefficient and error-prone approach because you might forget that you changed some files or might list the wrong versions. It is easier to indicate which component baselines and activities

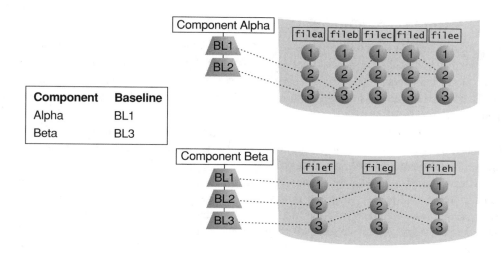

Figure 3-3 Example of component baseline selection.

you want to have in your stream and let ClearCase figure out the right files and versions to select. (The activities represent the "change" piece of the baseline + change model.)

In summary, you can determine any stream configuration in UCM by looking at its foundation baselines plus the activities that are being worked on or that have been worked on in the stream. Figure 3-4 illustrates a development stream configuration based on component baselines and activities.

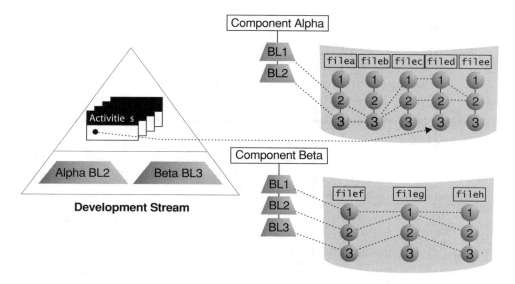

Figure 3-4 Baseline + change view/stream configuration artifacts.

3.4   What Is ClearQuest?

ClearQuest is an IBM Rational Software product that provides out-of-the-box support for recording, tracking, and reporting on all types of requests for change to a software system (such as defects and enhancement requests). Underlying ClearQuest is a customizable-workflow engine that enables organizations to define and enforce the process to which they want requests for change to conform.

ClearQuest has three key parts: a user interface (the client); a back-end core, which provides an interface to the data store; and a designer used to create and customize the change-request management interface and processes.

ClearQuest can be used to extend the UCM model with support for change request management. The UCM process diagram in Figure 3-5 shows two steps the project manager performs: assign and schedule work, and monitor project status. ClearQuest is the technology that supports these steps. With ClearCase alone, activities have only a name, a one-line description, and a change set. ClearCase maintains the essential configuration-management information, but not the change-request management information. To support change request management, additional data must be maintained, such as state, assigned user, a long description, priority, severity,

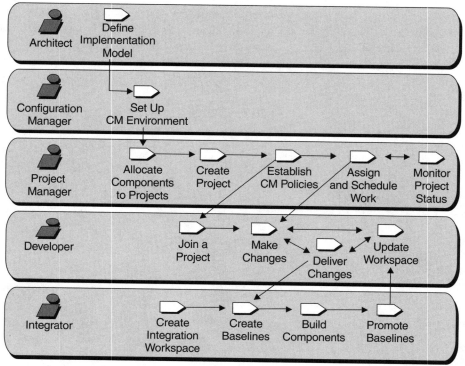

Figure 3-5   UCM process overview.

Source: This figure is based on the configuration and change-management core workflow of the Rational Unified Process [RUP 5.5 1999].

and so on. In a UCM environment, ClearQuest provides these capabilities. If you are interested in an integrated change-management solution, you need both ClearCase and ClearQuest.

With ClearCase UCM alone, activities are used as the mechanism to track a change set (see the section "Organize and Integrate Consistent Sets of Versions Using Activities" in Chapter 1). The primary difference between using ClearCase alone and using it in combination with Clear-Quest is the level of process centered on the activities.

If you are using ClearCase UCM by itself, activities are created at the point of use. That is, individual developers, working in their development stream, create activities when they check out files. These activities consist of a one-line description and so appear to the developer as kind of a metacomment for a change spanning multiple files. The section "Modifying Files and Directories" in Chapter 8, "Development Using the ClearCase UCM Model," goes into this in more detail. The bottom line is that ClearCase UCM without ClearQuest does not support the process for activities you need if you want to do change request management.

Chapter 11, "Geographically Distributed Development," provides detailed discussion of ClearQuest functionality and operation.

3.5 ClearCase UCM Process Overview

To provide an overview of the ClearCase UCM process, this section discusses it in terms of five roles and the steps these roles perform. The roles (in order of appearance in the process) are architect, configuration manager, project manager, developer, and integrator.

Your organization might use different names, but each role is key to successful SCM. A single individual might take on more than one role, or multiple individuals might share responsibility for a single role. The role(s) an individual performs usually depends on that person's technical background, the size of the project, and the size of the system being developed. You might want to map the ClearCase UCM roles to the individuals and roles in your own organization as you work through this book.

Figure 3-5, an overview of the UCM process, lists the roles involved and the steps they perform. For example, a developer's first step is to join a project. The main team members are listed, followed by the steps they perform. Arrows indicate the typical order of the steps.

3.5.1 The Architect

The architect has a deep understanding of the system architecture. In terms of SCM, the architect is responsible for determining how the system architecture should be physically realized (that is, how to group and map the various design objects to the physical files and directories that will implement the design).

3.5.2 The Configuration Manager

The configuration manager is familiar with an organization's configuration and change-management processes and with the SCM tools being used. The configuration manager is responsible for creating and maintaining the physical infrastructure necessary to implement the design. This primarily involves creating and maintaining repositories and importing existing files and directories.

(In some organizations the configuration manager is also responsible for things such as disk space allocation, network resources, and backup strategies as they relate to SCM data. The process described here allocates these activities to the system administrator.)

3.5.3   The Project Manager

The project manager understands an organization's change-management processes and project-management policies. In terms of SCM, project managers are responsible for assigning and scheduling work activities and scoping components to project teams. When components are scoped, the project manager for a given project is responsible for creating the physical ClearCase projects and for defining the SCM policies by which the project is governed. Policies are defined in terms of both written policies and SCM tool settings that define automation and enforcement policies supported by UCM.

> **NOTE**
> In some organizations, the configuration manager is responsible for carrying out the policy decisions made by the project manager.

In larger organizations, a project manager might be two different people. The traditional division is between a management-oriented role, which allocates the work and establishes the policies, and a technical-lead role, which creates and configures the project and carries out the work. (Other key activities of the project manager are to create, monitor, and maintain a project plan. These are project-management tasks and not part of the SCM process. With respect to SCM, the project plan should be placed under version control, and, in this capacity, the project manager acts as a developer.) Typically, project managers are also responsible for producing and maintaining an SCM plan. Because ClearCase and the UCM do not provide any specific automation for creating an SCM plan, this topic is not discussed here. (Refer to IEEE Standard 828-1998, *IEEE Standard for Software Configuration Management Plans,* for details on SCM plans [IEEE 828-1998].)

3.5.4   The Developer

The developer is responsible for finding out what activities need to be performed. Developers either receive activity assignments from the project manager or formulate activities on their own, depending on the formality of the organization's change-management policies. Developers are responsible for making changes to files and directories, to implement those activities and deliver those activities to the integrator.

The role of developer is defined here in a very broad sense. A developer is anyone who makes changes to any elements that are under version control. A developer can be a project manager modifying a project plan, a technical writer modifying a user manual, a tester modifying some test scripts, an architect modifying a design model, or a Web author modifying an HTML page.

3.5.5   The Integrator

The integrator is familiar with the build strategy and build tools being used on a project, with the SCM processes of an organization, and with the organization's SCM tools. The integrator accepts activities from developers, creates new component baselines, builds the components of the system (for small systems, this might be one component containing the entire system), ensures that the builds are tested (the integrator might or might not perform the actual testing), and promotes the new baselines when testing is complete. For large systems that have multiple projects per release producing multiple components, a system integrator is responsible for assembling components, performing system testing, and creating baselines for the entire system.

3.6   The Architect: Defining the Implementation Model

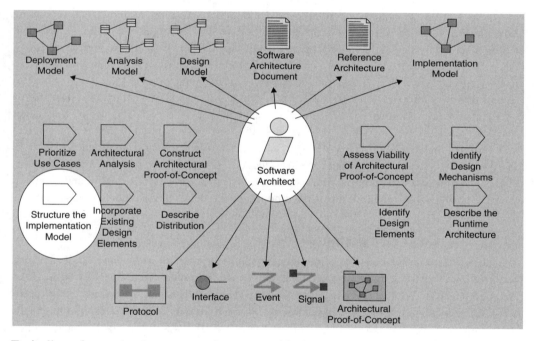

Typically, software-development requirements and budgets are established at product inception and evolve during product elaboration and development. The architect uses the requirements to create a software architecture or to modify an existing one. The software architecture serves as a logical framework to satisfy the requirements.

The concept of architecture has many facets, some that are relevant to software configuration management and others that are not. The authors of *The Unified Modeling Language User Guide* [Booch 1999] and *The Rational Unified Process: An Introduction, Second Edition* [Kruchten 2000] define architecture this way:

Software architecture encompasses the following:

- The significant decisions about the organization of a software system
- The selection of the structural elements and their interfaces by which the system is composed, together with their behavior as specified in the collaboration among those elements

- The composition of these elements into progressively larger subsystems; the architectural style that guides this organization, these elements, and their interfaces, their collaborations, and their composition

> Software architecture is concerned with not only structure and behavior, but also usage, functionality, performance, resilience, reuse, comprehensibility, economic and technologic constraints and trade-offs, and aesthetic issues. [Kruchten 2000]

In terms of SCM, architecture is concerned with the organization, grouping, and versioning of the physical files and directories of the system, both as they are organized in the development environment and as they are deployed on the target system. Some projects use high-level design documents to describe these aspects of architecture. More recently, models are being employed to visually represent the architecture, providing different architectural views of the system. (The term *view* as used here refers to an abstraction of a system architecture. An abstraction shown from a given perspective omits entities that are not relevant to that perspective. This use of *view* is not related to the ClearCase view object. Elsewhere in this book, any mention of the term *view* refers to a ClearCase view (see [Kruchten 1995]).) One of these views, the most important for SCM, is the *implementation view,* which maps logical system design objects (such as classes) to the physical files and directories that implement them. These files and directories are placed under version control. One of the jobs of the architect is to produce this implementation model of the system.

3.6.1   ClearCase Components

Terminology used for the decomposition of a software system varies widely and is not standardized. Humphrey defines five layers: system, subsystems, products, components, and modules [Humphrey 1989]. Whitgift defines three layers: system, subsystem, and elements [Whitgift 1991]. IEEE defines three layers: computer software-configuration items (CSCI), computer software components (CSC), and computer software units [IEEE 1042-1987]. The Rational Unified Process defines four layers: system, implementation (or component) subsystems, components, and files [RUP 5.5 1999]. For the purposes of SCM, ClearCase defines a general-purpose set of objects that can be used to represent any of the preceding models. These objects are composite baselines, components, and elements. (Details on UCM objects and the object model can be found in Chapter 4, "A Functional Overview of ClearCase Objects.")

Elements are the files and directories that are under version control in ClearCase. Components are used to group elements. A ClearCase *component* is a physical object that identifies a root directory, under which the elements that comprise the component exist. ClearCase components are versioned, shared (reused), and released as a unit. A large system typically consists of many components; a small system might be contained in a single component. A ClearCase *composite baseline* is a mechanism for grouping component baselines into a logical collection. This logical collection of versions of components can then be thought of as a subsystem.

3.6.2 Components in the Unified Modeling Language

The word *component* is one of those overused terms that means different things to different people in different contexts. One of those contexts is the Unified Modeling Language (UML). UML is a language for visualizing, specifying, constructing, and documenting a software system. The UML definition of the term *component* is relevant to our discussion here. In light of the broad adoption of UML in the market, it is worth a few words to explain how UML components relate to ClearCase components.

The authors of *The Unified Modeling Language User Guide* define a component as "a physical and replaceable part of a system that conforms to and provides the realization of a set of interfaces" [Booch 1999]. They also define three kinds of components: deployment components, work product components, and execution components. Deployment components are elements of the system as deployed on the target machine. Examples are executables, libraries, and other files needed to support a running system. Work product components are the elements that make up the development environment. Examples are source files, headers, and other files used to derive or build the deployment components. Execution components are those produced by the system executing on the target machine.

ClearCase components can be UML deployment components, UML work product components, both, or neither, depending on the elements being managed in the ClearCase component. However, UML components are generally too fine-grained to apply SCM controls (exceptions do exist). For a large system, you might be dealing with hundreds of UML components. Although this is certainly better than dealing with thousands of files, there is still significant SCM overhead.

UML also defines two higher levels of abstraction, systems and subsystems, that are better mapped to ClearCase components or to a ClearCase data structure called a *composite baseline*. A composite baseline is a ClearCase mechanism for grouping component baselines into a logical collection. Composite baselines are discussed in more detail in Chapter 4. A system, "possibly decomposed into a collection of subsystems, [is] a set of elements organized to accomplish a specific purpose and described by a set of models, possibly from different view points" [Booch 1999]. Systems and subsystems are rendered in UML as stereotypes of a package.

If you are using UML to model your system, ClearCase components or ClearCase composite baselines should relate, one to one, to the UML concept of systems or subsystems. Figure 3-6 shows the UML representation of systems, subsystems, and components, and how they map to ClearCase composite baselines, components, and elements. Mapping your system architecture to ClearCase composite baselines or components is not a requirement for using ClearCase UCM. However, a strong mapping between the organization of the system (the architecture) and the implementation of the system (the files and directories) reduces integration problems, eases build development (such as with makefiles), reduces the risk of accidentally violating the architecture, and facilitates integration. (How to map architecture to composite baselines or physical ClearCase components is discussed in more detail in the section "Defining the Implementation Model" in Chapter 5, "Establishing the Initial SCM Environment.")

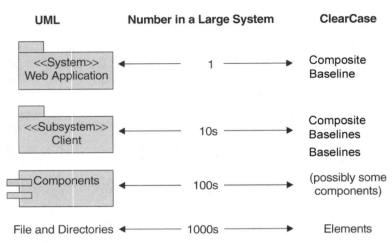

Figure 3-6   UML component mapping.

After the architect has completed the implementation model, the configuration manager physically creates the repositories, components, and directory structure where development will take place.

3.7   The Configuration Manager: Setting Up the SCM Environment

Before the first developer can start making changes, the configuration manager must establish the SCM environment. Two key steps are involved: establishing the hardware environment and establishing the development environment.

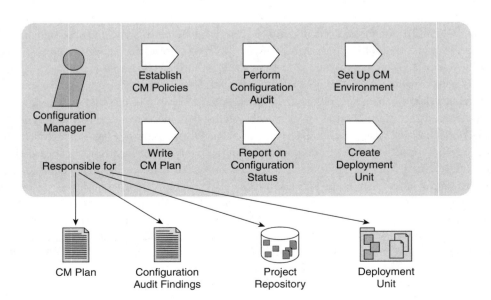

To set up the hardware environment, the configuration manager works with the system administrator to assess and allocate machine resources (such as designated servers and disk space). To complete the hardware environment, the configuration manager must work with the system administrator to install and configure the necessary software tools (such as ClearCase) on both server and client machines.

The second step, establishing the development environment, involves the following:

1. The configuration manager works with the architect to finalize the implementation model (the mapping of design objects to logical packages and then to ClearCase components).

2. The configuration manager determines where the components will be stored (which SCM repositories).

3. The configuration manager creates the repositories and the components.

4. The configuration manager creates the product directory structure.

5. The configuration manager imports any existing files and directories into the repositories, to create the initial set of versioned elements.

6. The configuration manager establishes an initial baseline for all components. A component baseline records a specific version of every element (files and directories) in a component.

7. If applicable the configuration manager establishes one or more composite baselines that record a set of baselines for inclusion in projects as subsystems.

After the configuration manager establishes the development environment, the project manager can create a new project.

3.8   The Project Manager: Managing a Project

A ClearCase project is created by the project manager and is used by a team to produce new baselines of one or more components. A ClearCase *project* is an object that contains the configuration information needed to manage a significant development effort. Project managers configure the ClearCase project to define the scope of work for the project (the set of components) and to set policies that govern how developers access and update the set of source files. A ClearCase project also defines a shared area where development changes are integrated.

The size of the overall development initiative influences the number of projects that are created to fulfill it. Small initiatives might have one project that is producing a new release of an entire system. Large initiatives have multiple projects working together to produce a single release of a system. It is important to distinguish between the product being produced and the project or projects producing the product.

The project manager does the following:

1. Creates the project

2. Identifies the components or composite baselines (already defined by the architect) needed by the project

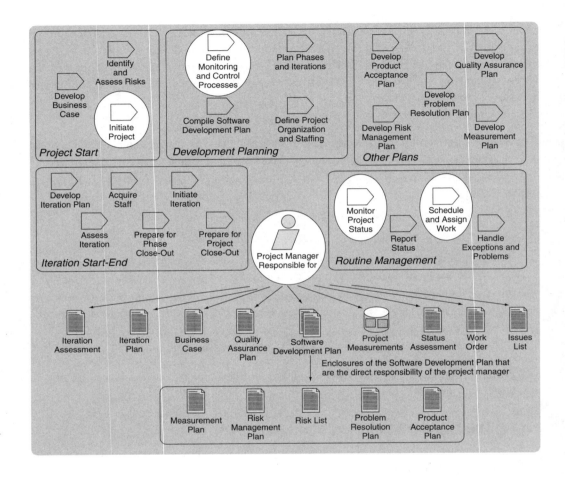

3. Identifies which components are to be modified (writeable) and which components are merely referenced (read-only) by the project

4. Identifies the baseline (version) of each subsystem or component from which developers will start their work

5. Defines the policies that govern how the usage model is applied to the project

Defining policies for a project means configuring how ClearCase will automate and enforce policies during development on that project, and defining other project policies, which might not be automated by ClearCase but must be documented and followed manually.

After the project manager has created the project, defined the scope of work for the project (indicating which components will be modified or referenced), and established the project's policies, developers can join the project and begin working.

3.9   The Developer: Joining a Project and Doing Development

Developers join one or more projects where they perform their work. The process of joining a project creates the developer's *workspace*. In ClearCase, a developer's workspace is comprised of a ClearCase view and a development stream. A ClearCase view provides a window into the files being managed. The stream defines the configuration for the view and determines which versions of the files will be displayed.

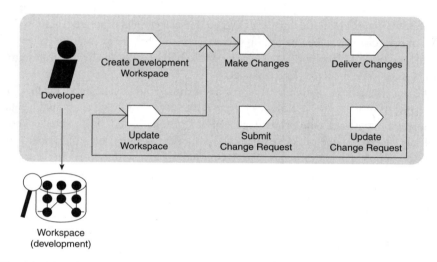

When developers join a project, they can work directly in their view or through any number of integrated development environments (IDEs—for example, IBM WebSphere Studio Application Developer, or Microsoft Visual Studio). In views, developers check out, edit, build, unit-test, debug, and check in file and directory elements as needed to accomplish their tasks. All modifications are associated with an activity, forming a change set.

Activities represent the tasks that developers work on. Examples include "implement feature A," "fix defect 109," or "redesign the search algorithm for orders." In UCM, the project manager can plan and assign activities if a change-request management tool such as ClearQuest is being used (see Chapter 12, "Change Request Management and ClearQuest"). Developers can also define activities when they start doing work if a project is using an informal change-management process. The developers need only track the change sets.

When developers complete an activity, they deliver their changes to the project's integration stream, making them available to the integrator for integration and inclusion in the next component baseline(s). Developers must also keep their own development stream current with changes being made by other developers on the project. ClearCase supports an explicit operation called *rebase* (short for *rebaseline*). Rebase incorporates new baselines created by the integrator into the development stream. After a rebase, developers will see new baselines that include changes that other developers have delivered and that the integrator has integrated.

After developers have created, tested, and delivered changes, it is time for the integrator to build and test those changes.

3.10   The Integrator: Integration, Build, and Release

The job of the integrator is to take changes that developers deliver, produce new baselines of components, and promote those baselines for internal project consumption or external use.

Each project has one integration stream into which developers deliver their activities. The integrator uses an integration view attached to the integration stream to create a working environment for performing the first step of the integration: creating a new baseline. The integrator creates an integration view, configured by the integration stream to select the previous project baseline plus all the new versions identified by the delivered (but as yet unincorporated) activities.

The integrator freezes the integration stream to ensure that the integration view will select a fixed set of versions and then builds the system. If the build succeeds, the integrator creates new baselines of the components that have changed.

If the system passes a certain level of testing, the integrator can promote the baselines. *Promotion* is a means of marking baselines as having either passed or failed a certain level of testing. For example, an integrator could promote a baseline to Built, Tested, or Rejected. These promotion levels are defined by the project manager as part of defining project policies and are largely used by external consumers of the baseline. By promoting project baselines to a certain level of quality, the integrator implicitly selects the baselines as the project's recommended baselines. The recommended baselines are the default baselines presented to developers when they join a UCM project or rebase (update) their development streams.

3.10.1 Releasing a Component

To release a component, the integrator places all project deliverables, which are artifacts, under version control. The product deliverables can reside in one of the development components or in a separate component reserved for deliverables. Deliverable components are components that contain elements that have been built and are shared with other teams. These elements are included in the build process (for example, statically linked libraries), are included in the final system's runtime environment (for example, executables, dynamically linked libraries), or make up the deliverable (for example, documentation).

The elements of a deliverable component are also included in a baseline of that component. Other development teams can select and share deliverable or source elements by referring to the appropriate component and its baseline.

3.10.2 System Integration

For large systems, there is likely to be more than one project producing modifications to many components, generating a need for system integration. System integration happens when component and subsystem (composite) baselines are assembled into a final system.

With the UCM, system assembly is done by creating a system project and selecting the baselines that are being produced by the various subprojects. In other words, all components for the system project are reference (read-only) components. The complete system can then be built and tested as a whole.

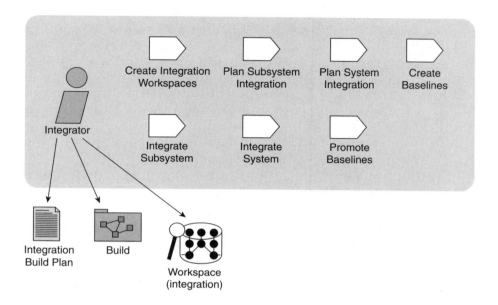

3.10.3 Releasing Systems and Subsystems

All of this work leads up to the release of the system or subsystem. A system integrator places all project deliverables under version control (including any additional deliverables produced during the system build). If a subsystem is being released, the system integrator creates a composite baseline that contains the entire set of individual component baselines and subsystem baselines that make up the released subsystem. The final composite baseline that represents the system or subsystem is promoted to the appropriate level to indicate it has passed all testing operations. The final step is to produce the necessary media or simply deploy the files on the target system (such as Web sites or internal production machines) and, in the case of subsystems, to publish the composite baseline identifier for inclusion in other UCM project definitions.

3.11   Summary

UCM provides the software-configuration management tools and processes to achieve effective, efficient software development. It does this by building upon a model that unifies the activities and artifacts upon which projects are built and progress. This model serves to raise the level of abstraction at which development is done; to provide stability for projects and individual contributors; to manage, track, and control the flow of changes in a project; and, finally, to provide facilities for automated project metrics as well as real-time communication about a project's activities and artifacts. UCM is built upon the foundations of ClearCase and ClearQuest to manage the project's artifacts and activities, respectively. You have seen that the UCM process can be described in terms of five roles: the architect, the configuration manager, the project manager, the developer, and the integrator.

A Functional Overview of ClearCase Objects

This chapter provides an overview of ClearCase objects and concepts. It serves as a bridge between general SCM terminology and ClearCase-specific terminology.

4.1   The Repository: Versioned Object Base

At the heart of any SCM system is the object repository. ClearCase repositories are called *versioned object bases,* or VOBs. The ClearCase online help reads, "A VOB is the permanent data repository in which you store files, directories, and metadata." Anything that can be represented as a file or directory can be managed in a ClearCase VOB.

ClearCase VOBs support all of the characteristics listed in the first SCM best practice: The SCM repository must be scalable, fault tolerant, distributable, and replicable (see Chapter 1, "What Is Software Configuration Management?"):

- **Scalable**—ClearCase VOBs can grow from hundreds of files and directories to many thousands of files and directories. Files and directories in a ClearCase VOB can be moved between VOBs if a VOB becomes too large. VOBs can be split and joined.

- **Fault tolerant**—ClearCase VOBs have an internal database that does not require additional database management. The VOB database and ClearCase architecture ensure that transactions such as check-out on a file are atomic and so ensure that the permanent datastore does not get corrupted.

- **Distributable**—ClearCase VOBs can be distributed across different servers in the network transparently to the end user. Because VOBs can be moved, you can distribute the load as needed to meet project demands.

- **Replicable**—ClearCase VOBs can be replicated in two or more sites. Replication means full copies are made and kept up-to-date (in sync) with each other at different geographic sites. This is critical for geographically distributed development, where the network between sites is often not as reliable or often does not have as high a bandwidth as the local area network.

ClearCase VOB technology has an interesting twist not found in traditional SCM systems. In systems such as the revision control system (RCS), the repository and the file system are two separate entities. With ClearCase, you can combine the two.

Instead of being a black-box repository from which things need to be inserted and extracted, the ClearCase repository displays its contents as files in a file system, which can be operated on in the same way as you would files in the native file system. In the same way you add disks to a file system, you can create as many ClearCase VOBs as required. The VOBs can be distributed across many machines but referenced as if they were one single repository. Figure 4-1 shows two servers and three VOBs, and how the VOBs plug into the native file system. A scalable solution such as this one is particularly critical for large organizations.

ClearCase VOBs store files and directories. In ClearCase terminology, these versioned objects are called *elements*. Figure 4-2 shows the relationships between VOBs and elements in UML format.

> **NOTE**
> See UML Diagram Format in the "Conventions Used" section in the preface if you are unfamiliar with UML format. See [Booch, 1999] for more complete information on UML.

Along with elements, VOBs store metadata associated with the version control environment, as well as user-defined metadata. *Metadata* is data associated with an object. It supplements the object's file system data, providing important information about the object, such as who created it,

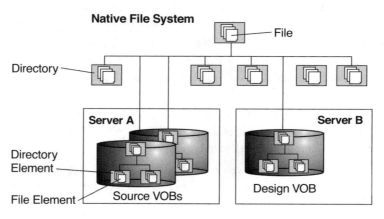

Figure 4-1   Distributed VOB architecture.

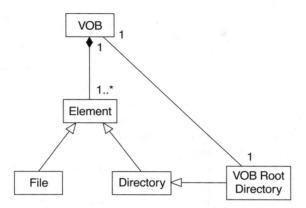

Figure 4-2   VOB and element relationships.

when, and why. Metadata can also be used to implement, enforce, or automate certain aspects of the development process.

ClearCase has two primary types of VOBs. The first is the standard VOB, as described earlier. The second type is called a *project VOB* (PVOB). PVOBs hold objects associated with the project environment, such as projects, components, activities, and baselines, all described later in this chapter. The PVOB is basically the central point of administration for a set of projects working on a set of components. For example, in the development of the ClearCase product itself, there is one PVOB, which contains all the projects working on the 40-odd components that comprise the ClearCase product family source base. In short, VOBs store and organize the objects that make up the system being developed, whereas PVOBs store the objects used to organize and manage the projects doing the development. For information on a range of topics related to VOBs, see Chapter 5, "Establishing the Initial SCM Environment."

4.2   Workspaces: Snapshot and Dynamic Views

One of the essential functions of an SCM tool is to establish and manage the developer's working environment, often referred to as a *workspace,* or "sandbox." In ClearCase, workspaces are called *views.* The primary purpose of the view is to provide developers with a stable and consistent set of software, where they can make changes and perform unit testing. ClearCase views select the appropriate versions of the files and directories, as defined by a set of configuration rules, from all available versions in a VOB. For example, a view might select all versions that were used to build Release 2 of a system.

The view makes the files and directories available for browsing, modifying, and building. The versions selected in a view should be stable (the versions of the files and directories you are working on should not change without warning) and consistent (the versions of multiple elements selected should be complementary). For example, if you are fixing a bug in Release 1, you don't want to select some element versions from Release 1, some from Release 2, and some of the latest element versions. Instead, you want all the Release 1 element versions plus your own modifications.

Every ClearCase view contains a set of rules that define the configuration for that view (that is, that define which versions should be seen). These rules are called a *configuration specification,* or config spec. For projects that use the UCM model, ClearCase automatically generates these config specs (for a discussion of streams, see the section "Project Management: Projects, Streams, and Activities," later in this chapter). For projects that do not use UCM, you can use the default config spec, generate config specs by hand, or automate config spec generation using scripts.

ClearCase provides two main types of views, *snapshot* and *dynamic*. A third type of view is really a subtype of a snapshot view. This third type of view, the *Web view*, is used by the ClearCase Web Client and the ClearCase Remote Client. Each type has its own advantages, and you should expect to use both snapshot views and dynamic views to maximize the benefits of ClearCase. Snapshot views have copies of the files loaded into them from the VOB. Although they take longer to set up and require more disk space than dynamic views, build performance is better because there is no dependency on the network to access the files. Web views are like a snapshot view, maintaining copies of files loaded from the VOB. However, instead of locating the database portion of the view on the ClearCase Web client, where the files are loaded, this database is located on the ClearCase Web server. Dynamic views reference files directly out of the VOB. No copies are made, so setting up a dynamic view is fast and takes very little disk space. The following sections go into more detail on each type of view.

4.2.1   Snapshot Views

Snapshot views are similar in approach to traditional development sandboxes (that is, they are uncontrolled copies of a software system's files and directories). When you create a snapshot view, you specify a local directory into which the files and directories you want to work on are copied. This is referred to as a `Get` operation or a read-only check-out by some SCM tools. ClearCase refers to this as loading a snapshot view.

The use of ClearCase snapshot views differs from the traditional approach of local file copies in a number of ways. Snapshot views have a database that keeps track of what versions have been loaded into the working directory. Snapshot views mirror the directory structure as part of a load/update operation. They keep track of when a developer changes the read-only bit on a file and modifies it without issuing a check-out command. This is called hijacking the file. During update operations, hijacked files are not overwritten and can be turned into check-outs.

Another difference from traditional sandboxes is that snapshot views can be updated in a single operation. Instead of performing `Get`s on individual files or directories, a snapshot view user performs a single `Update` operation. The `Update` does the following: checks for hijacked files, asks the user if he or she wants to check out these files, and compares the versions of the files in the snapshot view's local directory to the versions that are selected in the VOB based on the view's config spec. If these are different, it copies only those files that have changed into the snapshot view. This `Update` operation is crucial for maintaining consistency in the developer's working environment.

Generally, you might not want to make a copy of all the files that make up the system (unless, in fact, you need the entire system to do your work). For example, you might want to copy only the files associated with the component you are working on. This is done by specifying a set of load rules in the configuration specification, which define what pieces of the system are interesting. This information is used to limit the set of elements copied from the VOB to the snapshot view. A GUI interface can also be used to specify what pieces of the system get loaded into the snapshot view.

Another aspect of keeping the development environment consistent is ensuring that the right elements get loaded. This might change over time based on the activities the developer is performing. The snapshot view Update operation not only downloads new element versions, but also "unloads" files that have been removed from the view's load rules or files that have been renamed, deleted, or moved from one directory to another.

For example, imagine that you're working on component A fixing a bug, so you load component A into your snapshot view and do your work. When you're done, you're assigned to fix a bug in component B. You can change your load rules to select component B and deselect component A. Component A will be unloaded at the same time component B is loaded. This frees up disk space and ensures that you do not introduce any unknown dependencies between components A and B.

4.2.2   Web Views

Both the ClearCase Web Client and the ClearCase Remote Client use Web views. Web views are similar to snapshot views, with the exception that the management component of the view (the view storage area) is located on the ClearCase Web Server. Like snapshot views, you specify and load ClearCase-controlled elements into a directory on your local machine, but the full ClearCase client software does not need to be installed on your local machine. Instead, all interaction with the Web view must occur through a Web browser or ClearCase Remote Client interface. If you have ClearCase client software installed on your local machine, you still must use the Web browser or ClearCase Remote Client interface to interact with Web views.

4.2.3   Dynamic Views

Like snapshot views, dynamic views establish a developer's workspace by providing a set of element versions based on the config spec rules. Unlike snapshot views, dynamic views do not copy elements to a local storage directory. They provide access to element versions by using a virtual file system that refers to elements directly from the VOB (see the section "The Repository: Versioned Object Base," later in this chapter). The virtual file system mechanism provides transparent version control. Existing tools can open files without creating separate copies or ever removing the files from the repository. The dynamic view approach to development workspaces is unique to ClearCase.

How does this work? Dynamic views deal directly with the operating system and the file system. The implementation supports the operating system's file system interface and user environment. Because of this, dynamic views are presented differently depending on your development platform (for example, UNIX or Windows).

When full ClearCase is installed, a file system called the *multiversion file system* (MVFS) is installed as well (see the section "The Multiversion File System" in Chapter 5). The MVFS uses standard operating system protocols to add a new file system type. Multiple file system types are common: Windows NT has FAT and NTFS; UNIX has NFS and DFS. When you are in the MVFS file system space and you access a file using a tool such as an editor, the MVFS intercepts the file Open call, determines what view the user is working in, determines the right version of the file to select, and opens that version of the file.

UNIX Example

Here is a UNIX example. Let's say you have a software system under version control. Using the hello world project example, here is the project directory structure:

```
/vobs/hw
/vobs/hw/Makefile
/vobs/hw/src/hello.c
/vobs/hw/inc/hello.h
```

Let's say two developers, Ann and Jim, each have their own dynamic view: ann_view and jim_view. Ann is working on fixing a bug in Release 1. Jim is working on Release 2.

Ann performs the following commands, (setview, as seen in this code, establishes the view context for the shell session in which the setview command is issued. You can also do things such as cleartool setview -exec <application> to start an application in the context of a view. For UNIX gurus, setview is performing a chroot operation to a directory structure maintained by ClearCase that mimics the entire UNIX directory tree. This directory is located under /view on UNIX and under a specific drive letter (usually configured to M: or V:) on Windows.)

```
noview>     cleartool setview ann_view
ann_view>   cd /vobs/hw/src
ann_view>   cat hello.c
main {
    printf("hello world\n");
}
```

Jim performs the following commands:

```
noview>     cleartool setview jim_view
jim_view>   cd /vobs/hw/src
jim_view>   cat hello.c
main {
    printf("You are now running with \n");
    printf("the power of version 2\n");
    printf("hello world\n");
}
```

Ann's view and Jim's view see different output from the cat command even though they are in the same directory: This is because they are using different configuration specifications and, in the case of `hello.c`, are selecting different versions of the file. This is what is meant by "transparency with dynamic views." Tools can work with the files in place, and makefiles do not have to be tailored to support search paths and other user-specific settings.

The result of using dynamic views is that Ann and Jim can work in isolation without impacting each other. Many benefits can be gained by using dynamic views. First, the software is not being copied to various places in the network. Multiple software copies consume disk space and cause confusion. Second, there is no need to specify which pieces of the software need to be copied or loaded. With dynamic views, you have access to all the software all of the time. Third, build problems that result from builds being performed in different environments/directory trees are avoided. Finally, dynamic views provide unique build support, such as audited builds and derived object sharing. These features are covered in the section "Building: Clearmake, Derived Objects, Configuration Records," later in this chapter.

Windows Example

On Windows, dynamic views are presented consistently with the Windows file system (and are therefore presented differently from how they are presented on UNIX). In the example, Ann runs Windows Explorer and performs the menu command File, Map Network Drive. As seen in Figure 4-3, she selects her dynamic view and a network drive to which it will be mapped.

Ann can now access her project through Windows Explorer on drive F. She could also use any other interface, such as Microsoft Visual Studio. Using the `hello world` example, Figure 4-4 shows Ann's view accessing the `hello world` VOBs from within the Explorer.

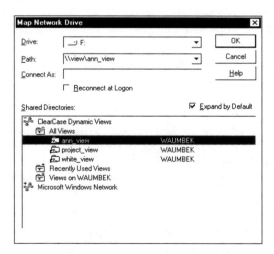

Figure 4-3 Mapping a dynamic view to a network drive.

4.2.4 Differences Between Snapshot and Dynamic Views

Dynamic views provide a global view on the source base without the need to have a full copy of the entire source tree. This means that they can be created very quickly. Updates occur automatically

Figure 4-4   Ann's Explorer window.

and do not require the copy time associated with snapshot views. Dynamic views provide significant build capabilities such as derived object sharing and build audits. Snapshot views cannot do so.

Snapshot views provide two key benefits over dynamic views. Because files are copied to the local disk, the build performance is faster than in dynamic views. Also, because of the local copies, it is possible to work offline with snapshot views. This is usually referred to as disconnected use. It is particularly important for people using laptops at home or while traveling. Table 4-1 summarizes the differences between snapshot and dynamic views.

Snapshot and dynamic views each have advantages and disadvantages. You should expect to use both types to maximize the benefits from ClearCase. Use dynamic views when you need to conserve disk space, require all the source code, desire frequent and automatic updates, or want to take advantage of ClearCase's build facilities. Use snapshot views when you want to work offline, require only a small subset of the code, or want to maximize your build performance.

Table 4-1 Differences Between Snapshot and Dynamic Views

Snapshot	Dynamic
Copies loaded from VOB	Transparent access to VOB
Periodic updates	Fast creation and immediate updates
Capability to load a subset of the code	Global view of code base
Fast local build speed	Derived object sharing
Capability to work offline, disconnected use	Audited builds

4.3   Project Management: Projects, Streams, and Activities

Because of the complexity and size of software-development efforts, project managers need automation and tools to help organize and manage large software projects. ClearCase UCM has objects and automation that assist in the management and organization of software projects: projects, streams, and activities (see Figure 4-5).

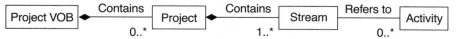

Figure 4-5   Projects, streams, and activities.

4.3.1   Projects

The Project Management Institute defines a project as follows:

> Projects are performed by people, constrained by limited resources, and planned, executed, and controlled. A project is a temporary endeavor undertaken to create a unique product or service. Temporary means that every project has a definite beginning and a definite end. Unique means that the product or service is different in some distinguishing way from all similar products and services. Projects are undertaken at all levels of the organization. They may involve a single person or many thousands. They may require less than 100 hours to complete or over 10,000,000. Projects may involve a single unit of one organization or may cross organizational boundaries as in joint ventures and partnering. Projects are often critical components of the performing organization's business strategy. [PMI, 1996, p. 4]

A ClearCase *project* directly maps to this definition. A ClearCase UCM project represents a group of individuals collaborating to produce new baselines of one or more components of a system (or perhaps the entire system). A ClearCase project is an object whose attributes define the scope of work for that project (which components are being worked on), the policies that govern the work for that project, the workspaces (streams and views) used on that project, and which activities are being worked on by the team members.

Project objects are created in PVOBs and can be organized into folders. A Project Creation Wizard is used to create a new project, and a Project Explorer is used to browse and modify projects.

4.3.2   Streams

A workspace is a logical concept in ClearCase UCM that is implemented with two objects: a *stream* and a view. A stream defines the working configuration for the view (or views) associated with it. It contains the information needed to automatically generate a configuration specification for the view. Unlike base ClearCase users, ClearCase UCM users do not have to create or modify the config specs. Streams logically define configurations in terms of baselines and activities.

Figure 4-6 illustrates how this works. The VOB shown on the left contains many elements and many versions. In the middle, the triangle represents a stream. The base of the triangle lists one or more foundation baselines for the stream. The upper portion of the triangle lists a set of activities (along with their change sets). The view (shown on the right) uses the stream's activities and baselines to display particular versions of elements stored in the VOB.

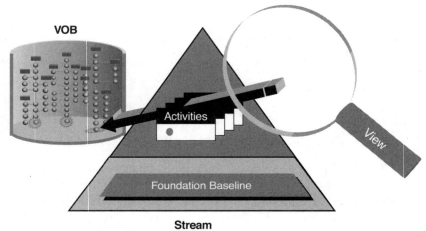

Figure 4-6   Stream/view relationship.

Types and Purposes of Streams

Streams can be classified into two modes of policy and use: development and integration. A stream that refers to the activities being worked on by a developer is called a development stream. A stream that contains the combined activities of all developers for a given project is called an integration stream. Each project has one integration stream and multiple development streams (see Figure 4-7). Each UCM project, in turn, has policies that govern the specifics on how these streams will be configured and used in the context of that project.

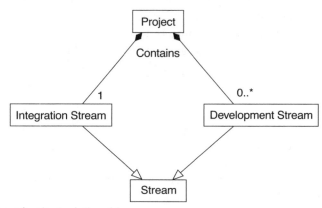

Figure 4-7   Stream/project relationships.

CLEARCASE PRO TIP

In some cases, it is necessary to have more than one view sharing the same configuration (stream)—for example, with multiple development views attached to the project's integration stream. This allows developers to deliver their changes in parallel.*

Two cases that require multiple views attached to a single development stream are cross-platform builds and small-team collaboration. For cross-platform builds, you might need to build your system on both Windows NT and UNIX. To do this, you need to have a UNIX view and an NT view, but both must select the same versions of the files (at least, if you are writing portable code). This is accomplished by having two views attached to the same development stream.

For small-team collaboration, you might have two or more developers cooperating closely. Because the activity is part of the stream configuration, both developers can associate a view of their own with the same development stream and work semi-isolated from one another, recording changes against their activities. The check-in operation, in this case, makes changes visible to those members who are sharing the development stream. This mode of work gives up some of the benefits of isolation that UCM provides by making possibly untested changes immediately visible to all the members collaborating on the common stream. Furthermore, this mode of work requires that the collaborating members check in all of their changes and test them in a single view before delivering activites from the shared stream.

* True, this may lead to element contention, but allowing parallel deliveries was felt to be a better option then disallowing them just to avoid contention. The deliver operation ensures that all necessary files are checked out before proceeding so that no deadlock situations are encountered.

Streams also serve two primary purposes:

- **They configure the views attached to them.** That is, they configure the view to select the right versions of the files for doing work on that project in that stream (see Figure 4-8). ClearCase users will understand that the stream supplies the appropriate configuration specification to its attached views.

- **They physically store the activities that developers have worked on in their view.** When a developer checks in a new version, it is recorded in the stream in the activity he or she is working on. In this way, streams behave like ClearCase branches. (In fact, the implementation of a stream in ClearCase 4.0 includes a branch type per stream. View profile users could think of streams in terms of a view profile combined with a private branch. Branches are described in the section "Versioned Objects: Elements, Branches, and Versions," later in this chapter.)

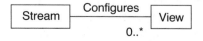

Figure 4-8   Stream/view relationship.

Stream objects are created and stored as child objects to the project object. Integration streams are automatically created as part of project creation when the Project Creation Wizard is used (see "Creating a ClearCase Project" in Chapter 6, "Project Management in ClearCase"). Development streams are created when developers join a project (see "Working on a Project" in Chapter 8, "Development Using the ClearCase UCM Model").

Relationships Between Streams

Streams are not just isolated entities in a project structure. They exist along with other streams in a project, and the relationships between streams are important to how UCM tracks and manages the flow of activity within a project. Three possible relationships exist between UCM streams:

- **Unrelated streams**—These are streams that exist in different UCM projects where there is no ancestral relationship between the projects. An example of unrelated streams is a development stream in Project A and a development stream in Project B where neither Project A nor Project B is an ancestor or descendent of the other project. In this case, the integration streams for Project A and Project B can be thought of as unrelated streams or as peer streams. Figure 4-9 illustrates unrelated streams.

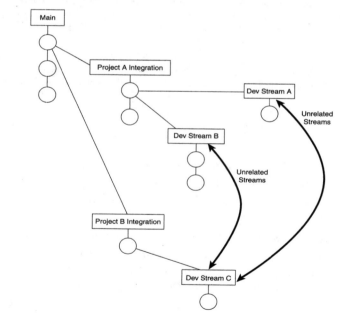

Figure 4-9   UCM streams that are unrelated.

- **Peer streams**—Peer streams are streams that share a common parent stream. One example of peer streams is a development stream X and a development stream Y, both in Project A, where both streams share Project A's integration stream as their parent. The integration streams of unrelated projects can also be thought of as peer streams. Figure 4-10 illustrates peer streams

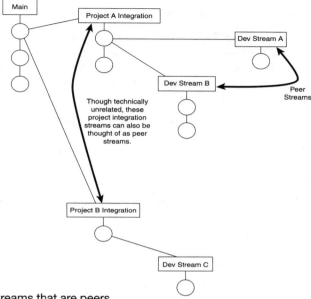

Figure 4-10   UCM streams that are peers.

- **Parent/child streams**—UCM makes extensive use of the concept of parent/child relationships between its streams. Stream Y is said to be a child of another parent Stream X if the default target stream for UCM delivery operations from Stream Y is Stream X. Conversely, child Stream Y looks for its parent Stream X as the default source stream for UCM rebase operations. Figure 4-11 provides an illustration of parent/child streams.

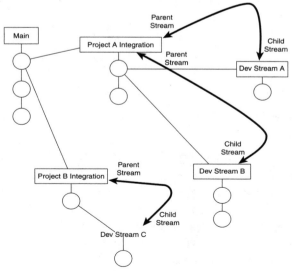

Figure 4-11   Parent/child stream relationships in UCM.

Parent/Child Stream Relationships Within Projects

The most common use of the parent/child relationship between streams is to manage the flow of UCM activities between development streams within a project and the project's integration stream. There is no limit to the number of levels of parent/child stream relationships. This flexibility allows UCM to manage highly complex flows of activities within a project. Figure 4-12 provides an illustration of complex intraproject parent/child relationships.

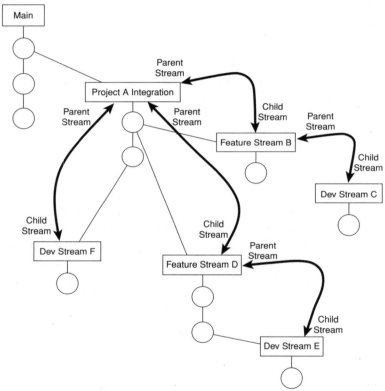

Figure 4-12   Hierarchical UCM parent/child streams.

Parent/Child Stream Relationships Between Projects

Projects can also make use of the parent/child relationship structure to govern project or subproject process flows. For example, if Project A already exists, you can create Project A_1 using a baseline on the Project A integration stream as the foundation for the new project. This establishes the integration stream for Project A_1 as a child stream of the integration stream for Project A. With such a structure, the default target stream for a UCM deliver operation from Project A_1 is the integration stream for Project A. Likewise, the default target stream for a UCM rebase operation from Project A_1 is the integration stream for Project A.

This structure can be useful for managing maintenance projects that are derived from a release baseline in an existing project. Bug fixes and maintenance releases could be done in the context of the maintenance project, and then those UCM-managed bug-fix and maintenance activities could be easily delivered to the parent project.

Figure 4-13 provides an illustration of these parent/child relationships between UCM projects.

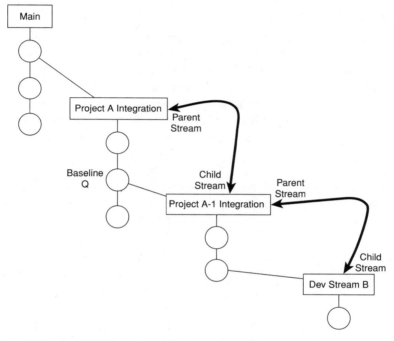

Figure 4-13   UCM parent/child relationships between projects.

Extended Stream Relationships

Although UCM uses parent/child relationships between streams to govern certain default operations for rebase and delivery operations, it currently makes no use of extended relationships such as grandparent/grandchild streams.

4.3.3   Activities

One of the primary advantages that UCM provides to individuals working on a development project is in the notion of activity-based development. Most software configuration management systems perform version control operations on individual files, but they require the individual developer to keep track of those changes. They also require the developer to keep track of which changes are associated with which tasks. Clearly, if a developer is working on several tasks simultaneously, this record-keeping requirement can become more onerous than the actual development tasks being undertaken and is prone to errors. UCM automatically associates the changes made to files, folders, and directories with the specific activities for which the changes are made. This relieves individual developers of this burden and allows developers to concentrate on the work to be done to advance the project rather than administrative work. The following paragraphs discuss the UCM concept of an activity.

The Conceptual UCM Activity

The concept of "activity" in the UCM model differs depending on the project context. In the development of the UCM model, one of the key ideas is that the model itself could scale without changing the way a developer interacted with the system. For example, the UCM model is designed to scale around the importance of the activity object.

In general, there are three components to the initiation of work in a project: an issue, a response, and a result. An issue forms the stimulus for work. For example, an issue could be the discovery of a defect or a request for enhancement from a customer. Second, there is a response to the stimulus. This takes the form of a task or action on the part of someone. For example, a developer is assigned to fix the defect. Finally, the work response culminates in some result, such as new element versions that fix the defect (such as the change set). Depending on the complexity of your environment and the tools you employ, different physical objects often represent these concepts, and, in many cases, they overlap (see Figure 4-14).

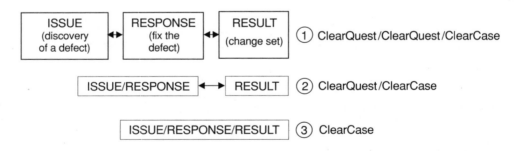

Figure 4-14   Activity objects and their relationships.

In a very complex development environment, each one of these objects (issue, response, and result) is physically recorded and tracked independently. For example, a defect record is filed when the defect is found. When the organization decides to work on the defect, a task record is created in a project-management or workflow product to track the assigned work. This task is associated with the defect record in the defect-tracking system. Finally, a change set is created in the SCM system that is linked to the workflow/project-management task object.

In less complex environments, the issue and response are often combined into one object that reflects both the defect data and the task progress data. For example, a defect is recorded in a defect-tracking system. The defect record is then assigned to a given user and goes through a set of states to indicate work progress on fixing the defect. In these cases, the defect record is tracking both the issue and the response. Often the change set information is also recorded in the defect record.

In SCM-centric environments, where there is no defect-tracking system or a highly disconnected approach to defect tracking, a change set object is created to track the change set for SCM purposes only. The relationship between the change set object and any issue or task might be recorded loosely in a textual description.

Based on the complexity of your software-development environment, any of these approaches can be effective and efficient. Designers of the UCM model needed to take into account all three approaches and allow for increased activity information as a project grows in size and complexity. In UCM, a developer is always working with an activity. That activity could be a simple change set, or it could be a more complex object that represents a defect or task.

ClearCase Activity Objects

An *activity* tracks the work required to complete a development task. It includes a text headline, which describes the task, and a change set, which identifies all versions that you create or modify while working on the activity. Activity objects are created in a PVOB in the stream in which they will be used.

In ClearCase UCM, the activity object combines all three concepts just discussed: issue, response, and result. However, the primary job of the ClearCase activity object is to track the change set or result. If defect-tracking or activity-management software (such as Rational Software's ClearQuest) is used, then the change set portion of the activity lives in the PVOB, but all other activity data resides in the ClearQuest database. With ClearQuest, the UCM model can then support the other two approaches shown in Figure 4-6.

In any case, the developer simply works with activities. For information on activity-based SCM, see the section "The Developer: Joining a Project and Doing Development," in Chapter 3, "An Overview of the Unified Change Management Model." For information on how activities are exposed to the developer, see "Making Changes," in Chapter 8. For information on how ClearQuest extends the UCM model, see "Change Request Management and ClearQuest," in Chapter 12.

4.4   Versioned Objects: Elements, Branches, and Versions

The atomic object put under version control in ClearCase is referred to as an *element*. Elements are file system objects: files and directories. Every element records versions of the file or directory it represents. So, when a user checks in a file, a new version is created for that element. These element versions are organized into branches. A *branch* is an object that specifies a linear sequence of element versions. They are used for many purposes, such as doing parallel development and maintaining variants of the system.

Each element starts life with a main branch and a null zero version that does not have any content. This is represented in ClearCase as `/main/0`. The first new version checked in creates Version 1 on the receiving branch or stream. In a UCM environment, this first version of an element is created on the UCM stream associated with the ClearCase view in which the user is working. The organization of versions into branches provides a time-ordered representation of each element's history. The relationship between the repository (VOB), the elements it contains, and each element's branches and versions can be seen in UML notation in Figure 4-15.

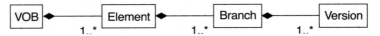

Figure 4-15   VOB, element, branch, and version relationships.

ClearCase provides both a command-line way and a graphical way to view an element's branches and versions, both called a *version tree*. A graphical example of a version tree display is shown in Figure 4-16. Boxes indicate the branches. Circles indicate time-ordered versions as they are checked in. The arrows indicate merges of changes from one branch to another. The text next to a version indicates a label that has been applied to that version.

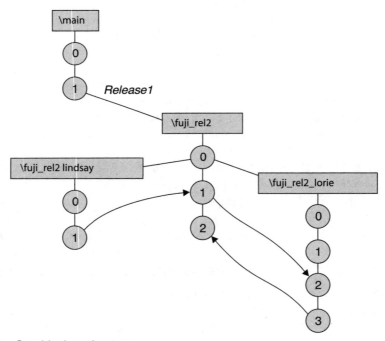

Figure 4-16   Graphical version tree.

The following is the same version tree as shown in Figure 4-16, displayed from the text-based command line:

```
prompt> ncleartool lsvtree example.c
example.c@@/main
example.c@@/main/0
example.c@@/main/1 (RELEASE1)
```

```
example.c@@/main/fuji_rel2
example.c@@/main/fuji_rel2/0
example.c@@/main/fuji_rel2/fuji_rel2_lorie
example.c@@/main/fuji_rel2/fuji_rel2_lorie/0
example.c@@/main/fuji_rel2/fuji_rel2_lorie/1
example.c@@/main/fuji_rel2/fuji_rel2_lorie/2
example.c@@/main/fuji_rel2/fuji_rel2_lorie/3
example.c@@/main/fuji_rel2/fuji_rel2_lindsay
example.c@@/main/fuji_rel2/fuji_rel2_lindsay/0
example.c@@/main/fuji_rel2/fuji_rel2_lindsay/1
example.c@@/main/fuji_rel2/1
example.c@@/main/fuji_rel2/2
```

4.4.1   Directory Versioning

Directories are also versioned in ClearCase primarily to allow rebuilding of previous versions of a software system. Directories define the namespace for files. This allows files to refer to other files either absolutely or relatively. Being able to rebuild previous versions of a software system is typically necessary to fix a bug in a previous release. Often if the directory structure has changed between releases, the build tools (make or clearmake) might not work unless the old directory structure is restored. Similarly, internal file references might be broken if files have since been renamed, deleted, or moved.

Like files, directories are checked out and checked back in whenever they are modified. Directories are modified during the following operations: renaming an element, moving an element from one directory to another, adding a new element, removing an element, or removing the name of an element. (Removing an element's name [rmname] is a ClearCase-specific operation because of the support for directory versioning. The command rmname removes the element from the current version of the directory, but not from the VOB itself [as does rmelem]. In this way, earlier versions of the directory will have the element and later versions will not. You almost always want to do an rmname instead of an rmelem.)

Typically, in Windows, the process is automated through the GUI. For example, if you select a file and click the right mouse button to bring up the ClearCase context menu and select "Add to source control," ClearCase checks out the directory, creates the new element, and checks in the directory, all in one operation.

On UNIX, this is done specifically by checking out the directory itself, as follows:

```
prompt> cleartool checkout -c "adding new.c" sources
prompt> cd sources
prompt> cleartool mkelem -c "first version" new.c
prompt> cleartool checkin -nc .
```

In the last line, `-nc` stands for "no comment." ClearCase automatically comments all directory operations for you because it knows what you are doing. The period is UNIX shorthand for the current directory.

Versioning of directories is a feature of ClearCase that is not avialable in most SCM systems. As a result, it is a new concept for most people and can be the source of some confusion if not understood. In particular, consider the case in which a particular directory, Foo, is checked out by two different developers working on their own private development streams. Each developer adds a new version-controlled element to his or her working copy of the directory, and each names this new element `bar.c`. One of the developers delivers the activity containing his changes to directory Foo to the project's integration stream. When the second developer delivers her changes to directory Foo to the proejct's integration stream, ClearCase detects and flags a merge collision. That collision, of course, is that an element with the name `bar.c` is already cataloged in the version of directory Foo that is in the project's integration stream. This situation happens often enough (especially at sites new to ClearCase) that it has a name: the evil twin scenario. When this first happens to a developer, it usually causes a great deal of hand-wringing, but happily, the recovery is simple. If the two elements `bar.c` are meant to be the same, the second developer simply chooses one and completes the delivery. If the two elements are not meant to be the same and the name collision was accidental, the second developer needs to cancel out of the delivery, change the name of the element to some noncolliding value (say, `xyzzy.c`), and then reinitiate the delivery. Some ClearCase installations have developed triggers that parse the contents of all versions of a directory on all branches and streams to detect and prevent the evil twin scenario. The challenge in developing such automated approaches is to make sure their performance remains satisfactory as the number of elements, branches, and streams grows. Other sites simply rely on user education to deal with the evil twin scenario.

4.4.2 Element Types

In ClearCase, each element placed into a VOB is of a specific element type. Element types can be used for a number of purposes:

- To define what storage/delta mechanism is used for the element
- To scope which versions are selected in a configuration (for example, "show me Release 1 of all the design documents")
- To scope policy rules (see the section "Process: Labels, Attributes, Hyperlinks, Triggers," later in this chapter)
- To define the mechanism used for comparison and merging

ClearCase has predefined element types, which are primarily used to determine the storage, or delta, mechanism that should be used for the type. The predefined elements types are as follows:

- **File (`file`)**—Each new version of file elements is stored as a complete copy. No delta computation is used for disk space savings.

- **Text file (`text_file`)**—This element type identifies the file as a text file and uses inline delta storage1 to store only the changes made between one version and the next. This is the primary type used for most text files.

- **Compressed text file (`compressed_text_file`)**—The compressed text file element type uses the same delta storage mechanism as the text file but additionally compresses the delta file after changes are added. This element type is used to maximize disk space conservation.

- **Compressed file (`compressed_file`)**—The compressed file element type is used for files to which you do not want to have any delta mechanism applied but you want to conserve some disk space. Elements of this type are identical to type file, in that they are stored as a complete copy of each version. They differ in that each complete copy version is compressed.

- **Binary delta file (`binary_delta_file`)**—The binary delta file element type uses a delta mechanism that efficiently computes and stores only the differences between one version of a binary file and another. This type manager can significantly reduce disk space consumption if large binary files are being versioned regularly.[1]

- **Directory (`directory`)**—New versions of directory elements are stored directly in the VOB database, using an internal format. This element type is used to identify and manage directories.

Element types can have supertypes. For example, you could define an element type of `c_source` that identifies C files. This element type might have a supertype of `text_file`. In this way, the element type `c_source` inherits the storage characteristics of the `text_file` element type. The purpose of defining your own element types is to use them in queries, configuration specification rules, and triggers.

Some additional predefined types build on the basic element types and have their own specialized compare/merge capabilities. These are as follows:

- **Hypertext Markup Language (`html`)**—This element type is used to identify and manage HTML-formatted files. The supertype of an `html` element is `text_file`, so it also uses inline delta storage.

- **Microsoft Word (`ms_word`)**—This element type is used to identify and manage Microsoft Word documents. The type manager uses Microsoft Word's compare/merge tools. The supertype of an `ms_word` element is file, so the whole copy is stored.

- **Rose models (`rose`)**—This element type is used to identify and manage Rational Rose diagrams. The type manager uses the Rose model integrator to perform compare/merge operations. The supertype of a `rose` element is `text_file`, so storage is via inline deltas.

- **Extensible Markup Language (`xml`)**—This element type is used to identify and manage XML files. The type manager uses new XML compare/merge tools to support parallel development of XML files. The supertype of an `xml` element is `text_file`, so storage is via inline deltas.

1 This differs from the forward delta or reverse delta storage mechanisms and is felt to be the more efficient mechanism for significant development efforts (see Delta Storage Mechanism in Chapter 2).

If you are an advanced ClearCase user, you might want to take advantage of the capability to define your own type manager for files that have specific compression/delta mechanisms that are proprietary to your company. Type managers also define how to handle comparing two (or more) versions and how to merge two (or more) versions.

4.5   Component Management: Components and Baselines

UCM provides the capability to group together files, directories, and folders that should be controlled and versioned as a unit into UCM components. UCM also provides the capability to define versions of individual components as UCM baselines. UCM further provides the capability to group baselines into logical groups called composite baselines. These UCM constructs and how to use them are discussed in this section.

4.5.1   Components

A ClearCase *component* groups files and directories that should be developed, integrated, baselined, and released together. The files and directories grouped into a ClearCase component usually implement a reusable piece of the system architecture (although this is not enforced).

Components are defined by identifying a root directory. That directory and all files and subdirectories are considered to be part of that component. For more details, see "The Architect: Defining the Implementation Model," in Chapter 3.

4.5.2   Baselines

A version of a component is a *baseline*. A component baseline identifies zero or one version of each element that is contained in that component. Component baselines are used to configure a stream and ultimately to provide the right information to the view to determine what versions of the files and directories should be displayed.

> **NOTE**
> Components have baselines the way elements have versions. When you change an element, you create a new version of that element. When you change elements in a component, you create a new baseline of that component. A stream groups together a set of component baselines. When you perform a baseline operation on the project's integration stream, you are creating a new set of component baselines, one for each component that has been modified. Composite baselines provide the functionality of a project-wide baseline by defining a single baseline that encompasses all the relevant individual component baselines required to define a stable project configuration.

Each baseline has a user-defined quality or promotion level. That is, with ClearCase, a company can define different levels of testing and can mark baselines indicating the level of testing that each has passed. This makes it easier to perform reuse because other project teams can determine what level of quality any given component baseline has reached.

Figure 4-17 shows the relationship among the project VOB, components, and baselines.

Figure 4-17 Project VOB, component, and baseline relationships.

Composite Baselines

A composite baseline is a UCM structure that logically associates baselines together. This logical collection is called the composite baseline, and the baselines that are part of the collection are referred to as members of the composite baseline. Figure 4-18 illustrates Baseline A that has Baselines B and C as members.

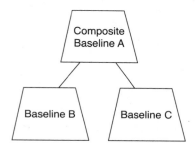

Figure 4-18 A composite baseline containing two component baselines.

Baselines that are members of a composite baseline can themselves be composite baselines. There is no limit on the number or the depth of composite baseline dependency trees. Figure 4-19 illustrates a hierarchy of composite baselines where composite baselines contain other composite baselines as members.

Composite baselines make managing baselines for projects easier. If your project uses several components, as part of the initial configuration for the project, you need to specify individual baselines within those components to serve as the foundation for your project. In these cases, you could simply create a composite baseline that contains as members those component baselines you want to serve as the foundation for your project. This enables you to use your own project-naming scheme to define the foundation baseline and makes it easier to understand the project structure.

A more compelling use for composite baselines lies in the capability to use them to define versioned subsystems and then to use those versioned subsystems as building blocks for more complex systems. These subsystems can contain single UCM components or, more likely, several UCM components. This enables you to start organizing your projects to produce and manage code for reuse and to take advantage of the significant development savings that can be realized through reuse. For example, say you have three different projects that produce reusable artifacts, as follows:

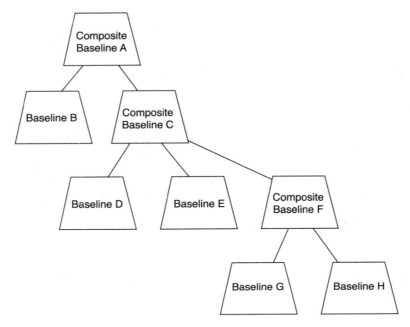

Figure 4-19   A composite baseline containing component baselines as well as other composite baselines.

- **Core project**—Creates artifacts that implement core objects or functionality
- **GUI project**—Creates artifacts that provide standardized GUI look-and-feel building blocks for your organization's applications
- **Database project**—Creates artifacts that provide standardized database functionality and interfaces for your organization's applications

Using the functionality of UCM baselines and composite baselines, each of these projects can be managed independently with independent release cycles. When each project reaches a release point, it would create a baseline with an appropriate release name and publish its release notes and baseline name to the entire development organization. These released baselines could themselves be composite baselines and could be used as a foundation for an application-development project. Further discussion on ways to use composite baselines can be found in the discussion "The Assembly Project," in Chapter 9, "Integration." Figure 4-20 provides an illustration of how composite baselines would be used in such situations.

In this figure, composite baselines have been used to define versioned subsystems that are then usable as a unit by other projects. Specifically, the higher-level application project foundation is based on Release 3 of the GUI subsystem, Release 15.1 of the core subsystem, and Release 22 of the database subsystem. The GUI subsystem and the database subsystem are themselves based on other baselines that denote specific versions of components and subsystems.

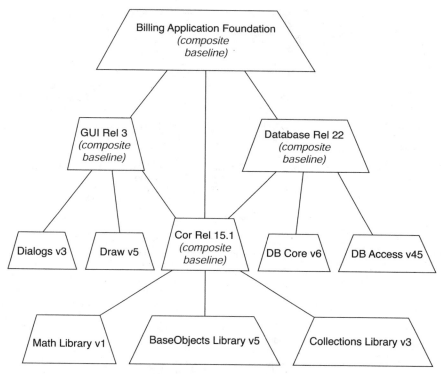

Figure 4-20 Composite baselines allow definition and control of complex interproject dependencies.

Issues with Composite Baselines

You have seen how composite baselines provide the capability to define and use versioned subsystems composed of lower-order baselines and composite baselines. The flexibility and power of this structure can also lead to the possibility of baseline conflicts.

If a composite baseline doesn't include another composite baseline in its member set, there is no possibility of a conflict. If, as you saw in Figure 4-20, a composite baseline contains other composite baselines, there is a potential for baseline conflict. Specifically, consider Figure 4-21.

In this diagram, you see a variant of Figure 4-20. In this case, however, the top-level Billing Application Foundation composite baseline contains the Core Rel 15.1 baseline, while the GUI Rel 3 composite baseline contains the Core Rel 14 baseline and the Database Rel 22 composite baseline contains the Core Rel 12.5 baseline, each of which uses a different version of the BaseObjects Library component. In this structure, it is not clear to UCM which version of the BaseObjects Library to use, so it represents a baseline conflict. UCM detects this conflict and requires the creator of the Billing Application Foundation composite baseline to explicitly specify which version of the BaseObjects Library component to use in the Billing Application Foundation composite baseline. This selection will then override the versions of the BaseObjects Library components specified by the composite baselines that make use of the BaseObjects Library.

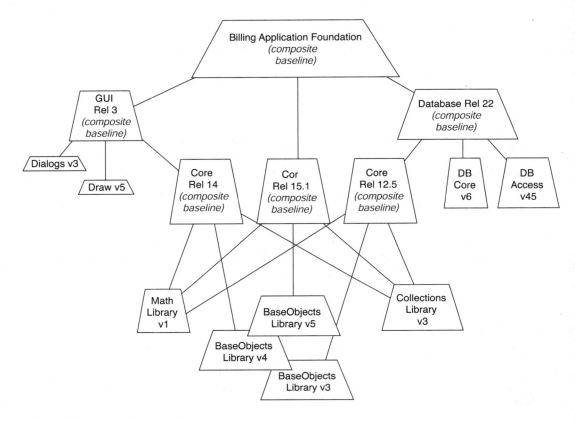

Figure 4-21   Baseline conflict in composite baselines.

In Figure 4-22, a specific version of the BaseObjects Library has been specified and, as a result, overrides the versions specified in the conflicting member composite baselines.

A feckless approach to defining subsystems and the composite baselines that denote them will greatly enhance the likelihood of encountering many such confusing conflicts. To avoid such scenarios, care should be taken to organize your projects and components to allow for maximum reuse with as few such conflicts as possible.

> **NOTE**
>
> An excellent paper titled "Best Practices for Using Composite Baselines in UCM," written by Jim Tykal, is available on the IBM DeveloperWorks site (http://www-128.ibm.com/developerworks/rational/library/5134.html). This paper provides significant detail on the UCM operations that define and use composite baselines as well as scenarios that can be used to reduce the potential for conflicts between composite baseline definitions.

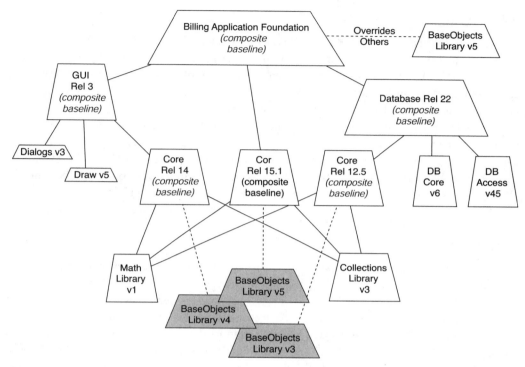

Figure 4-22   Resolution of baseline conflicts in composite baselines.

Composite baselines enable you to define and use complex subsystems using a single UCM structure. This, in turn, enables you to organize your projects and artifacts for reuse and provides the potential of substantial reduction in both time to develop new applications and costs involved in such development. The more complex your systems or subsystem is, however, the greater the potential is for conflicts between subsystems. By understanding how composite baselines work and developing a strategy for how they should be defined in your organization, you can minimize the risk of conflict and greatly enhance the productivity of your organization.

4.6   Process: Labels, Attributes, Hyperlinks, Triggers

ClearCase provides a number of additional objects that are useful for a wide variety of purposes. In many cases, these are used by ClearCase itself to implement specific functionality, but they are also available to you when you want to automate or enforce project processes and/or record additional data and relationships between objects in the system. The major objects, which are often referred to as *metadata,* are labels, attributes, hyperlinks, and triggers. These objects have been used to implement specific project policies as part of UCM.

4.6.1   Labels

A *label* is an instance of a label type and is attached to a version of an element. A *label type* is a named tag that can be used to identify a consistent set of element versions. For example, you could create a label type called `RELEASE1` and attach a label of that type to all the versions of the elements that make up Release 1. In and of themselves, labels do not represent any semantics between elements other than those your organization defines.

In general, UCM users will be using components and baselines, and should not need to create and manipulate labels themselves (this is handled by UCM automation). However, if a project using UCM needs to share code and interact with a project using base ClearCase, labels would be used. The UCM project would identify the label associated with a given component baseline for sharing outside that project. For sharing internally, a ClearCase label can be imported as a UCM baseline. Figure 4-11 shows how labels are displayed in the Windows version tree browser.

4.6.2   Attributes

Attribute types form a name/value data set that can have *attribute* instances attached to almost any ClearCase object. For example, you might create an attribute type called `review_status` that has one of the values of `passed`, `failed`, or `pending`. An instance of this type can be attached to each version of an element, indicating the code review status of that version.

Basically, attributes can be used to associate arbitrary data with objects in the system. Attributes can be attached to elements, baselines, branches, versions, hyperlinks, projects, components, and activities.

Attributes are defined to contain one of these data types:

- **Integer**—Integer values
- **Real**—Floating-point values
- **Time**—Date/time values
- **String**—Character string values
- **Opaque**—Arbitrary byte sequence values

Any of these can also have an enumerated list to restrict the legal values. For example, a string attribute type named `priority` could be defined as a string, enumerated type `HIGH`, `MEDIUM`, and `LOW`.

4.6.3   Hyperlinks

Hyperlinks define relationships between objects. For example, a predefined hyperlink type `Change` links versions to activities as part of the change set implementation. (When writing custom automation tools, you should not use this internal implementation for getting the change set. Use `cleartool lsactivity` or the ClearCase Automation Library.) Another predefined hyperlink type `Merge` defines merge relationships between versions on different branches.

You can define hyperlinks and use them to establish relationships between objects in your system. For example, if you store your detailed design documents in ClearCase, you could link these documents to the source code that implements the design or to the component containing the source code.

4.6.4   Triggers

Triggers are user-defined events that fire when ClearCase operations occur. Coupled with attributes and hyperlinks (as just described), triggers enable you to automate the creation of interobject relationships, attach data, and enforce policies based on ClearCase events.

Triggers are of two different types: pre-event and post-event. Pre-event triggers fire before a ClearCase event occurs and can cancel the triggering event. They are typically used to enforce policies. For example, a pre-event trigger could disallow a check-in if the `review_status` attribute on that version was not set to `passed`. Post-event triggers are typically used for notification. For example, after an event has occurred, e-mail could be sent notifying a project team that a key system header file was modified.

Most ClearCase events, including UCM operations, are triggerable. This capability to apply a programmatic action to a CM event provides the capability to implement powerful contol constructs to govern how software is to be developed in a project or an organization. Examples of such triggers might be to enforce naming conventions for baselines or to restrict the ability of developers to deliver activities to the project based on change control board decisions.

> **NOTE**
> The line between useful control constructs, such as enforcement of change control board decisions, and control constructs that are convoluted, arcane, and unintelligible can be very fine. We have noted that many organizations move too quickly to develop complex automated processes that ultimately are (or should be) abandoned because they prove to be too slow to execute or they provide irresistible incentive for users to find ways around them or, worse, to sabotage them. Therefore, care should be taken to avoid overengineering such controls.

4.6.5   Creating and Managing Types

Use of any of the metadata types is a two-step process. The first is defining the type. The second is creating instances of the type. Element types and branch types also behave similarly. So, for example, you have to create an element type before you can create an element instance of that type.

ClearCase provides both GUI and command-line access to creation and management of types. With UNIX, administrators usually use the command-line interface. The key command-line operations are as follows:

- List type:

```
cleartool lstype -<XX>type
```

• Make type:

```
cleartool mk<XX>type
```

- Make instance of a type:

```
cleartool mk<kind>
```

Where <XX> is as follows:

- el: Element type
- br: Branch type
- lb: Label type
- at: Attribute type
- hl: Hyperlink type
- tr: Trigger type

Where <kind> is as follows:

- element: Element instance
- branch: Branch instance
- label: Label instance
- attr: Attribute instance
- hlink: Hyperlink instance
- trigger: Trigger instance

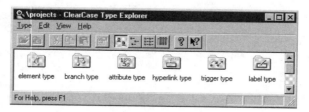

Figure 4-23   ClearCase Type Explorer.

On Windows, the Type Explorer application is generally used for managing types (see Figure 4-23).

4.7   Building: Clearmake, Derived Objects, Configuration Records

One aspect of configuration management that is often overlooked is build management. ClearCase provides significant functionality aimed at supporting reproducible builds, object sharing between developers, parallel builds, and distributed builds. ClearCase supports these best when you are using make technology as your build engine. The key build features are described in the following subsection.

4.7.1   Build Audit

Typically, when a software system is built, many object files, libraries, and executables are produced. ClearCase calls these *derived objects*. Often the traceability between the derived objects and the versions of the source used to produce them is lost, making it impossible to reproduce builds. This can lead to an inability to maintain, debug, and patch releases being used by your customers.

ClearCase provides a make-compatible build tool called *clearmake*. When clearmake is used to build derived objects, a record is kept of who built each derived object, when it was built, on what platform it was built, and, most important, what files and what versions of those files were referenced during the build. This information is called a *configuration record*. All the configuration records for all derived objects that are part of a build make up the *build audit*. ClearCase provides the capability to generate a bill of materials for any build (that is, what versions of what files were referenced for the entire build).

When some other type of build tools, such as Ant, CruiseControl, and customized programmatic build scripts are used, ClearCase provides the `buildaudit` command. The `buildaudit` command is used in conjunction with these other types of build tools to produce a configuration record and can generate a comprehensive bill of materials for any build.

> **NOTE**
> For further information on using ClearCase with Ant, you can review the materials at http://ant.apache.org/manual/OptionalTasks/clearcase.html.
> Information on using ClearCase with the CruiseControl build tool can be found at http://www.buildmeister.com/articles/cruisecontrol-clearcase.php.

The build audit can be used to compare builds, enabling you to see what versions of what files are different between two builds or even what compiler options might have changed. A frequent problem in debugging is having an error show up in code that everyone is convinced was not changed. One of the big advantages of being able to compare two builds is the ability to quickly determine which files or build options changed from one build to the next.

4.7.2   Object Sharing

By keeping a configuration record for each derived object, it becomes possible to automate sharing of derived objects. This means that instead of rebuilding the same object, library, or executable over and over, it can be shared between developers. This happens automatically when using clearmake because clearmake can determine that the derived object you are about to build uses the same versions, same compiler, same compiler switches, and so on as one that already exists. This derived object sharing can significantly reduce both the development build times and the amount of disk space required for each developer's workspace.

4.7.3   Parallel and Distributed Builds

Clearmake supports parallel and distributed builds on UNIX platforms. Parallel building is the capability to run multiple compiles simultaneously by understanding the build order dependency graph described in the make file (that is, the order in which files must be built, based on their dependencies). (See [Oram, 1993] for more information on using make to build your software projects.) Distributed builds enable you to use multiple machines to perform build steps. This is often advantageous for performing nightly builds because there are usually quite a few idle CPUs after normal working hours. For each machine that might be used in a distributed build, you can specify at what hours and what load limits that machine should be used. Clearmake uses this information to determine if and when it can use any given machine.

4.7.4   Clearmake versus Classic Make

Typically, make build environments use a "make depends" step, which stands for "make dependencies." This step parses the source files looking for language-specific constructs (such as `include file.h`) that indicate dependencies. These dependencies are used to construct the appropriate dependency rules in the makefile. When using clearmake and dynamic views in ClearCase, this is not necessary because ClearCase records these dependencies in the configuration record. This eliminates an extra build step (which is sometimes forgotten) and is more accurate because it is based on the files that are actually opened during the build instead of a parse scanning for language-specific `include` constructs.

Another advantage of clearmake over classic make is that clearmake uses the version information of the files to determine when a rebuild needs to take place. Classic make uses the date/time to determine whether a rebuild is required. So, for example, if you decide to reconfigure your view to see an older version of a file, clearmake will rebuild, but classic make will incorrectly conclude that a rebuild is not necessary.

> **NOTE**
>
> For a more detailed explanation of how dynamic views work and the benefits of transparent file access, refer to a paper by the creator of ClearCase, David Leblang, entitled "The CM Challenge: Configuration Management That Works" [Leblang, 1994]. It is part of the book *Configuration Management*, edited by Walter Tichy [Tichy, 1994]. This paper is particularly useful for UNIX-based teams evaluating ClearCase as a potential SCM tool.

4.8   Summary

This chapter explored the ClearCase objects that make up a ClearCase UCM environment and the relationships between them. From the versioned object base at the highest level to individual streams, baselines, and activities, you have also seen how these constructs can be used to provide a project with structure, control and tracking, and management of the assets under development.

CHAPTER 5

Establishing the Initial SCM Environment

The quickest way to get started using ClearCase is by creating one project VOB (PVOB) and one source VOB, and importing your existing source code. However, this is effective for only small projects and small systems. For most projects, some advanced planning is advised. This chapter covers the information you need to know to do this planning and the steps you must take to set up the initial SCM environment. We cover the basics of ClearCase architecture, discuss the hardware resource requirements for ClearCase, suggest some guidelines for taking a system from its logical design to its physical implementation, cover the creation of ClearCase VOBs, and discuss setting up component baseline promotion levels.

ClearCase installation and other administrative details are not covered in this book. It is expected that you will consult the ClearCase documentation set for installation and administration. Another resource that is full of practical advice on how to successfully deploy and implement a ClearCase environment is *The Art of ClearCase Deployment* [Buckley and Pulsipher, 2004].

5.1 ClearCase Architecture Basics

The first step in creating any SCM environment is to obtain or allocate the necessary hardware and install and configure the SCM tool. This section gives you a high-level overview of the ClearCase architecture and makes some hardware configuration recommendations. Admittedly, the information provided here is a simplified view of the actual ClearCase architecture. (The ClearCase administration manual provides much greater detail.) However, you should find it sufficient for basic planning purposes.

ClearCase is a multiserver, distributed SCM tool that allows for a great deal of flexibility and scalability in hardware configuration. To understand the hardware resource requirements for ClearCase, you should start with a basic understanding of the ClearCase architecture. ClearCase is specifically designed to spread the workload across multiple machines. During evaluations, it is certainly possible to install and configure one machine to use ClearCase, but typically a ClearCase environment consists of at least one server and several clients.

When determining your hardware environment for ClearCase, you must find a home for six types of processes and the multiversion file system (MVFS). The processes are as follows:

- License server
- Registry server
- VOB server (In fact, three types of servers are associated with a VOB. The actual number of server processes running depends on the load being placed on the VOB. ClearCase automatically starts additional server processes when needed and stops these processes when demand drops.)
- View server
- ALBD server
- Client processes (such as cleartool)

The multiversion file system is a client-side requirement and is used on platforms that support dynamic views.

5.1.1   The License Server and Registry Server

The two administrative processes are the *license server* and the *registry server*. The purpose of the license server is to manage license keys and ensure that the licensing constraints are not violated. (ClearCase includes its own license manager. ClearCase licensing is truly per user. A single user can be using ClearCase at his or her desk on a Windows machine and in a test lab on two UNIX machines, and consume only one ClearCase license. ClearCase licenses are floating and have a default timeout period of 1 hour.) The purpose of the registry server is to maintain the directory and machine locations on which all view and VOB data is being stored. In this way, any ClearCase client can locate any ClearCase data, regardless of where in the network this data is stored. The license server and registry server require very little in the way of server resources. The primary consideration is that the machine on which these servers reside should be very reliable. Often the license and registry servers are placed on the same machine as the primary VOB server processes.

5.1.2   The VOB Server and View Server

ClearCase VOBs store all the files and directories being managed by ClearCase. As such, they are a global resource that most clients will need to access. Each VOB has a set of VOB server processes associated with it that handle read and write traffic to the VOB. For small projects at small companies, you might start with only one VOB. Large numbers of projects at large companies might have hundreds of VOBs. A single VOB can contain from zero to tens of thousands of elements (files and directories). The number of elements you place into any given VOB depends largely on three factors: how many people will be accessing the data concurrently, whether you take advantage of ClearCase's build capabilities, and the size of the machine on which the VOB server will be running.

ClearCase views provide a working set of files for a developer. ClearCase views have a small database associated with them, the view database, that keeps track of what files are being changed and what files should be visible to the user. ClearCase views tend to be used by a single individual. The number of ClearCase views you need depends on how many users and how many projects are underway at any given time.

The storage location for VOB or view data determines where ClearCase VOB and view servers will be running. Both the VOB server and view server processes run on the same machine that physically contains the VOB and view databases.

Three basic configurations exist for VOB and view storage: (ClearCase offers additional options, such as splitting source code, build objects, and caches into multiple pools, that can be distributed across multiple disks or put onto high-end machines optimized for file services. These more complex scenarios are covered in the ClearCase administration manual.)

- VOBs and views on the same server machine
- VOBs and views on different server machines
- VOBs on a server machine and views on client machines

These configurations are discussed in the section "Example Hardware Configurations," later in this chapter.

VOBs and Views on the Same Server Machine

It is possible to store both VOBs and views on the same server machine (refer to Figure 5-3 later in the chapter). This is usually done for demonstrations and evaluations of ClearCase. It also can be done for smaller teams that have limited client-side computing power. In this configuration, one server holds both the VOBs and views, and the client machine runs the ClearCase client processes. In general, this configuration is suitable for a limited number of small projects.

The primary reason not to store views and VOBs on the same machine is that both VOB and view servers cache data and will compete for memory resources. ClearCase is designed as a distributed system, and one of the assumptions is that the VOB and view servers will be running on different machines. With the VOB and view servers on the same machine, both processes will compete for memory, I/O, and CPU resources. The problem you might encounter if you choose this configuration is slow performance. Typically, increasing machine memory or I/O capacity will alleviate the issue. However, ideally, the VOBs and views should be on different machines.

VOBs and Views on Different Server Machines

In this configuration, the VOBs live on one or more dedicated VOB server machines, and the views live on one or more dedicated view server machines (refer to Figure 5-6 later in the chapter). Users interact with ClearCase running client processes on their desktops. This configuration is primarily used by larger development organizations. It is appealing to organizations that prefer common central servers with lightweight desktop machines. This approach allows ClearCase server capacity to be easily increased. As more users come on board, you simply add more view server machines. As more source code is managed, you simply add more VOB server machines.

This configuration also has the advantage of making it easier for the administrator to back up view storage directories because these reside on a central server rather than on multiple desktop machines. This approach has two drawbacks. The first is the cost of purchasing one or more additional server machines. In the long run, this cost is small compared with the improved development productivity and reduced administration costs. Second, when an organization is using dynamic views, you might experience performance problems on the view server machine because of the MVFS, particularly on Windows operating systems. This configuration is recommended when using snapshot views in the split mode, where the view's database lives on the view server machine and the storage directory for the files resides on the client.

VOBs on a Server Machine and Views on Client Machines

In this configuration, the VOBs live on one or more dedicated VOB server machines, and the views live on the client machines. This configuration was the basis for the original ClearCase design and remains the preferred configuration for ClearCase (refer to Figure 5-5 later in the chapter).

In this configuration, views live on the desktop machine and communicate directly with the client-side processes. The benefits of this configuration are that you do not need to maintain another server machine and you reduce the amount of network traffic ClearCase generates. This could result in a performance improvement if you have a heavily loaded network. Another benefit is that users are generally better at managing their own disk space if the view storage resides on their desktop machine. The disadvantage to this approach is that it is much harder to back up view storage. As long as users check in their changes frequently, this is usually not a problem. However, if users rarely check in changes, the need to back up view storage becomes more critical. (It should be said that the practice of not checking in changes regularly should be discouraged. Key to this is ensuring that check-in is not also used as a means to promote the change to group visibility.)

In short, a single server is recommended for the evaluation process, VOB and view servers are recommended for large organizations that have dedicated IS/IT groups using snapshot views, and VOB servers with views are recommended for clients in small- to medium-size projects that maintain their own servers and large organizations that primarily use dynamic views.

Of course, mixed configurations are possible. For example, you could store user views on desktop machines while storing project build views on the VOB server machine.

5.1.3   The ALBD Server and Client Processes

The client machine is the primary machine for the ClearCase user. It offers a variety of end-user client processes, ranging from the cleartool command-line interface to many GUI interfaces, such as the ClearCase Project Explorer or graphical merge tool. These client processes communicate with the license, registry, view, and VOB servers to perform their functions and provide the information a ClearCase user requires.

The ClearCase ALBD (ALBD stands for the Atria Location Broker Daemon—Atria was the name of the company that originally designed and developed ClearCase) server is a broker between ClearCase processes and data. It provides other ClearCase processes with the information needed to locate and communicate with other ClearCase processes, regardless of where in the network the processes exist. Typically, the ALBD server is set up as part of every ClearCase installation. (The exception is a client-only install on the Windows platform. This installation favors snapshot views, where the snapshot view server is *not* running on the client. In this mode, there are no servers running on the client and, thus, no need for the ALBD server.)

5.1.4   The Multiversion File System

As discussed earlier, ClearCase supports two types of views: snapshot and dynamic (see "Workspaces: Snapshot and Dynamic Views" in Chapter 4, "A Functional Overview of ClearCase Objects"). Dynamic views do not have copies of the shared read-only files; they provide them to the user directly from the ClearCase VOB. The mechanism used to deliver the files is the multiversion file system. The MVFS is unique in the industry to ClearCase.

Most operating systems provide a file system interface that enables you to plug in different types of file systems (see Figure 5-1). For example, NFS is the network file system that can be plugged into a UNIX or Windows system. NFS is dominant on UNIX. On Windows, the NTFS and FAT file systems plug into the Windows file system interface. ClearCase uses this file system interface to plug the MVFS into the operating system. That is, the MVFS supports the operating system's file system interface, as does NFS, NTFS, SMB, and FAT. The result is that the MVFS appears similar to the predominant file system on both the UNIX and Windows operating systems.

The key difference between the native OS file system and the MVFS is that the MVFS understands versioning. When a user opens a file, the MVFS uses the rules in the user's view to determine which version of the file to open. Because the processing is done at the OS file system level, any application, such as Emacs, Vi, Notepad, or Word, can seamlessly retrieve the right version of the file. In marketing-speak, this is called transparency. In other words, the version control and version selection are done in a way that is transparent to the end user and to any application accessing the data (see Figure 5-2).

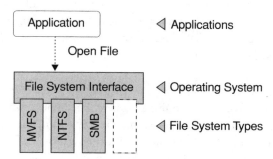

Figure 5-1   File system interface.

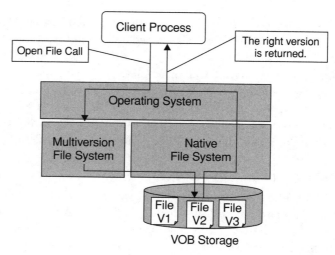

Figure 5-2   The multiversion file system.

The MVFS and dynamic views offer significant advantages, the first of which is transparency. Others are the time saved in updating or creating a workspace (because files are not copied) and the capability of build auditing (during the build process, it is possible to accurately track what files are opened and read for any step in the build).

From an architectural basics standpoint, the key thing to note is that the MVFS is a client-side piece of ClearCase that does its thing on the client machine. To be clear, if you never create or use a ClearCase view on a VOB server machine, you will never need the MVFS on the VOB server.

5.1.5   Example Hardware Configurations

This section examines the hardware configurations of four common distributions of the processes just discussed.

Evaluation Environment

In an evaluation or demonstration environment, it is possible to install all ClearCase processes on the same machine. You should select a "server" configuration during the installation process. The evaluation machine and the ClearCase server processes are shown in Figure 5-3. This configuration is not recommended for use in a production environment.

Basic Environment

For a smaller site, a basic environment configuration is the simplest when using ClearCase in a production environment. In this configuration, there is one ClearCase server machine and multiple client machines. The server machine holds all of the VOBs and administrative processes. The client machine has disk space to hold the views and runs both view server processes and ClearCase client processes. This basic environment is shown in Figure 5-4.

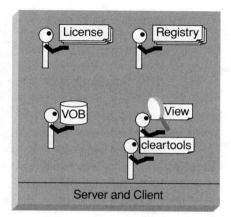

Figure 5-3 Evaluation environment.

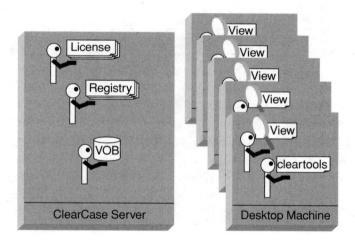

Figure 5-4 Basic environment.

Modest Environment

The modest environment is easily scalable to larger project teams. You can add multiple ClearCase servers and distribute the VOBs across these servers. In this configuration, the clients still run the ClearCase client processes and the view servers for the views stored and used on the client machine. A modest environment is shown in Figure 5-5. The modest environment is also recommended for large teams that are primarily using dynamic views.

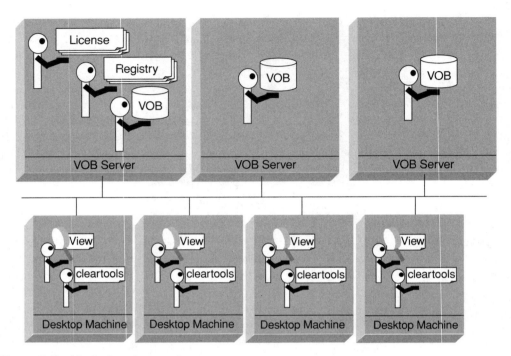

Figure 5-5   Modest environment.

Complex Environment

For very large sites, it is often useful to introduce dedicated view servers. This makes administration easier because view servers are centralized. Larger environments might also have dedicated build machines used for project-level building. A more complex ClearCase environment, with dedicated view servers, is shown in Figure 5-6. This environment is recommended for large teams that are primarily using snapshot views.

5.2   ClearCase Hardware Resource Requirements

One of the questions most often asked is what kind/size/make/model/type of machine should be used for a VOB server. The answer invariably is, "It depends." Many factors contribute to what type of machine will be best for your company (including amount of data, type of data, number of concurrent users, and build strategy). The information in this section and the following section on the client should be viewed as a starting point in your quest for the perfect environment.

The key to a well-performing ClearCase environment is a well-performing server machine. How do you ensure that your server machine (or machines) performs well? Easy: Buy the most loaded and most powerful machine you can. Sooner or later, you will grow into (or out of) it, and you never know whether your budget will get cut next year. However, if your company is like most,

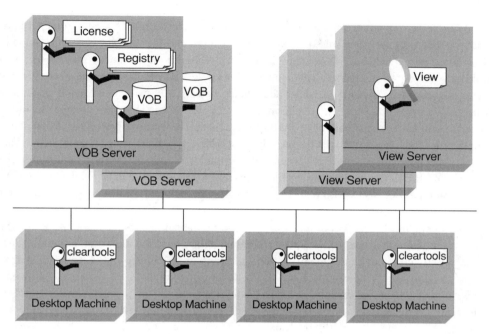

Figure 5-6   Complex environment.

hardware resources are not always easy to acquire, and you might need to start with what you already have. So, it is useful to understand where to apply your dollars with respect to ClearCase.

Typically, the VOB server processes make the most demands on system hardware. The VOB server machine is also the most critical piece of a ClearCase network as far as performance monitoring and tuning are concerned. A VOB server machine is a machine that is dedicated to running VOB server processes. There might be more than one VOB on a single VOB server machine, and there might be more than one VOB server machine in the network. The key resources to consider when sizing a VOB server are memory, disk I/O, network bandwidth, and CPU. These are listed in order of priority to ClearCase performance, with memory being the most important and CPU being the least.

5.2.1   Memory Requirements

VOB server processes, view server processes, and the MVFS do a lot of caching and background data writing. The best thing you can do to make sure you have a well-tuned ClearCase environment is to ensure that your server and client machines have enough main memory. When a machine starts paging ClearCase data to disk, you can guarantee that performance will suffer. Memory is the cheapest way to improve ClearCase performance. Lack of sufficient memory is the most common cause of poor ClearCase performance.

VOB server machines should have a minimum of 1GB. (As of this writing, this pertains to ClearCase v2003.06.14.) The rule of thumb is that you add all the database space consumed by VOBs stored on a machine and divide by 2. This is the minimum amount of main memory you should have on a dedicated VOB server machine (see the "Other Recommendations" section, later in this chapter, for more on what "dedicated" means). You can use cleartool space or the ClearCase administration console to determine this amount. So, in short, for every 2MB of database space you have, you should have 1MB of main memory. The assumption here is that half of the data in a ClearCase VOB will be actively accessed at any given time. A more conservative approach, and one recommended if you have the resources, is to have 1MB of memory for every 1MB of VOB database size. This allows the entire set of the VOB data to be available in memory at any given time. Because VOBs will continue to grow over time, it is also good practice to have extra memory on a VOB server machine.

For client machines, a minimum of 512MB of main memory is recommended. Many people might feel this is too high, but this recommendation covers a minimum amount of memory for a software developer's client machine rather than specifically for ClearCase. There is clearly a trend toward Windows machines on the desktop, and often developers need many applications running at the same time. For example, a developer might have a defect-tracking tool such as ClearQuest, a design tool such as Rose, and an IDE such as Microsoft Visual Studio all open at the same time. If you add one or two ClearCase views and some ClearCase client processes such as the difference tool or version tree browser, the memory requirements quickly add up. To keep ClearCase views from paging their caches to disk, you need to ensure that sufficient main memory is available on the client machine.

In summary, memory is the cheapest and easiest way to boost ClearCase performance, particularly on the ClearCase VOB server machine. Check the size of your VOB databases periodically, and make sure you have a minimum of half of this available in memory for the VOBs.

> **NOTE**
> For ClearCase 2003.06.14, Rational Software documents a minimum configuration of 128MB on the server and 64MB on the client. Smaller sites (with a small number of VOBs and a small number of users) may experience acceptable performance with this minimal configuration, but because of the low cost of memory, I recommend starting with substantially more.

5.2.2   Disk I/O Requirements

The second possible performance bottleneck in a ClearCase environment is the speed at which data can be written to disk. The key is to ensure that you have sufficient I/O resources on your VOB server machines. This is critical if you have a large number of VOBs on a single machine actively being written to. VOBs that are predominantly being referenced will not contribute to the need for fast disk I/O (unless you do not have enough main memory, and then I/O speed will influence the disk caching). Writing to the VOB takes place when you are using ClearCase's build facilities (such as clearmake) and during operations such as check-in, deliver, and baseline creation.

The following two recommendations will help you reduce I/O performance issues.

- **Do not place busy VOBs on the same disk partition.** Use multiple disks to balance the load. Technically, there is no reason why you cannot place multiple VOBs on the same disk. However, it is better to plan ahead and distribute the VOBs that are most often accessed on multiple disks.

- **Make sure you have sufficient controllers to service busy disks.** For busy read/write VOBs, there should be one controller per disk. Disk striping, disk arrays, and RAID systems can also improve performance. Having many disks daisy-chained to one channel is not recommended because data can be transferred to only one disk at a time. It is better to have controllers that support multiple channels if your controller is servicing more than one disk. Optimal performance results from having one dedicated controller and channel per disk.

5.2.3　Network Bandwidth and Reliability

Because ClearCase is a distributed application, adequate network capacity and reliability are required for good performance. Some pieces of ClearCase are more dependent on the network than others. For example, to use ClearCase, you need access to the license server. When you use dynamic views, files are accessed directly over the network from the VOB. Clearmake makes extensive use of the network to reduce build times by sharing binary files that have already been built in other views. Using snapshot views can reduce the reliance on the network—at the cost of not using other ClearCase functionality.

　　If you find that limited capacity or reliability of your network are causing your ClearCase environment to be suboptimal, a few recommendations can solve this. Machines hosting views and VOBs should be on the same subnet (there should be no router hops to get from one machine to another). If the local area network (LAN) is too saturated (that is, you are seeing messages for RPC timeout and the NFS server not responding), you might need to add a subnet for ClearCase machines or increase network capacity. In general, collisions greater than 10 percent are a problem in a ClearCase network. In short, you need to have a reliable network with sufficient capacity when using ClearCase.

5.2.4　CPU

In general, ClearCase is not a CPU-intensive application. Before you increase your CPU capacity, make sure you are really having a CPU problem on a server machine. (This is fairly easy to determine by looking at CPU loading and which processes are consuming CPU.) UCM use tends to utilize more CPU resources compared to base ClearCase. However, the most likely scenario you will encounter with ClearCase is that many active VOB server processes are running on the same machine or that the VOB server machine is being used as a build machine. In the first case, you can try adding processors to the machine if it supports this. The most likely solution, however, is to move some VOBs to another server machine. In the second case, simply stop using the VOB server machine as a build machine.

ClearCase is a multiprocess application and, as such, can take advantage of multiple processors on a machine. However, you are not likely to experience improved performance past four processors.

5.2.5   Other Recommendations

Beyond the mechanical measures of what kind and how much hardware to use is the area of how that hardware should be used. We have found that adherence to the following usage "best practices" further optimizes the efficiency of the hardware used in a ClearCase installation.

Dedicated ClearCase Servers

VOB server machines should be dedicated to ClearCase. (To be clear, there is no technical reason why you cannot run other processes on a VOB server machine.) Dedication means the following:

- No compiles, builds, or testing are performed on the VOB server.
- No ClearCase views are stored or used on the VOB server.
- No third-party tools other than ClearCase (such as Oracle or Sybase) are used.
- The VOB server does not act as a file server (no user home directories).
- The VOB server does not act as a mail server.
- The VOB server does not act as an NIS master or DNS service.
- The VOB server does not act as a Web server (such as HTTPD or IIS).
- There are no direct user logons.

The VOB server machine can act as a license server or registry server without any significant impact. In fact, for sites with one VOB server machine, it makes sense to have the single VOB server act as the ClearCase registry and license server, to reduce the points of failure.

VOB Disk Space

When determining VOB storage location, allow room for disk space growth. New VOBs should have at least 50 percent free space on their disk partitions.

There is no universal guidance on how much storage to allocate for a VOB. This is because the size of a VOB depends on many factors. Such factors include what kind of objects will be version-controlled (for example, binary files will likely be larger than text files), how many objects will be in the VOB, how many versions of each object will be in the VOB, and so on. The best approach is to determine the initial size of the objects you will be placing under version control and allocate enough space to contain a best-guess multiple of that size based on the criteria just noted. After that, monitor the size of the VOB at a reasonable frequency and adjust your space allocation if you determine that the VOB is likely to grow beyond the bounds of your initial estimate. There are four areas of VOB growth to monitor: database storage, source pools, clear-text pools, and derived object pools. The size of the database and VOB pools can be found using cleartool space or the ClearCase administration console (see Figure 5-7).

These are the four areas of VOB growth:

- **Database storage**—Every VOB has a database, which grows slowly over time. The size of a VOB database depends on a number of factors, such as the type and amount of metadata used, event record history, the number of directory element versions, and clearmake usage.

- **Source pools**—Every VOB has one or more source pools, which contain all the versions for the files stored in ClearCase. The size of the source pool depends on the number of elements stored and the number of element versions. The amount of new data stored for each version depends on the size of the change itself and the type manager being used. For example, a `whole_copy` type manager stores an entire copy of an element for each new version, whereas a `text_file` type manager stores only the delta between the new version and the previous version.

- **Clear-text pools**—Every VOB has one or more clear-text pools, which are file caches that store the most recently accessed versions of elements (this is called the working set). The size of the clear-text pool depends on how many versions of how many elements are being accessed over a period of time. This cache is predominantly used to support dynamic views. A ClearCase scrubber process is configured to control the size of this pool by determining how long unreferenced element versions remain in the cache.

- **Derived object pools**—Every VOB has one or more derived object pools, in which ClearCase stores shared built objects, referred to as derived objects (for example,

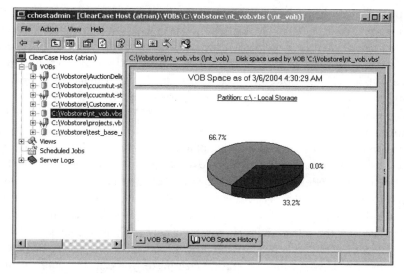

Figure 5-7 ClearCase administration console—VOB space example.

libraries or executables). The size of this pool depends on the size of the system being built and the number of derived objects being shared between views. A ClearCase scrubber process is used to control the size of this pool.

5.2.6   User, VOB, and View Limits

The ClearCase architecture allows for a high degree of scalability because it can take advantage of additional hardware resources as the size of the system and the team grows. Very few physical limits exist in the ClearCase application itself. For example, there are no technical limits on the number of users, VOBs, views, or elements. The maximum number of concurrent users any given VOB can support is highly dependent on many variables, such as the type of data in the VOB, how it is accessed, what the working set is (what elements are being accessed concurrently), what users are doing with the data, how and if clearmake is being used, the ratio of elements to derived objects, the amount of metadata in the VOB, and, of course, size of memory, disk I/O, network bandwidth, and CPU. A certain amount of system and administrative overhead is associated with each VOB, so typically you should try to minimize the number of VOBs you use.

Ultimately, good performance is relative, subjective, and highly dependent on your own configuration and usage patterns.

5.2.7   VOB Sizing Considerations

The number of VOBs you need depends on the number of files and directories that make up the system you are managing, the number of concurrent users accessing those VOBs, whether users are using clearmake, what hardware server resources are available, what type of data is stored in the VOB, and the number of components in your system. The number of variables involved makes it very difficult to provide any general-purpose recommendations. However, this section looks at some suggestions that should help you get started.

If you have fewer than 3,000 files and directories in your software system and fewer than 20 developers, you can skip this section. Almost any machine being sold today will be a good-enough VOB server machine for small numbers of files and developers, and you should be able to put all your files into one VOB, as a bonus. However, if your project doesn't fall within these parameters, read on.

The type of data in a VOB affects concurrent usage patterns and, ultimately, performance. When looking at the type of data, explore two extremes: a VOB containing source code and a VOB containing documentation. In the case of source code, these files are changing and being built daily by some number of concurrent users. In the case of documents, these are files primarily being referenced and changed only occasionally. (*Note:* We would place HTML files that are changing frequently in the source code category.) In short, an active read/write source code VOB can accommodate fewer elements than a documentation VOB with no build traffic and fewer writes.

For example, if your VOB is holding source code and your team is doing software development using clearmake, the rule of thumb is approximately 3,000 elements per VOB. Clearmake makes use of a lot of VOB server resources to provide derived object sharing and the build audit configuration records. If your team is not using clearmake, you can store more elements in that particular VOB—say, approximately 5,000 elements. If you are storing HTML pages or Word documents and these are primarily being referenced (that is, the majority of the work being done by the VOB server is servicing read requests, not check-out/check-in requests), a VOB can easily support more than 10,000 elements. We've seen VOBs whose primary purpose was to store design and process documents hold upward of 40,000 elements, with no performance issues.

> **NOTE**
> The number of lines of code and the size of the source code files do not have a significant effect on ClearCase performance. The number of elements (files and directories) makes the biggest difference.

The number of anticipated concurrent users can also affect performance, but that number is largely related to hardware resources. That is, the more concurrent users you have, the more hardware you might need. Also, when you have a few VOBs being accessed by a large number of users, it is often necessary to place them on different servers or at least make sure that they are on separate disks with multiple I/O controllers.

5.3   Monitoring and Tuning for ClearCase Performance

Many interdependent pieces in a development environment play a role in ClearCase performance. Additionally, exactly how these pieces interact depends on how an organization uses ClearCase. This can lead to some confusion about how to even approach the problem of monitoring and tuning to optimize ClearCase performance. Here are three simple principles to keep in mind when approaching ClearCase performance monitoring and tuning.

1. ClearCase performance depends on the interoperation of several different server roles. Figure 5-8 provides an illustration of this interoperation.

   In this figure, the ClearCase VOB server, the view server, and the ClearCase client form the vertices of a triangle. The edges of the triangle represent the connectivity between the ClearCase roles. When monitoring and tuning ClearCase environments, you need to pay attention to each vertex on this triangle as well as each edge. Furthermore, you need to measure the performance characteristics of the connections to a set of commonly used network resources; the ClearCase registry server, the ClearCase license server, network name servers, and network authentication. Often one machine will be configured to fill two or more roles. For example, a ClearCase client is often also a ClearCase view server, or a VOB server often also fills the roles of the ClearCase registry server and the ClearCase license server.

   Performance on each individual server depends on the interoperation of the memory, disk, network, and processor subsystems on that server.

2. Partition your analysis on each server and client into manageable pieces. One successful partitioning scheme is illustrated in Figure 5-9.

   This figure illustrates three general areas to examine when monitoring or tuning systems to optimize ClearCase performance: the OS and hardware level, the ClearCase parameters level, and the application level.

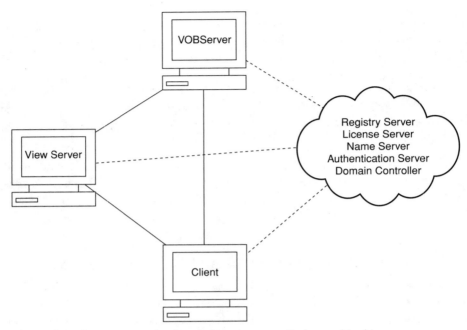

Figure 5-8   ClearCase server roles for performance monitoring and tuning.

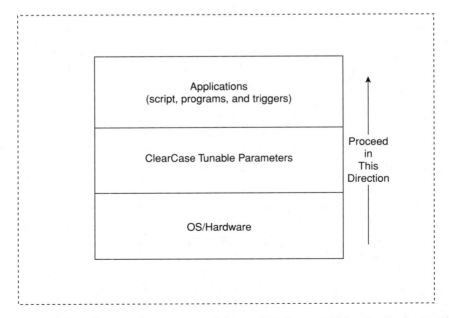

Figure 5-9   The ClearCase performance stack for partitioning monitoring and tuning tasks.

At the lowest level is the OS and hardware. Here you manipulate kernel parameters as well as hardware configurations. The middle level represents MVFS and view caching parameters in the ClearCase system that can be adjusted. The top level is the application space, the set of scripts and programs that are created by CM administrators and users to interact with ClearCase to achieve some desired SCM-related function.

Generally, as you move from a lower level to the next level up, the impact of your changes increases by an order of magnitude. For example, if you spend 1 hour tuning the OS and hardware, you might improve performance of a desired ClearCase operation by 1 second; if you spend 1 hour tuning ClearCase parameters, you might improve ClearCase performance by 10 seconds; and if you spend an hour optimizing or rearchitecting your SCM scripts, you might improve your performance by 100 seconds.

Reading this, you might then think that you should just skip the bottom two levels and start immediately at the top level. Don't make this mistake. A pathological configuration, such as a memory shortage or a poorly configured database cache, at one of the lower levels will impact everything in the layers above it. Also, it is usually possible to measure and tune the bottom two layers quickly, enabling you to move on to the area with the largest potential payback with a solid foundation beneath you. Also, the top layer is much more difficult and time-consuming to address; if you start there, you might never get to the lower layers.

3. Performance monitoring and tuning is iterative. Measure your selected area of performance, make a change based on your best assessment of where a performance bottleneck might be, measure again to see if you made things better or worse, and then repeat the process. If you don't follow this procedure, you will never know whether you are making things better or worse. This iterative process is illustrated in Figure 5-10.

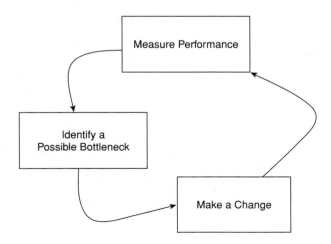

Figure 5-10   Performance tuning is a cycle of measuring, identifying, and changing.

5.3.1   Measuring the Lowest Level

The lowest level of the performance stack is the OS and the hardware. The most important thing to remember at this level is that memory is king. In fact, the most common cause of ClearCase performance degradation is a shortage of memory on a VOB server. A memory shortfall will affect all other aspects of system performance and will make it appear that the other disk, processor, and network areas are completely overwhelmed. Measure for and fix memory shortfalls first, and then move on to the other areas. The second most common area that affects ClearCase performance is the network. ClearCase is a client/server application that depends on a robust, speedy network for proper operation. Poor connectivity or large latency times will severely impact your perceived ClearCase performance. Take special note that network latency matters more to overall ClearCase performance than bandwidth. Simply stated, latency is the amount of time it takes an individual network packet to travel from the source machine to the destination machine. Factors that affect latency include the number of routers, or hops, between the source and the destination. Over long-haul networks or satellite connections, physical distance also affects network latency simply because the speed of light provides an upper bound to how fast the packet can travel from point to point.

Unfortunately, there is no standard set of tools for measuring memory, network, disk, and processor utilization. Each hardware and OS vendor has its own mix of utilities to accomplish these types of measurements. Table 5-1 gives some of the commonly used utilities for measuring the various system resources that matter to ClearCase.

Table 5-1   System Utilities for Measuring Various Resources by Operating System

Performance Resource Measured	Utility	Operating System
Memory	vmstat	UNIX variants
	Sar	Linux, UNIX variants
	Sysmon	Windows
Disk	iostat	UNIX variants
	Sysmon	Windows
Processor	vmstat	UNIX variants
	Top	Linux, UNIX variants
	Ps	Linux, UNIX variants
	Sysmon	Windows
Network Connectivity and Latency	ping	All ClearCase-supported platforms
	Traceroute	Linux, UNIX variants
	Tracert	Windows

A thorough discussion of monitoring and tuning ClearCase performance is contained in the ClearCase administration manual. Additionally, these articles on the IBM DeveloperWorks Web site specifically discuss the principles examined in this section:

- "Principles and Techniques for Analyzing and Improving IBM Rational ClearCase Performance, Part 1": *http://www.106.ibm.com/developerworks/rational/library/ 1107.html*
- "Principles and Techniques for Analyzing and Improving IBM Rational ClearCase Performance, Part 2": *http://www-106.ibm.com/developerworks/rational/library/content/ RationalEdge/sep03/t_principlescc_tm.pdf*

5.3.2   Measuring the Middle Level

The middle level of the performance stack consists of the caching characteristics of the MVFS and view servers. Both the MVFS caches and the view caches are located on view servers. Recall that the MVFS is used only for ClearCase dynamic views. If you aren't using dynamic views, you don't need to worry about MVFS caches. All views types, however, have view caches. You are looking for caches that are 100 percent full but that have a low utilization or hit rate (less than 85 percent). You can get this information directly from ClearCase with the commands shown in Table 5-2.

Table 5-2   Caches and Commands to Measure Them

Caches Measured	Command	What This Command Measures
MVFS caches	`cleartool getcache -mvfs`	How full the MVFS caches are
	`cleartool mvfsstat -cl`	The hit rate for the MVFS caches
View caches	`cleartool getcache -view` *viewname*	How full the view caches are and the hit rate for the specified view

If you detect a cache that is not being optimally used, you can adjust the size of the cache with the cleartool `setcache` command. For view caches, this value becomes persistent; that is, the view will remember the value. You can use the cleartool `setsite` command to establish a default cache size for all views created in your ClearCase region. You can also use the cleartool `setcache` command to adjust MVFS cache sizes. However, the size of the cache will revert to its default size the next time the machine is rebooted. The procedure to make MVFS cache size settings persistent varies depending on the operating system, so you should review your ClearCase documentation for more details on permanently setting the sizes of the MVFS caches.

Tuning these caches is important not only for individual ClearCase client performance, but also for the performance of your entire local ClearCase network. This is because if a ClearCase client can't find the information it needs in the MVFS or view caches, it must go all the way back to the VOB server to get the required information. This, in turn, adds traffic to your network and it causes your VOB servers to work harder than would be required if the client caches were properly sized.

5.3.3   Measuring the Top Level

The uppermost level in the performance stack consists of the applications that you use to implement higher-level SCM functions. These are usually scripts or programs that combine multiple ClearCase commands to manipulate or read SCM data and then to act on that data in some way. These scripts or programs can also be used in ClearCase triggers used to enforce a custom process or to report on some SCM activity. The scripts and programs used at this layer are often encoded in an interpreted language such as Perl or a command interpreter shell. If you are using Perl, you can potentially improve performance of your applications by using the ClearCase::CtCmd package created by IBM Rational Software or one of the other ClearCase packages created by David Boyce, available in the CPAN Perl archive at *http://www.cpan.org*. Performance of Perl scripts can also likely be improved by converting your Perl program directly to an executable using a utility such as perlapp from ActiveState, at *http://www.activestate.com*.

The application level of the performance stack is the most difficult, time-consuming area of performance measuring and tuning. This is so because, first, any measurement that you do is likely an intrusive programming project on its own, requiring you to modify the programs or scripts in question to insert the measurement code. Second, this layer is difficult and time consuming because the scripts and programs in question typically implement or enforce some kind of desired development process. Thus, any attempt to change or optimize this process will likely need significant justification and testing before it is adopted.

5.4   Defining the Implementation Model

Defining the implementation model involves going from the logical design to the physical implementation of the system. Logical design elements, such as classes, are grouped into physical files and organized into physical directories. The Rational Unified Process calls this structuring the implementation model, whose purpose is the following [RUP 2003.06.13 2004]:

- To establish the structure of the implementation model
- To adapt the structure of the model to reflect team organization or implementation language constraints
- To define dependencies between subsystems
- To add test artifacts to the implementation model
- To update the implementation view of the software architecture document

Moving from logical design to physical implementation is a very important step and, if done incorrectly, can cause problems. In *Large-Scale C++ Software Design,* John Lakos discusses this issue in a section entitled "Physical Design Concepts":

> Developing a large-scale software system in C++ requires more than just a sound understanding of logical design issues. Logical entities, such as classes and functions, are like the flesh and skin of a system. The logical entities that make up large C++ systems are distributed across many physical entities, such as files and directories. The physical architecture is the skeleton of the system—if it is malformed, there is no cosmetic remedy for alleviating its unpleasant symptoms. [Lakos, 1996, p. 97]

This instruction applies to any large-scale software system, not just one implemented using C++. When defining the implementation model, it is important to take SCM into account. This is done by having a clear mapping between the high-level design entities and the high-level SCM entities used to manage groups of files.

When using ClearCase, you must establish a mapping between the architecture and ClearCase components. In UML terms, this means establishing a mapping between the logical design packages (implementation subsystems) and the ClearCase components that contain the files that will implement those packages. (The Rational Unified Process defines this as the implementation view of the architecture. See [Kruchten 2000].) The mapping should be at a high level in the architecture, usually the subsystem level; as noted in the RUP formulation, it should include test artifacts. For small systems, there might be only one ClearCase component and no further decomposition. Systems with hundreds of components should not be mapped directly, one to one, to ClearCase components. Instead, you should identify a higher level in the architecture by grouping the hundreds of components into a smaller set of subsystems (refer to Figure 3-3).

For both SCM purposes and good architecture, there must be a high degree of cohesion between internal elements of a ClearCase component and a low degree of coupling between ClearCase components. This is key for successfully mapping architecture to versioned components. David Whitgift explains, "Each item within the hierarchy should be cohesive: It should possess a single defining characteristic that relates its [elements]. The coupling between items in different parts of the hierarchy should be weak; in CM terms, this means that dependencies should be minimized" [Whitgift 1991]. Dependencies here refer primarily to build-time dependencies.

The implementation subsystems, managed in ClearCase components, should have clearly defined interfaces with other parts of the system and should be independently buildable and testable, which allows for independent and parallel development of major parts of the software system by independent teams. This can significantly speed up development, as well as improve reuse and ease of system maintenance.

5.5   Creating the VOBs

When you have determined how many ClearCase components you will need, you are ready to actually create the project VOB, source VOBs, and the components. This section provides an overview of creating ClearCase VOBs and the use of administration VOBs. It is not a replacement for the ClearCase administration manuals. When actually creating VOBs, refer to these manuals for more detailed information. The purpose of including this information here is to give you a better idea of how ClearCase really works, which will aid in understanding later chapters.

As discussed in the section "The Repository: Versioned Object Base" in Chapter 4, there are two types of VOBs: standard and project. Any VOB can also act as an administration VOB, which stores metadata (for example, branch types or label types) that is shared among a set of linked VOBs. This section provides an overview of how VOBs are created on different platforms and discusses the use of administration VOBs.

5.5.1   Creating the PVOB Using the Command-Line Interface

In this example, you will create a PVOB using the command-line interface. This example uses UNIX syntax, but the command-line interface is also available on the Windows platform. The first step in creating a PVOB is determining where it will be stored. This means both which machine the PVOB server will run on and which disk partition it will physically be stored in. Second, you must determine where in the UNIX file system the VOBs mount point will be created. Unlike Windows, the mount point for a VOB on UNIX can be anywhere in the file system. Typically, VOBs are mounted under a common mount point, such as `/vobs`.

For an example, let's say that you will create a PVOB mounted under `/vobs` with the name projects. The PVOB storage will be on a machine called ccserver1 in a directory that has been exported as `/ccserver1_store1`.

To create the project VOB, you would log onto the machine ccserver1 and issue the following command (all on one line):

```
prompt> cleartool mkvob
   -tag /vobs/projects
   -ucmproject
   -c "My New PVOB"
   -public /ccserver1_store1/projects.pvb
```

Let's break this down:

- `cleartool mkvob` is the ClearCase command.
- `-tag /vobs/projects` is the flag that determines the mount point for the PVOB. That is the point in the UNIX directory structure where end users will go to access the data in the PVOB.
- `-ucmproject` is the switch that indicates that this VOB should be a UCM project VOB instead of a regular VOB that contains only file and directory elements.
- `-c "My New PVOB"` is the comment you enter that will be stored and displayed as the description for this PVOB.

- `-public` is the flag indicating that this PVOB will be used by a group of users on many machines. When using this flag, you are required to enter the public VOB password set by the administrator when ClearCase was installed. This allows the VOB to be mounted on multiple machines automatically.

- `/ccserver1_store1/projects.pvb` is the storage directory for the PVOB data. The storage location must be a directory that is globally available from all client machines. If the local directory on the server machine (ccserver1) is different from the global mount point for the storage directory, then you can use specific options to the `mkvob` command to indicate this.

5.5.2   Creating the PVOB Using the Graphical User Interface

In this example, you will create a PVOB using the Windows graphical user interface. You can also create PVOBs graphically on UNIX with a similar Motif-based interface. To begin, from the ClearCase Host Administration tool, select the VOB's entry with the right mouse button and choose New, VOB, as shown in Figure 5-11. This starts the VOB Creation Wizard (used for creating any type of VOB); the first step is illustrated in Figure 5-12. In this illustration, we have called the PVOB projects, filled in a comment field describing the PVOB, and checked the box Create as a UCM Project VOB, thus identifying this VOB as a PVOB. We have also checked the box This VOB will contain UCM components. This allows the VOB to serve double duty as a repository for project artifacts, if you choose to do so. In this example, the PVOB will store all the ClearCase projects for a fictitious company called Classics Inc.

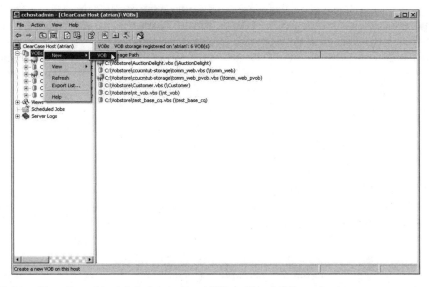

Figure 5-11   ClearCase Host Administration Utility—New VOB context menu.

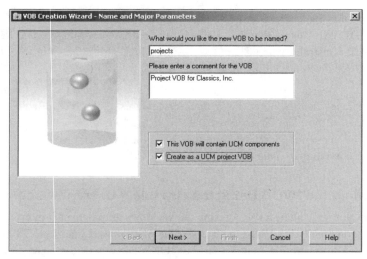

Figure 5-12   PVOB Creation Wizard.

5.5.3   Using Administration VOBs

ClearCase supports the capability to manage common metadata by using a single administration VOB. The ClearCase online help defines an administration VOB as "a VOB containing global type objects which are copied to client VOBs on an as-needed basis when users wish to create instances of the type objects in the client VOBs" (see "Creating and Managing Types" in Chapter 4 for more details on types and type instances). In short, common data for a set of VOBs can be stored in an administration VOB. ClearCase manages getting these common (or global) definitions of data types into each of the respective VOBs.

For a UCM environment, the PVOB serves as the administrative VOB for common metadata shared between the other VOBs containing component elements. See Figure 5-13 for an illustration of this.

If you are an existing ClearCase user and have already established an administration VOB for your site, the PVOB and VOBs containing component data can use the existing administration VOB (see Figure 5-14).

5.5.4   Using More Than One PVOB

As you review your ClearCase site configuration, you might determine that, for security, performance, or other reasons, you would like to use more than one PVOB. If you decide to use multiple PVOBs you should designate one PVOB to serve as the top-level administrative VOB for all the PVOBs. This is required for projects in PVOBs to share and modify components defined in other PVOBs. If your PVOBs don't share a common administrative VOB, they will be able to read but not modify components defined in other PVOBs. Figure 5-15 illustrates this hierarchy.

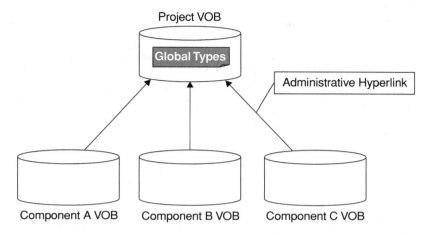

Figure 5-13   The PVOB acting as the administration VOB.

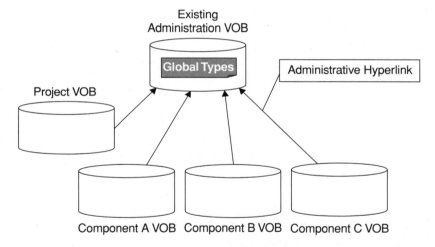

Figure 5-14   Using an existing administration VOB with a UCM PVOB.

In Figure 5-15, multiple PVOBs share a common administrative VOB. In the illustrated case, the administrative VOB is also a PVOB. You should create your administrative VOB or PVOB first and then create your other PVOBs. When you create your other PVOBs, you can specify the administrative VOB as illustrated in Figure 5-15.

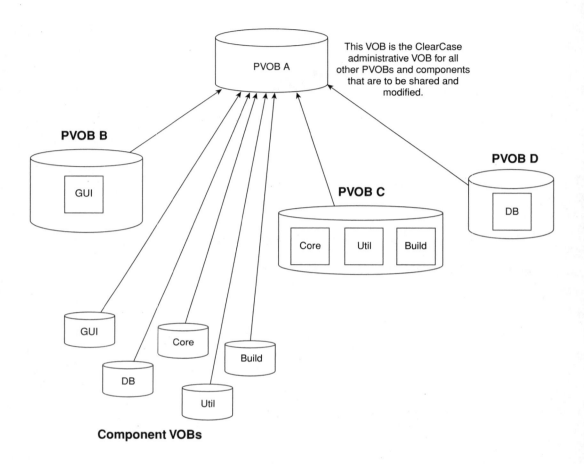

Figure 5-15   A PVOB can also serve as an administrative VOB for other VOBs.

5.5.5   Creating VOBs and Components Using the Command-Line Interface

In this example, you will create a VOB and a new component using the command-line interface. This example uses UNIX syntax, but the command-line interface is also available on the Windows platform. VOBs are created just like PVOBs, except that the `-ucmproject` flag is not used (see the section "Creating the PVOB Using the Command-Line Interface," earlier in this chapter).

For example, imagine that you want to create a VOB mounted under `/vobs` with the name `gui_comp`. The VOB storage will be on a machine called ccserver1 in a directory that has been exported as `/ccserver1_store1`. To create the VOB, you log onto the machine ccserver1 and issue the following command (all on one line):

```
prompt> cleartool mkvob
   -tag /vobs/gui_comp
   -c "My GUI Component VOB"
   -public /ccserver1_store1/gui_comp.vbs
```

(Refer to the section "Creating the PVOB Using the Command-Line Interface," earlier in this chapter, for a detailed description of the command-line options shown here.)

When using the command line, you create the component object independently from the VOB. To create the component object that points to the newly created VOB /vobs/gui_comp, you issue the following command:

```
prompt> cleartool mkcomp
   -c "GUI Component"
   -root /vobs/gui_comp
   gui@/vobs/projects
```

Let's break this down:

- `cleartool mkcomp` is the ClearCase command.
- `-c GUI Component` is the comment for the component creation.
- `-root /vobs/gui_comp` is the root directory of the component. Remember that this must be the root directory of a VOB.
- `gui@/vobs/projects` indicates that the name of the component is `gui` and the project VOB in which the new component object should be stored is `/vobs/projects`.

CLEARCASE PRO TIP
The relationship between an administration VOB and a client VOB is established by creating a special hyperlink between the VOBs. This is done automatically on Windows when using the VOB Creation Wizard. From the command line, it must be done separately from the VOB creation action.

5.5.6   Creating VOBs and Components Using the Graphical User Interface

This section picks up from the previous example, in which you created the PVOB called projects. The fictitious company Classics Inc. has a system that contains three components: database, core, and gui. The database component has all the code needed to isolate the database technology from the application. The core component has all the business logic and isolates the user interface from the key application algorithms. The gui component contains the graphical user interfaces. So, in this case, you need to create three VOBs to support these three components. Let's work through the creation of the gui component. From the ClearCase Host Administration utility, you select the VOBs entry with the right mouse button and select New, VOB (refer to Figure 5-11).

Unlike the command line, the VOB Creation Wizard can automatically create the component object when you create the VOB. In this case (see Figure 5-16), leave the box This VOB will contain UCM components checked. Name the VOB gui. This will be used as both the VOB tag and the name of the component. Add a comment, such as "Graphical User Interface software for Classics Inc." Because this VOB will not contain project data, do not check the box Create as a UCM project VOB. Click Next.

The next step (see Figure 5-17) is determining whether this VOB will contain multiple UCM components or whether the VOB will be a single UCM component. If it is to contain multiple UCM components, they must be defined later using the cleartool mkcomp command-line utility.

The next step, shown in Figure 5-18, is to determine where the VOB data will be stored. The decision does not involve a user-visible storage location, but rather on which server and on which disk the VOB data will be maintained. VOBs must be backed up regularly. This storage directory needs to be backed up. On Windows, ClearCase maintains a registry for VOB storage locations. You are asked to pick one when creating the new VOB. If you do not see a suitable directory, you can create a new global storage location or just use the Browse button to locate the correct directory. In this example, we are using a predefined server storage directory, \\atrian\Vobstore. ClearCase VOB storage must be in a shared directory so that it can be accessed from the client machines.

In the final step (see Figure 5-19), you specify the administration VOB. Note that the VOB Creation Wizard offers you the project VOB as the recommended administration VOB. Take this as the default for the purposes of this example. Refer to the "Using Administration VOBs" section, earlier in this chapter, for more information on other configuration options.

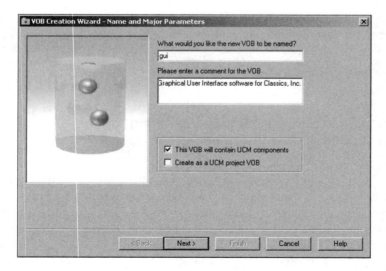

Figure 5-16   Step 1: creating a VOB.

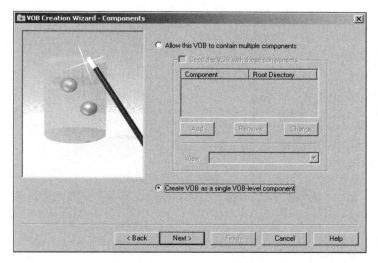

Figure 5-17   Step 2: specifying whether a VOB will be a single UCM component or will contain multiple UCM components.

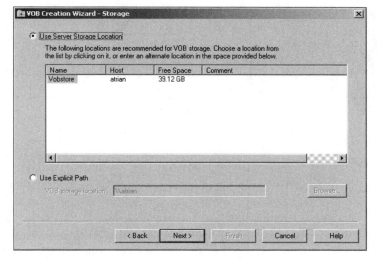

Figure 5-18   Step 3: specify a VOB storage directory.

CLEARCASE PRO TIP

Note that we have also checked the box Make this a public VOB. The public designation for a VOB is important only if you are going to use ClearCase dynamic views. If you are using ClearCase LT, which doesn't support dynamic views, the public designation for a VOB is meaningless. The public designation for a VOB behaves differently on UNIX than on Windows.

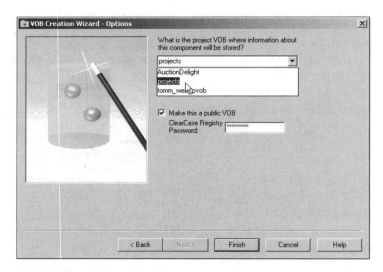

Figure 5-19   Step 4: specifying the administration VOB.

On UNIX and Linux machines, public VOBs are mounted as a group on ClearCase clients at boot time.

On Windows machines, public VOBs are mounted as a group when you issue the `cleartool mount -all` command. If you use the `-persistent` option to this command, `cleartool mount -all -persistent`, all public VOBs will be mounted each time you log on.

Click the Finish button, and you have created your first VOB and component all at once.

5.5.7   Importing Existing Source Code

Usually, new software projects are not at the beginning stage when you introduce a new tool such as ClearCase. Often projects are underway, using no version control or an inadequate version-control tool. ClearCase provides support for importing data both from the file system and from other tools. (As of this writing, ClearCase supports conversion from nonversioned operating system files and directories and these other SCM tools: SCCS, RCS, CVS, PVCS, and Visual Source Safe.)

Importing data is a two-step process. First, an export tool called clearexport_X is run, where X is the type of export you are doing. Specific export tools exist for Visual SourceSafe, RCS, CVS, PVCS Version Manager, and SCCS. The clearexport tool produces a data file that is then used by the import tool clearimport.

The second step is to run clearimport, which creates new elements in the specified VOB and duplicates the directory structure and file elements that match the flat file directory structure. The import automation from existing tools such as SCCS or PVCS is more intelligent and attempts to retain as much of these tools' metadata as possible.

If you have your software set up in a pre-existing directory structure not under version control, you would use the flat file import tool clearfsimport. This tool is also used if you are using a version-control tool that doesn't have a specific exporter for ClearCase. In these cases, you can create a workspace or sandbox containing the configuration of files you want to transfer into ClearCase and then use the `clearfsimport` command to import that configuration into ClearCase.

If you use the export/import procedure multiple times, ClearCase knows how to create new versions for any preimported elements. This multiple import approach is the one used when managing third-party software components in ClearCase.

5.6 Baseline Promotion Levels

When using ClearCase UCM, you must perform one final administrative setup task: defining the promotion levels for component baselines. A baseline is a single version of a component. The quality or status of that baseline is indicated by a baseline promotion level. All components stored in a project VOB share a common set of legal promotion levels. This is to ensure a consistent definition of promotion level across multiple projects.

> **NOTE**
> If different projects cannot agree on a set of promotion levels, they must be stored in separate project VOBs. However, this is not recommended practice if these projects will be sharing components. A common understanding of baseline promotion levels is key to effective project communication.

ClearCase UCM predefines a set of component baseline promotion levels, illustrated in Figure 5-20. Baseline promotion levels are linear. You can move a baseline upward or downward. You must define the promotion level where a new baseline will begin its life. Within the out-of-the-box promotion levels, this is named INITIAL.

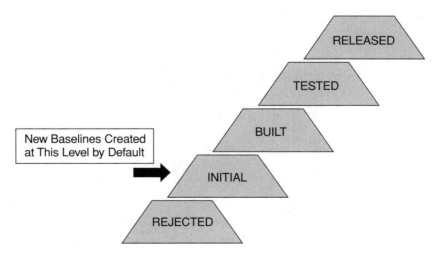

Figure 5-20   Predefined baseline promotion levels.

From the command line, you redefine the promotion levels using the command `cleartool setplevel`. See the command-line reference page in the ClearCase manual for details, including the steps on how to rename an existing promotion level.

From the ClearCase Project Explorer, you can redefine the promotion levels by selecting the project VOB top-level folder and selecting the Define Promotion Level menu, as shown in Figure 5-21.

You can then define your promotion levels using the dialog box shown in Figure 5-22. When you have established your promotion levels, you have finished setting up the initial SCM environment.

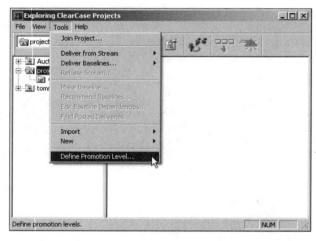

Figure 5-21   ClearCase Project Explorer: defining promotion levels.

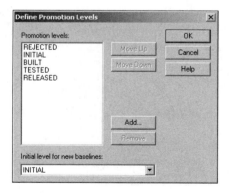

Figure 5-22   Defining baseline promotion levels.

5.7 Summary

This chapter has reviewed the fundamental architecture of a ClearCase environment. We discussed each of the server roles upon which ClearCase depends, as well as some possible ways to organize these roles in several kinds of environments. We considered the hardware requirements for these server machines, and we discussed how to approach monitoring and tuning an environment for optimal ClearCase performance. Finally, we showed how to create VOBs and PVOBs and how to manipulate baseline promotion levels. Now a project can be created and development can begin.

CHAPTER 6

Project Management in ClearCase

This chapter discusses creating, configuring, and managing a ClearCase project and how the SCM project relates to an overall project for teams of various sizes. The ClearCase project policies are also discussed, including when and why you use each of them.

6.1 What Is a ClearCase Project?

Every organization has its own definition of a project. So, what is a ClearCase project conceptually? A ClearCase project consists of one or more people who are working together on activities to produce one or more artifacts. Typically, a ClearCase project represents a large development effort such as a major release or major iteration of a set of components or of an entire software system.

A ClearCase project defines the following:

- Who is making changes
- What is being changed
- How changes are made
- How changes flow from a developer's workspace into a release

6.1.1 Who Is Making Changes?

A ClearCase project organizes a set of people who are collaborating to produce new software component baselines. Depending on the size of the overall development effort, there might be one or more ClearCase projects.

ClearCase project use can be discussed using the five project categories defined earlier (see "Five Project Team Categories" in Chapter 2, "Growing into Your SCM Solution"):

- **Individual**—The ClearCase UCM parallel development process might not be appropriate for an individual developer. In this case, the developer can opt to use base ClearCase functionality or can use UCM and work on only one stream. The advantages that ClearCase UCM provides to the individual developer lie in the area of tracking the developer's changes and associating those changes with specific UCM activities. This tracking and association provides specific detailed information that enables developers to determine their progress against their goal and to ensure that the functionality they set out to build is actually implemented. This auditability can be an important advantage if the software is being developed for another organization.

  Working on a single stream in ClearCase UCM is trivial. First, you can do it by convention—that is, create a UCM project and then choose to work only on the project's integration stream. This mode of work still allows development streams to be created as child streams of the integration stream if that level of project organization becomes necessary. Another way to work on only a single stream is to let UCM enforce that policy. A UCM project can be created as a single-stream project. If a project is so designated, ClearCase UCM will create the project-integration stream and will enforce the policy that no other stream can be created in the project. In either scenario, the developer gets all the advantages that UCM activity tracking provides, but without the overhead of delivering and rebasing activities.

- **Small**—A small project team would have one ClearCase UCM project created for each major release of the product it is producing. For teams like this, it is important not to confuse "project" and "product." For example, a project might be Release 3 of product X. In ClearCase, the project Release 3 identifies a group of individuals working together to produce this major release. The team is working on product X, which is physically realized in one or more components. Very small teams, such as individual developers, might determine that a single-stream development model would serve them best. In this case, they can choose to work on only the project's integration stream, leaving the door open to a later expansion of the project into parallel development, or they can define their project as a single-stream project and then let UCM enforce the single-stream policy for them.

- **Modest**—Like small teams, modest teams would have one project created for each major release of the product or products on which they are working.

- **Major**—Major projects consist of multiple teams collaborating on a release of one or more products. In this case, each team would have its own ClearCase project. There would then be one central project, which would be used to collect the changes from each individual project. So, for example, if there were three components of the system—the database component, the core component, and the GUI component—there would be four projects defined for each major release. These projects might be called Release 4 GUI project, Release 4 Database project, Release 4 Core project, and Release 4 Integration project.

- **Extreme**—Like major projects, extreme projects would have multiple teams defined for each release, but they would have even more projects per release than major projects. Extreme project teams might even have some projects that do not live for the life of an entire release, but only for the life of an intermediate iteration.

6.1.2 What Is Being Changed?

ClearCase projects define the scope of the work in terms of what part of the product a certain project team will be modifying. A project manager declares which components will be available for the project members to modify and which components will be available only as reference. This is covered in more detail in the section "Identifying Your Components and Baselines," later in this chapter.

6.1.3 How Are Changes Being Made?

ClearCase projects also define how work will be performed on the project and what project defaults ClearCase should assume. Project policies are designed to provide a nonscripting, intuitive way for the project manager to determine how UCM will behave for his or her project. An example of a project policy, as noted earlier, is whether the project will be a single-stream project or whether it will be enabled for parallel development. Project policies are covered in more detail in the section "Determining Your Project's Policies," later in this chapter.

6.1.4 How Do Changes Flow and Get Integrated?

ClearCase projects define a fixed flow of change within the project. Each project has one integration stream in which all the work for that project is collected. In single-stream projects, this is the only stream that the project will ever have. In projects that are not single stream, typically each developer who joins that project has a development stream and development view where he or she does work. When developers are done with the development and unit testing of their assigned work, they deliver their work to the common project-integration stream. This movement from development stream to integration stream defines the flow of change within the project.

In terms of configuration management, each project is insulated from changes going on in other projects. That is, each integration stream is isolated from other project-integration streams (just as project-integration streams do not see changes made in development streams until they are delivered). One project will not see changes from another project until you explicitly update it to a new component baseline or specifically merge changes from the other project. See later chapters, such as Chapter 8, "Development Using the ClearCase UCM Model"; Chapter 9, "Integration"; and Chapter 10, "Building, Baselining, and Release Deployment," for more details.

When defining your own ClearCase projects, keep these points in mind:

- For each project, you should define a project manager (or technical leader) who has ownership of the project.
- Be clear about the project/product distinction.
- Create only the number of projects you need to manage your development.

6.2   Creating a ClearCase Project

A Project Creation Wizard walks you through the creation of a new ClearCase project. This is shown in an example in the section "Creating Your Project," later in this chapter. However, before you run the wizard, you should understand the decisions you will be asked to make when setting up a new project. The steps you will take are as follows:

1. Identify the project manager for the project.
2. Identify the components and baselines that form your project's foundation.
3. Determine the policies that govern your project's work.
4. Determine the UCM project properties that structure your project.
5. Determine where the physical project object will be located.
6. Create your project.

6.2.1   Identifying Your Project Manager

Someone must create the project and be responsible for it. (The role of the project manager is described in "The Project Manager: Managing a Project," in Chapter 3, "An Overview of the Unified Change Management Model.") For ClearCase projects, the project manager should be a technical individual who understands SCM and the UCM model. Some organizations might refer to this person as a technical lead, project integrator, or configuration manager.

In any case, you must identify the person who is responsible for creating and maintaining the project. This person will make decisions about how the project will be run and what parts of the system will be worked on. This person also will actually create the ClearCase project. (It is possible to have an administrator or tools engineer create the project for another individual. However, after project creation, a number of ClearCase objects must have their ownership changed. Therefore, it is more straightforward for project managers to create projects themselves.)

6.2.2   Identifying Your Components and Baselines

One of the challenges of managing software projects is ensuring that team members are working on the "right" things—what pieces of the software system should be modified and what version of those pieces should be used as the starting point for those modifications. As was discussed in Chapter 3, one of the key benefits of UCM is that it uses a baseline + change model. This model provides a framework that ensures that only consistent changes move through the system.

When you start a new ClearCase project, you must decide which components will be needed to perform the activities planned for the project and which versions of those components will be used as the starting point (see "Component Management: Components and Baselines" in Chapter 4, "A Functional Overview of ClearCase Objects," for more information on components).

The components and component baselines define the scope of work for your project, or what components that project must reference and modify. The baselines of the components you select are referred to as the foundation baselines for your project. Specifically, the *foundation baselines* define the initial configuration for your project's integration stream.

You define components either one component at a time or by specifying an existing project and inheriting that project's component list (for an example, see the section "Creating Your Project," later in this chapter). You can also modify the component list or which baselines are being used by going to Project Explorer, bringing up the property sheet on the project's integration stream, and then going to the Configuration tab, shown in Figure 6-1.

Another aspect of defining the working configuration is deciding whether a component is read-only or modifiable. This is done as part of defining a project's policies and is covered in the next section.

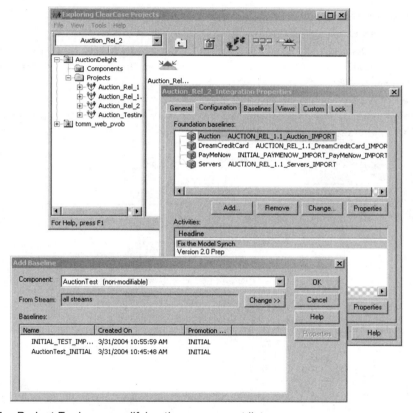

Figure 6-1   Project Explorer: modifying the component list.

6.2.3 Determining Your Project's Policies

One of the aims of the UCM design is to make it easy for a project manager to determine how UCM works. That is, you should be able to configure the UCM model without a lot of script writing. The means to do this in UCM is determining project policies. UCM defines a set of policies that can be configured for each project by the project manager. Any person working on that project is then governed by those policies.

The list of project policies has grown since the initial release of UCM and will continue to grow to make UCM scalable both to smaller projects and to enterprise-level projects. Figures 6-2 through 6-5 show the project policies available at the time of this writing. Each policy and its various settings are covered in the following sections.

Component Policies

The Components tab in the project policy applet is shown in Figure 6-2. Here you determine how your project will use the UCM components that have been defined.

Modifiable and Read-only Components

Each UCM project has a list of components to which it subscribes. When identifying these components, the project manager must indicate whether they are modifiable or read-only when working in the context of that project. This policy provides a great deal of flexibility in how organizations manage their software development.

Read-only components are typically used during runtime testing, during the build process of the components being changed, or for sharing between projects in a producer/consumer model (that is, one project produces or creates a component while another consumes or utilizes

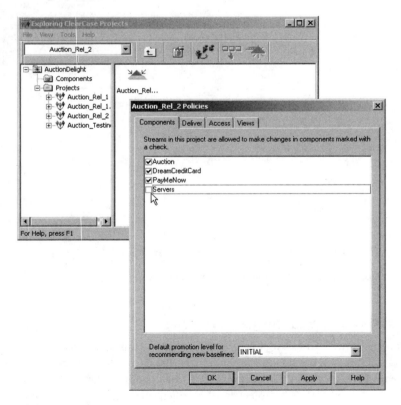

Figure 6-2   Project component policies.

the component). Figure 6-2 shows the project's Components tab and how to mark some components as modifiable and some as read-only.

Recommended Baseline Promotion Level

Each component baseline has a defined promotion level, which typically labels its quality characteristics. (These levels are defined by the configuration manager, to ensure consistency across projects in a project VOB [see "Baseline Promotion Levels" in Chapter 5, "Establishing the Initial SCM Environment"].) For example, the UCM default promotion levels are Rejected, Initial, Built, Tested, and Released. An initial baseline promotion level is assigned for all new baselines. For the UCM default, the level of Initial is assigned to newly created baselines.

The recommended baseline policy is used to define new baselines that are ready for use by developers on the project. That is, when developers go to update their development streams using the rebase operation, the recommended baselines become the default baselines.

You define a recommended baseline by choosing the promotion level at which a baseline may be used by developers. The latest baseline promoted to the level you chose becomes the recommended baseline for any given component and is offered as the default for rebase operations. Your choice of promotion levels depends on your own definition of them and how you perform building and baselining. Here are two typical examples:

- You lock the integration stream at some point at night and then run a system build and smoke test automatically. If the smoke test passes, your scripts create a new baseline and then unlock the integration stream. You ask your developers to perform a rebase every morning because you want everyone to keep up-to-date with each other's changes. In this case, you want the latest baselines to be recommended as soon as they are created. To do this, you would select the Initial level in the default UCM promotion model.

- Let's say that your build/test cycle is less automatic. You create a new baseline before you build. Your nightly build process and test scripts cannot automatically determine whether it was successful. Instead, a tester is responsible for verifying the quality of the built baseline before it becomes recommended. In the UCM default model, you would select the Tested promotion level as recommended. In this way, baselines could be created yet would not be offered during rebase operations until after someone had verified the build and promoted the baselines to the Tested state.

The Recommended Baseline Promotion Level policy setting also determines the promotion level to which to promote the latest component baselines when the Promote Baselines operation is selected from the Project Explorer. Promotion levels can also be used for reporting purposes and to indicate the latest baselines that are in production in internally managed systems or Web sites.

Deliver Policies

These policies apply to deliver operations. As shown in Figure 6-3, each of these policies can be enabled or disabled for all streams in the project, or the project can allow the policy to be defined for each individual stream. UCM checks the policy settings on the deliver operation's target

Figure 6-3   Project deliver policies.

stream, as well as the project's deliver policies. If the settings are different, the project's policy
settings take precedence.

Policies for All Deliveries

The first section of the Deliver tab includes two policies that apply to all deliveries:

- **Do Not Allow Deliver to Proceed with Check-Outs in the Development Stream.** This
  policy controls whether a developer can deliver a change while files in an activity's
  change set are still checked out. Only the checked-in changes get delivered, so this
  means that the change set that is being delivered might not have been tested. This is
  known as delivering a partial change. This policy relaxes the consistency checking that is
  performed in the UCM model.

  In one use case it would be useful to allow partial delivery of changes: A developer is
  implementing a new feature and gets it partially implemented and working. She checks
  in all the files to save this intermediate working version. She continues working by
  checking out the files again. The next day, the project integrator asks if the feature is
  ready. The developer says that it is partially complete and is good enough for others to

use. In this case, the developer would deliver the change (essentially delivering her own checkpoint versions) without delivering the changes she currently has checked out. When she completes her changes, she would simply redeliver the activity.

If you have less experienced developers, allowing this to happen might cause problems. For example, if a developer left a file checked out when he was done with a change and ignored the warning that the deliver operation provides, a partial and potentially problematic change could be delivered.

This, like all policies, is left to a project manager's discretion. We recommend that you do not allow this flexibility unless you find that your project team needs to use this feature. If you do allow it, make sure people are trained on when it is appropriate to perform partial deliveries.

- **Require Development Stream to Be Based on the Project's Recommended Baseline(s) Prior to Deliver (Require Rebase Before Deliver).** The purpose of this policy is to allow the project manager to tune how often developers are required to incorporate updates from other developers into their own private development streams. This policy basically says that, for developers to deliver changes to the project's integration stream, they must have their foundation baselines set to the project's recommended baselines or more recent baselines.

This policy, in combination with the frequency at which you promote new baselines, will enable you to tune the UCM model during the development cycle, allowing more or less isolation for individual developers.

When you set this policy, developers must rebase to the recommended baselines before performing a deliver. In effect, you are requiring developers to integrate others' changes into the development stream and make sure they work with changes before delivering their changes. This policy reduces the number of build and integration problems that are discovered in the integration stream. It also assists in creating a more stable and buildable integration stream.

When this policy is not set, developers do not ever need to rebase. This works well if you are trying to develop as quickly as possible and project builds are not yet being performed. Usually, this occurs early in the development cycle. However, the longer this situation persists, the farther apart each developer will get from working against the same code base and the more difficult integration will become.

We recommend that you always have this policy set and that you use baseline promotion to control the amount of rebasing on your project.

Policies for Intraproject Deliveries

The next section of the Deliver tab also lists two policies:

- **Deliver Changes from the Foundation in Addition to Changes from the Stream.** This policy prevents hidden deliveries of changes that have been made to a stream's foundation baseline. The classic example of this occurs when a delivery is attempted from a stream to another stream that is not the default target for a delivery. If this policy is enabled, developers must exercise caution to prevent unintended deliveries of changes to the target stream. Disabling this policy prevents such deliveries. For this reason, we recommend disabling this policy.

- **Allow the Deliver Even Though Target Stream Is Missing Components That Are in the Source Stream.** This policy governs whether deliveries will be allowed that contain changes in components that are not included in the target stream. If this policy is enabled, the delivery will be allowed, but the changes made to the components not in the target stream will not be included in the delivery. Enabling this policy opens the project to the possibility that only a partial set of changes made to an activity will be delivered. These partial deliveries can undermine the integrity of delivered activities that are very difficult to troubleshoot. For this reason, we recommend disabling this policy.

Policies for Interproject Deliveries

The final section of the Deliver tab includes four settings:

- **Allow Interproject Deliver to Project or Stream.** This policy governs whether deliveries will be accepted from streams in other projects.

- **Deliver Changes from the Foundation in Addition to Changes from the Stream.** This policy is identical to its counterpart described earlier in the policies for intraproject deliveries. In this case, though, it applies to deliveries coming in from streams in other projects. Enabling this policy opens the project to what amounts to an unintended partial migration to a new foundation baseline, which can cause project instability. For this reason, we recommend disabling this policy.

- **Require that all source components are visible in the target stream.** Similar to the policy for intraproject deliveries, this policy governs whether deliveries will be allowed that contain changes in components that are not included in the target stream. If this policy is disabled, the delivery will be allowed, but the changes made to the components not in the target stream will not be included in the delivery. Disabling this policy opens the project to the possibility that only a partial set of changes made to an activity will be delivered. These partial deliveries can undermine the integrity of delivered activities that are very difficult to troubleshoot. For this reason, we recommend enabling this policy.

- **Allow the Deliver Even Though Modifiable Components in the Source Stream Are Nonmodifiable in the Target Stream.** This policy is identical to its counterpart described earlier in the policies for intraproject deliveries. In this case, though, it applies to deliveries coming in from streams in other projects. Enabling this policy opens the project to the possibility that only a partial set of changes made to an activity will be delivered. These partial deliveries can undermine the integrity of delivered activities that are very difficult to troubleshoot. For this reason, we recommend disabling this policy.

Access Policies

Figure 6-4 shows the two policies available on the Access tab:

- **Allow All Users to Modify the Project.** This security policy governs who can make changes to the UCM project. If this policy is disabled, only the project owner, the owner of the PVOB, or a ClearCase privileged user is allowed to make changes to the UCM project.

- **Allow All Users to Modify the Stream and Its Baselines.** This security policy governs who can make changes to UCM streams and baselines in those streams. If it is disabled, only the stream owner, the owner of the PVOB, or a ClearCase privileged user is allowed to make changes to a UCM stream or baselines in that stream. This is a policy that can be enabled or disabled for all streams in a project, or it can be set individually for each stream.

Figure 6-4 Project access policies.

View Type Defaults

Two of the essential functions of ClearCase are establishing and managing the developer's workspace. As discussed earlier, workspaces are called *views* in ClearCase, and two types of views are offered: snapshot and dynamic. Each type has specific characteristics that make it the best choice for different situations (see "Workspaces: Snapshot and Dynamic Views" in Chapter 4 for details).

The view type default policy sets the default type of view presented when a developer first joins the project. The purpose of this policy is to enable you to optimize the choice of view type for both development and integration views on either UNIX or Windows platforms. This enables new developers to get started using ClearCase without having to understand snapshot and dynamic views and to decide between them themselves.

If you do not set this policy, UCM uses its own internal default settings. These are dynamic views for both development and integration views on UNIX platforms. On Windows platforms, they are snapshot views for development views and dynamic views for integration views (see Figure 6-5).

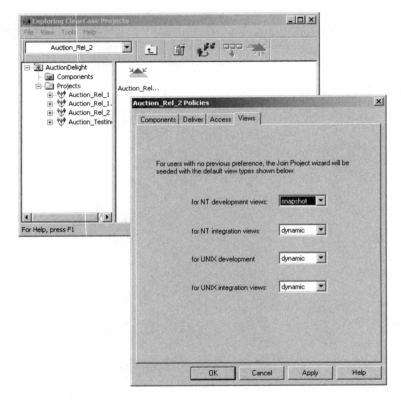

Figure 6-5   Project view policies.

6.2.4   Determining Your UCM Project Properties

In addition to the policies that govern the flow of changes in a project, UCM projects have properties that determine the structure of the project. These properties are accessed in a manner similar to the project policies, as shown in Figure 6-6.

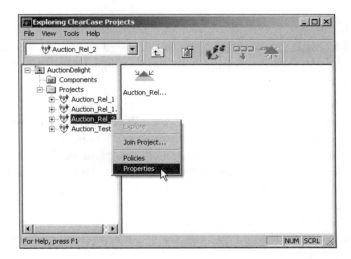

Figure 6-6 Accessing the properties of a ClearCase project.

General

The project name and description can be viewed or changed on the General properties tab, shown in Figure 6-7.

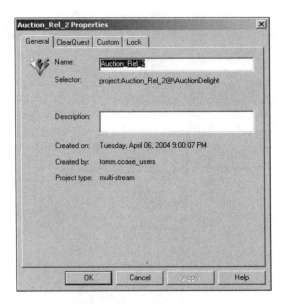

Figure 6-7 The General tab on the properties sheet.

ClearQuest

The ClearQuest project properties tab, illustrated in Figure 6-8, provides the mechanism to view or change the way UCM interacts with ClearQuest. As Figure 6-8 shows, there are a number of ClearQuest settings on this tab to discuss.

Project Is ClearQuest-Enabled

This policy simply indicates whether the project will be using ClearQuest, a software product that focuses on activity management, defect tracking, and request management. When this policy is enabled, your project will use ClearCase and ClearQuest together. This policy also enables additional UCM features, which are described in Chapter 12, "Change Request Management and ClearQuest." ClearQuest offers your project more rigorous change-management processes and additional policies.

It is possible to enable and disable this policy while a project is underway. For example, you could enable ClearQuest when your project is close to release and a more rigorous defect-tracking process is desired.

If you enable a pre-existing UCM project to use ClearQuest, the UCM activities that have already been defined in the project automatically are migrated into ClearQuest as a special Clear-Quest record type, `UCMUtilityActivity`, which can then be viewed and tracked using ClearQuest queries, reports, and charts.

If you disable the ClearQuest association with a UCM project, the linkage between the UCM activities and the ClearQuest records is severed. Re-enabling the project to use ClearQuest will not restore the linkage but will migrate the UCM activities into the `UCMUtilityActivity` record type.

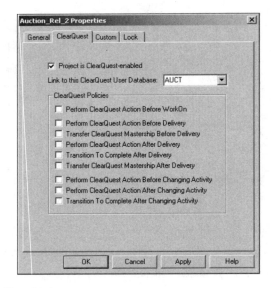

Figure 6-8   The ClearQuest tab.

Link to This ClearQuest User Database

This is the ClearQuest user database that contains the records associated with the UCM activities contained in the project. The ClearQuest database that is associated with a UCM project cannot be changed unless the project's integration with ClearQuest is first disabled by unchecking the Project Is ClearQuest-Enabled check box. Recall that this action severs the association with UCM activities and ClearQuest records. When the project is no longer ClearQuest-enabled, the project can then be linked to a different ClearQuest database by checking the Project Is Clear-Quest-Enabled check box. This results in the existing UCM activities being migrated to the newly associated ClearQuest database as `UCMUtilityActivity` records.

Perform ClearQuest Action Before Work On

If this policy is enabled, when a UCM user attempts to set to an activity, either through the command-line `cleartool setactivity` command or through a GUI action, UCM checks to make sure that the UCM user's username is the same as the name contained in the associated ClearQuest record's `Owner` field. If the names match, the UCM user is allowed to work on the activity. Otherwise, the UCM user is not allowed to work on the activity.

This policy can be modified to check for other criteria by modifying the ClearQuest hook that is associated with this policy.

Perform ClearQuest Action Before Delivery

The purpose of this policy is to enable you to implement an approval process in ClearQuest that is validated by ClearCase before allowing a delivery to proceed. This policy enables a ClearQuest global hook script that is executed before a ClearCase delivery. This policy is available only when you are using both ClearCase and ClearQuest. The default behavior for this policy is to allow all deliveries.

For example, you might implement a global hook script that checks to see if the code review field was filled in for any activity being delivered. The script would allow deliveries only of activities that had been code-reviewed. If the code review field was not filled in, the script would abort the delivery.

The ClearQuest script that is associated with the policy is a placeholder that does nothing. If you want to enable this policy, you need to add code the ClearQuest script to implement the actions you want it to take.

Transfer ClearQuest Mastership Before Delivery

This policy is meant to be used in an environment where ClearQuest MultiSite is being used and then used in conjunction with the Transition to Complete After Delivery policy described later. The nuances associated with this policy and the interaction between ClearQuest MultiSite and ClearCase MultiSite are described in the *Rational ClearCase Managing Software Projects* manual.

Perform ClearQuest Action After Delivery

The purpose of this policy is to enable you to implement a notification or other post-delivery process in ClearQuest at the end of a successful deliver operation. An example of such an action might be to send e-mail to a project integrator whenever a deliver operation successfully concludes so that the integrator can perform the necessary testing required to establish a new project baseline.

The ClearQuest script that is associated with the policy is a placeholder that does nothing. If you want to enable this policy, you need to implement the actions you want it to take.

Transition to Complete After Delivery

This policy uses the ClearQuest activity record's default action to transition it to a Complete state type at the end of a deliver operation.

NOTE

A state type is a category of states that UCM uses to define default state transition sequences. All ClearQuest states in a UCM-enabled ClearQuest record type must be based on one of four state types:

- Waiting
- Ready
- Active
- Complete

Multiple ClearQuest states can belong to the same state type. There must be at least one path of transitions that will move a record through the state types from Waiting to Ready to Active to Complete.

A full description of the mechanics of state types is in the ClearCase *Managing Software Projects* manual.

If ClearQuest fields must be filled out to perform that state transition and one or more of those mandatory fields are not filled out, this policy returns an error and the deliver operation is left in an uncompleted state. If the deliver operation was invoked from a ClearCase GUI, the ClearQuest record form automatically is displayed, enabling the empty fields to be filled out. While the deliver operation is in the uncompleted state, no subsequent deliveries can be initiated from the source stream until the required ClearQuest fields are filled out and the delivery is restarted and completed, or the delivery is cancelled.

Some caution should be exercised in enabling this policy. This is because sometimes an activity is not yet completed, but it is stable and some desired functionality in the incomplete activity should be delivered to the project's integration stream. In this case, if this policy is enabled, the incomplete activity automatically is transitioned to Complete after the delivery operation, even though there is work yet to be done on it.

Transfer ClearQuest Mastership After Delivery

This policy should be used only in conjunction with the Transfer ClearQuest Mastership Before Delivery policy, described earlier. It is meant to be used in MultiSite environments where remote delivery operations are performed and you want to transfer mastership of the ClearQuest activity back to the original replica when the deliver operation is completed at the remote site. The nuances associated with this policy and the interaction between ClearQuest MultiSite and ClearCase MultiSite are described in the *Rational ClearCase Managing Software Projects* manual.

Perform ClearQuest Action Before Changing Activity

The purpose of this policy is to enable you to implement a process in ClearQuest when a finish activity operation is attempted. The finish activity operation is used in single-stream projects and on the integration stream of multistream projects as the equivalent to a deliver operation.

The ClearQuest script that is associated with the policy is a placeholder that does nothing. If you want to enable this policy, you need to implement the actions you want it to take.

Perform ClearQuest Action After Changing Activity

The purpose of this policy is to enable you to implement a process in ClearQuest when a finish activity operation is successfully completed. Similar to the Perform ClearQuest Action After Delivery policy, this policy enables you to implement a notification or other process in ClearQuest at the end of a successful finish activity operation. An example of such an action might be to send e-mail to a project integrator whenever a finish activity operation successfully concludes so that the integrator can perform the necessary testing required to establish a new project baseline.

The ClearQuest script that is associated with the policy is a placeholder that does nothing. If you want to enable this policy, you need to implement the actions you want it to take.

Transition to Complete Action After Changing Activity

This policy uses the ClearQuest activity record's default action to transition it to a Complete state type at the end of a finish activity operation. If ClearQuest fields must be filled out to perform that state transition and one or more of those mandatory fields are not filled out, this policy returns an error and the finish activity operation fails.

6.2.5 Choosing the Location for Your Project

The ClearCase project explorer organizes projects into a hierarchy using folders. Before you run the Project Creation Wizard, you must determine where in the hierarchy you will create the project or whether you need to create a new folder in which to place the new project.

> **NOTE**
> For organizational purposes, it can be useful to create three high-level folders in the project VOB that organize the projects into ongoing, cancelled, and completed projects. This keeps ongoing work easy to access.

After you have created or located the correct folder for your new project, simply select it and choose File, New, Project to begin the process of creating the new project.

6.2.6 Creating Your Project

ClearCase UCM provides a Project Creation Wizard to assist you in creating a new project. This graphical wizard is available on both Windows and UNIX platforms. This section walks you through the Project Creation Wizard to give you a feel for what it takes to create a ClearCase project. For detailed information and instructions on creating a project, refer to the ClearCase documentation.

To start the Project Explorer from the command line, issue this command:

```
prompt> clearprojexp
```

Alternatively, you can access the Project Explorer from the ClearCase Explorer on Windows platforms and from the xclearcase GUI on UNIX platforms. Then perform the following steps:

1. From the ClearCase Project Explorer, select a folder or the top-level project PVOB in which you want to create a new project. Then select File, New, Project from the pull-down menu (see Figure 6-9). In this example, the AuctionDelight folder is selected. On Windows platforms, you can also access this function by selecting a folder with a right mouse click, as illustrated in Figure 6-10.

2. In the first step of project creation, you are asked for the name of your project, the integration stream name (UCM provides a default value based on the name of the project), a brief description, and whether you want the project to be a multistream project or a single-stream project. The title you select is used throughout the GUI interfaces. In this example, we are creating a project titled Auction_Rel_3. We will accept the default name for the project's integration stream, and we will specify that we want this project to be a traditional parallel development (multistream) project (see Figure 6-11).

3. After naming and describing your project, you define your project's scope of work or start configuration. On this page of the Project Creation Wizard, you decide whether you would like to pick each component and component baseline by hand or whether you would like to inherit the component and baseline definitions from a stream in an existing project. If you pick an existing project stream (as shown in Figure 6-12), you inherit that project's components and pick up the latest recommended baselines of those components. In our example, we have selected the Auction_Rel_2_Integration stream in the Auction_Rel_2 project under the Projects folder in the AuctionDelight PVOB as the basis for our project's Release 3 configuration.

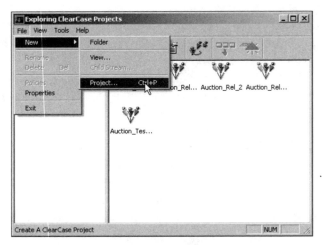

Figure 6-9   Creating a new project in the ClearCase Project Explorer.

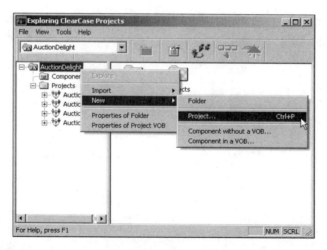

Figure 6-10 Creating a new project in the ClearCase Project Explorer on Windows.

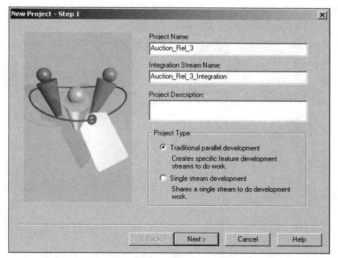

Figure 6-11 Selecting a project title, naming the integration stream, and defining the workflow model.

4. In the next step, you define the set of components your project will use and which baselines your project will start from. If you decided to inherit baselines from an existing project, this dialog box will already contain a set of components and component baselines. If you did not inherit from an existing project, it will be blank. At this point, you can add components, remove components, or change the baseline of any component by selecting a component and using the buttons at the bottom of the dialog box (see Figure 6-13).

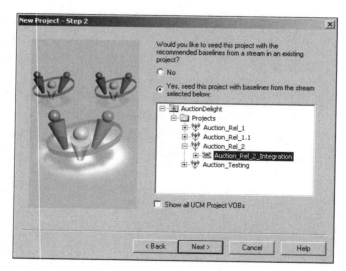

Figure 6-12   Opting to inherit component and baseline definitions from a stream in an existing project.

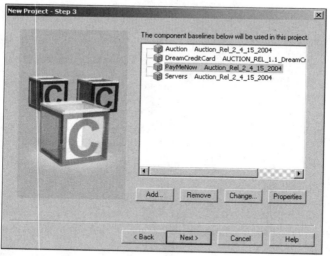

Figure 6-13   Modifying the component or baseline list.

5. In the next dialog box, you set the project policies that govern the work for your project. The component list can be modified later while the project is underway. In the example in Figure 6-14, you set the promotion level for baselines to become recommended and decide which components your project can modify. In our example, we picked the Initial promotion level, made the Auction, DreamCreditCard, and PayMeNow components modifiable, and made the Servers component nonmodifiable in the context of this project.

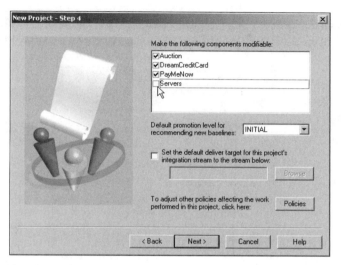

Figure 6-14   Setting the project policies.

6. In the final step, you decide whether your project uses ClearQuest (see Figure 6–15). In this project, you opt to use ClearQuest. When you choose this option, you must specify the ClearQuest database that will be associated with your UCM project. For this project, assume that your ClearQuest administrator has created a database named AUCT for you to use. You can also decide which ClearQuest policies you want to enable or disable. In this case, leave all the ClearQuest policies unchecked. Click the Finish button. UCM

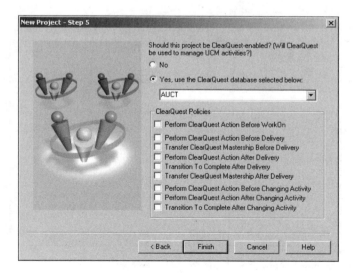

Figure 6-15   Opting to use ClearQuest.

presents a dialog box telling you what it will do (see Figure 6-16). When you click OK,
UCM will create your UCM project. You have created your first UCM project.

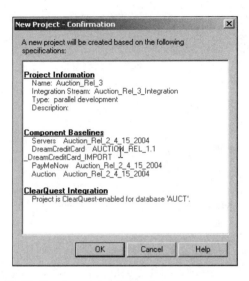

Figure 6-16   UCM project creation summary dialog box.

When UCM finishes creating the Auction_Rel_3 project, it immediately becomes visible
in the ClearCase Project Explorer, as illustrated in Figure 6-17.

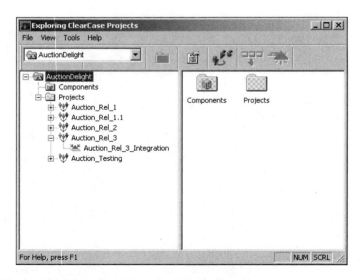

Figure 6-17   The project in the ClearCase Project Explorer.

6.3   Summary

This chapter discussed UCM projects and all the things you need to think about when you create one—things such as the size of the project team and how that will affect the dynamics of making changes, how those changes are to be made and integrated together, and UCM project policies, such as which components should be modifiable, which your project should simply use in a read-only form, how you want to recommend baselines for development, and much more. Finally, you learned how the UCM Project Creation Wizard guides you easily through establishing the initial properties and policies for your project. Subsequent chapters explore specific project scenarios and workflows, and how they work in a UCM environment.

CHAPTER 7

Managing and Organizing Your ClearCase Projects

To be competitive in today's market, you need to be prepared to effectively manage your software-development projects. If you don't, you might find your project encountering cost overruns, missed deadlines, low quality, and an incapability to respond to changing market conditions. Perhaps you will even face your project being cancelled. If you manage a small software-development project team (fewer than 5 people), it is fairly easy to keep on top of what the team is doing and how it is progressing toward the project's goals. However, as your software-development project team grows in size, it is harder to coordinate changes among the team, or sets of teams. And in today's world of software development, your software-development team might not only be large, but also geographically distributed across the world. If you can leverage the power of large software-development teams, manage to keep your project on track, and produce high-quality software that meets your customers' needs, you will win the game.

If you cannot keep track of a locally organized software-development project, then surely you will not be able to handle a geographically distributed development project. This chapter discusses large, multiproject development scenarios and other interesting project situations, including IS/IT application development, documentation-oriented project teams, and small project teams. It explores different strategies for organizing these teams and how to manage their integration activities. Chapter 11, "Geographically Distributed Development," extends these concepts to cover geographically distributed development in detail.

7.1   Coordinating Multiple Parallel Releases

As discussed in "Parallel Development Support" in Chapter 2, "Growing into Your SCM Solution," it is not often that you have the luxury of finishing one release before you begin the next. A project that starts from an existing ongoing project is called a follow-on project. Follow-on projects are supported in ClearCase UCM by creating a new project based on an existing baseline of a selected project's integration stream. To keep changes in sync between these projects going forward, you can rebase or deliver changes between the projects, depending on which direction you want the changes to flow. It is important to understand direction of change flow. For instance, you would not want to accidentally deliver future product enhancements back to a previous release's maintenance project. When you have multiple releases—and, therefore, multiple projects underway at the same time, it is good practice to establish a mainline project that is used to synchronize the source code. A mainline project is a project that serves as an integration and release point for multiple subprojects. Let's take a look at these types of projects.

7.1.1   The Follow-On Project

This section presents an example of creating a follow-on project. Suppose your development team needs to start working on the GUI_Rel2 project (note that this naming convention would indicate that this project is modifying the GUI component for Rel2 work). From the ClearCase Project Explorer, you would create a new project called GUI_Rel2. When asked in the Project Creation Wizard, you would answer yes to seeding the new project from the recommended baseline of an existing project. By selecting the baseline GUI_REL1 (from the GUI_Mainline project), you copy the GUI_REL1 component/baseline configuration to the GUI_Rel2 project. Work can now proceed on the GUI_Rel2 project (see Figure 7-1).

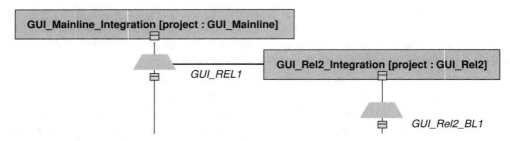

Figure 7-1   Follow-on project initial component baseline graph.

7.1.2   The Mainline Project

Regardless of team organization, you want to have a well-understood process of where to start an SCM project. Your teams should also have an idea of how to complete a project. With no guidance in this area, your teams will do whatever they think is right at the time they need to do it. This will lead to some serious problems over time. It is critical to develop a "rules of the road" document to agree on how your organization will behave while performing these operations. One of the ways teams tend to start a new project is by following on an existing project. This section discusses the problems with the cascading follow-on approach and how the use of a mainline project solves these problems. The primary problems with exclusively using the follow-on approach are losing changes, permanent divergence, and SCM tool failures because of infinite cascading branches. When you are managing many parallel releases, patch releases, and many operating system variants of a software system, it can be easy to lose changes or to allow parts of your system to permanently diverge. Most SCM tools use a mechanism to represent the structure of element versions. If you continue to branch off other branches, you set up an infinite cascading scenario. Most SCM tools other than ClearCase will reach some limit in branch naming as branches continue to cascade. Also, some development tools might not be capable of handling the long, extended pathnames generated by cascading branches.

The use of a mainline project avoids these problems by providing an approach to SCM that is well organized and includes points of convergence for the entire source code base. The approach is fairly simple: Major release projects converge at the mainline project when you finish a project, from which follow-on projects are started. Mainline projects should not be used for doing development. For environments in which security is more stringent, this mainline project can be owned by the production release team. This team would also want to own any maintenance projects because they would hold defect fixes for these releases.

7.1.3 Project Completion

Let's examine how the follow-on project scenario completes work when a mainline project is being used. When GUI_Rel2 is completed, you use the following procedure.

CLEARCASE PRO TIP

If ClearCase is used without UCM, the mainline project is usually managed on the `/main` branch. However, UCM does not use the `/main` branch, to allow UCM and non-UCM projects to share the same VOBs. So, in the case of UCM, although you still create a mainline project, the actual branch being used will not be `/main`.

The first step is to merge the baseline that constitutes the released artifacts from the GUI_Rel2 project to the GUI_Mainline project, as illustrated in Figure 7-2.

This can be achieved by delivering the baseline from the GUI_Rel2 project to the GUI_Mainline project. You can now create a new baseline on the GUI_Mainline project to reflect this configuration named GUI_REL2. (Note that GUI_Rel2 started from the GUI_Mainline project baseline named GUI_REL1.)

CLEARCASE PRO TIP

After a project completes to the mainline project, you can use `cleartool lock -obsolete` on the completing project and its objects to remove them from view of some of the ClearCase interfaces. Be sure to deliver any unfinished activities to a follow-on project's stream before performing this lock procedure (unless it is not applicable for that release).

7.1.4 Project Creation

You are now ready to create the follow-on project. In this case, you will create a project called GUI_Rel2_Fix. This will be a maintenance project for GUI_REL2. A maintenance project is used to perform bug fixes to a release. It is just like any other project, except that it is locked down

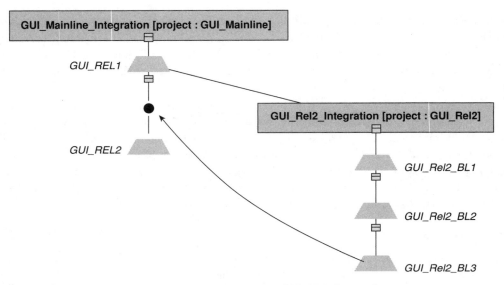

Figure 7-2 Delivering GUI_Rel2_BL3 changes to the GUI_Mainline project.

to allow only the developers who need to work on the defects that were reported against the release. When asked in the Project Creation Wizard, you would seed the GUI_Rel2_Fix project with baselines from the GUI_Mainline project. In this case, you want to pick GUI_REL2 baseline as the starting point for the GUI_Rel2 project. Figure 7-3 illustrates project creation using the mainline project.

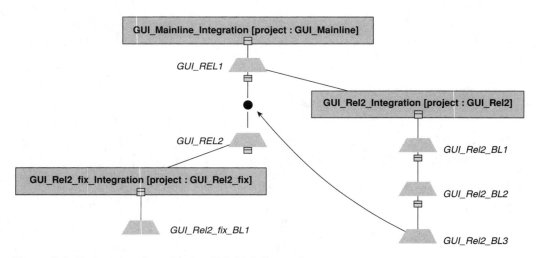

Figure 7-3 Project creation with the GUI_Mainline project.

7.1.5   Multiple Parallel Projects

The mainline project will hold only released artifacts. Any release-stabilization work should be done out on the development or maintenance project. You can always lock down any project to allow only certain people to make critical approved changes. If you have multiple parallel projects in progress at the same time, you can keep them in sync by delivering or rebasing changes between the projects, as appropriate. When organizing around component-based development teams (discussed later in this chapter), you will see that you can pick up changes for your project without ever having to merge.

When a project is ready to release, it merges its release baseline to the mainline project. At this time, any parallel projects can rebase from this release baseline on the mainline project. Until then, parallel projects should rely on performing deliver operations between the projects to stay in sync. If you were working on a maintenance project of an old release, you would never want to deliver changes from the maintenance project to the mainline project. This could potentially overwrite changes of a future release that have been delivered to the mainline project. Also, you would never want to rebase a maintenance project from a future delivery on the mainline project. This would introduce tomorrow's features into yesterday's release. This really depends on how many projects you have underway, how frequently they release, what you are committed to delivering to your customers, and whether you indeed have to support old releases. This is why maintenance projects should never be delivered back to the mainline project. They will just die out over time. Any changes to the maintenance project that also need to be included in future projects can be delivered to their development streams and integrated as part of the future release's regular integration effort. Figure 7-4 shows a parallel project baseline graph.

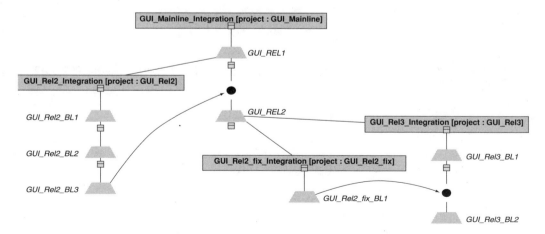

Figure 7-4   Parallel project baseline graph with mainline project.

Figure 7-5 shows a more complicated baseline graph.

For comparison's sake, Figure 7-6 illustrates a parallel project baseline graph that would result if a mainline project were not used.

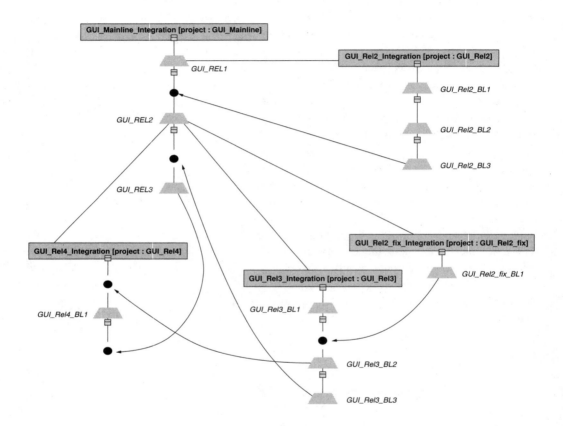

Figure 7-5 A more complicated baseline graph with multiple parallel projects spawned from the mainline project.

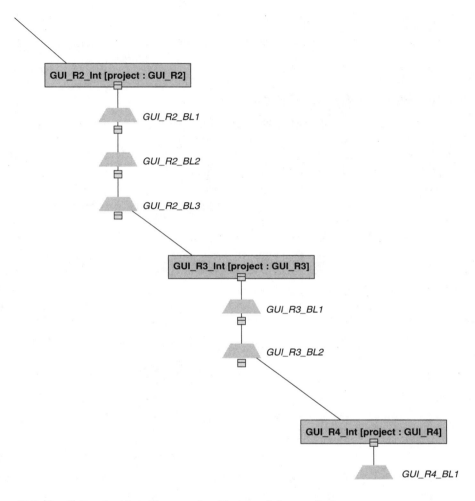

Figure 7-6 Parallel project baseline graph with no mainline project.

7.2   Organizing Large Multiproject Development Efforts

In large development efforts (major and extensive), multiple projects will be working together toward one single release of a software system. In very broad terms, there are two approaches to organizing your project teams: by architecture and by feature. Another pattern of organization in today's world is to get as much utilization as possible out of your software-development resources. This leads to many developers working on multiple projects and releases at the same time. Developers might be pulled off one project to help another, and so on. The organizational approach you take impacts how you do SCM on your project. Generally, over the life of a software system, a hybrid approach is employed.

> **NOTE**
>
> As related to SCM, the differences between architecture-oriented and feature-oriented project teams are significant only when a change affects multiple components.

7.2.1   Architecture-Oriented Project Teams

Architecture-oriented teams are organized along the same lines as the system architecture. There is no substitute for having good system architecture. You can avoid many SCM challenges with good architecture. If you don't have good architecture, it will be hard to organize your teams around architecture. You typically must logically break up your monolithic code base into components as a start, but you will find that your projects still have to change all components. You will most likely organize by feature if you fall into this category. So, in the simple example in Chapter 6, "Project Management in ClearCase," we have one component each for the database, the core, and the GUIs. For a large system, we would assign one team to work on the database component, another to work on the core component, and a third to work on the GUI component. The relationship between components and projects is not always one to one. In more complex systems, a single team might be responsible for more than one component. For example, each GUI interface in an application might be stored in its own component, but a single GUI team might be responsible for changes to any of the GUI components.

Architecture-oriented teams have the following characteristics and effects on SCM processes:

- The teams generally remain the same from release to release (barring major architectural changes).

- Team member knowledge becomes specialized the longer team members work in their product area.

- The integrity of the architecture is easier to maintain than with feature- oriented teams.

- The definitions and stability of component interfaces becomes very important to interteam coordination.

- Iteration planning is more complex because each iteration usually must demonstrate some feature. To demonstrate a feature that spans components, teams must produce baselines that implement pieces of the feature in their components. These components, when integrated, must implement an overall system-level feature.

- Integration is simplified because it involves assembling various component baselines rather than merging changes to common/shared code. This becomes even more important as your teams span multiple geographies.

- Component sharing and reuse is much easier to accomplish because component interfaces must be clearly defined. This generally leads to the capability to produce more product variants easier and faster.

- Testing of a feature is delayed until all changes required have been performed in all components.

Organizations that want to follow component-based development practices should organize their teams architecturally. The architecture approach requires more rigorous communication, planning, and coordination. If this is not feasible given organizational constraints, a feature-based approach is probably preferable. If the team is organized in a component team fashion, you will want to create your mainline project at the component team level. So, each component team will create its own mainline project. Also, it is a good practice for these teams to produce baselines of these components, while other projects consume these baselines. If you have multiple projects bound for the same release writing to the same components, your consuming projects must choose which baselines to use.

7.2.2   Feature-Oriented Project Teams

Feature-oriented teams are organized based on major pieces of functionality to be implemented in a system. For example, if you had three major features, A, B, and C, planned for the next major release of your product, you would have three project teams, A, B, and C.

Feature-oriented teams have the following characteristics and effects on SCM processes:

- The teams and team members change from release to release based on what needs to be implemented. Some organizations have pools of people who spin into teams as they come off one feature project and get assigned to the next.

- Team member knowledge becomes broader the longer team members work on the product.

- The integrity of the architecture is more difficult to maintain than with architecture-oriented teams. This is because team members are working across the entire system. They might know of functions they wrote or used in one component that would help them in work on another component. By making a function call in the code between components, they introduce a dependency between these components that might not already exist and might not be architecturally sound. Also, they might re-create a piece of functionality that already exists somewhere else in the component. For instance, more than one person can fix a discovered defect differently within the same component because there is no component ownership. This common mishap tends to occur more frequently with geographically distributed development.

- Iteration planning is simpler because iteration planning is usually feature-oriented and a single team is involved for each feature.

- Integration is more complex. Because all the source code could potentially be modified by any feature team, integration often involves merging changes made to shared source files. Integration should be planned and performed as early as possible. This type of integration becomes harder to do as the number of feature teams grows. This is why it is much easier to produce multiple product variants simultaneously using component-based teams.

- Component sharing and reuse are very difficult without employing a hybrid approach in which key individuals or teams are assigned to specific components.

- Features can be more easily deferred (that is, left unmerged), which is advantageous for risky features.

Feature-oriented teams are efficient for maintenance projects (those undergoing only defect fixes or minor enhancements). Feature-oriented teams are often the best approach for legacy systems with monolithic architectures when rearchitecting is not a viable option. The feature-based approach is also useful for IS/IT projects because it minimizes the planning and coordination required.

7.3   Coordinating Cooperating Projects: Independent Components

In many circumstances, you might have more than one project team cooperating on producing a final product release. For project teams that are organized architecturally (see the section "Architecture-Oriented Project Teams," earlier in this chapter), it is easy to define producer/consumer component relationships between projects because only one project team is making changes to any given component for any given release.

7.3.1   Project Creation

Here is an example. Let's say you have a product with a core component and a GUI component. You are working on producing Release 2 of this product. You have organized your teams architecturally so that you have a core team and a GUI team. For the core team, create a project that will modify the core component. Choose a baseline of the core component you want that project to work on—for example, Baseline 4.

CLEARCASE PRO TIP

When creating the project, be sure to seed it with baselines from the mainline project's integration stream for this component. You will be presented with a list of baselines. You should then pick the baseline from the list that you want to start this project from.

Allow the core component to be modified. For the GUI team, create another project (again, from the mainline project) and include two components: the GUI component and the core component. Pick the same baseline (Baseline 4) for the core component and a baseline for the GUI component. Mark the core component as read-only. You now have two projects whose component lists are illustrated in Figure 7-7.

7.3.2   Iteration Planning

The Rational Unified Process defines an *iteration* as "a distinct set of activities with a baselined plan and valuation criteria resulting in a release (internal or external)" [RUP 5.5 1999]. From an SCM standpoint, iteration planning is important because iterations usually mark key integration points. (For more information on iterative development, refer to the chapter in [Kruchten, 2000] entitled "Dynamic Structure: Iterative Development." For more details on the typical project-management aspects of iteration planning, refer to the chapter in [Royce, 1998] entitled "Iterative Process Planning.")

Let's look at iteration planning. As part of the work on Release 2 in this example, you must define internal iterations. Let's say that the application is a drawing application, and you would like to demonstrate to a customer a new feature to make sure it meets the customer's needs as

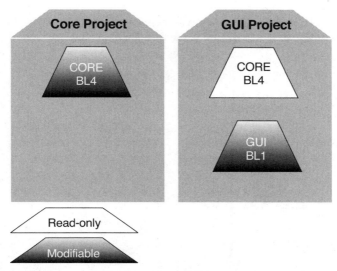

Figure 7-7   Initial GUI and core project component lists.

early as possible. You plan this feature for the first iteration (see Figure 7-8). This new feature is a drop-down dialog box that displays all the colors used so far in the drawing. Your architect determines that this feature will require the core team to implement a function that retrieves the colors in the drawing and returns the color list. The GUI team will then use this function and, based on the returned data, draw the colors in a drop-down menu.

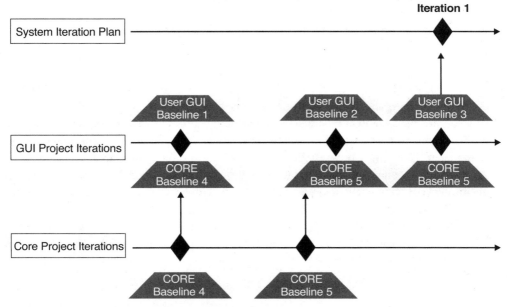

Figure 7-8   Iteration planning with multiple projects.

So, the core team implements a dummy function with the agreed-upon interface and creates the first baseline (Baseline 5). They test this dummy function, and it successfully returns a fixed set of colors. The core team's project manager contacts the GUI team's project manager and indicates that a new core component baseline is ready for their use. The project's component list at this point is shown in Figure 7-9.

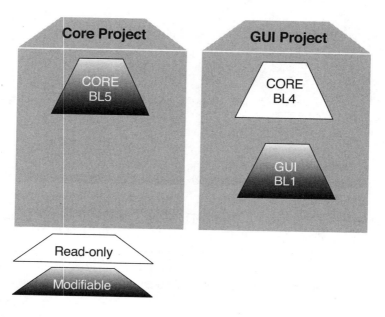

Figure 7-9　Project component lists. (Core team makes changes.)

7.3.3　Integration

The GUI team needs to see the new function in the new core component baseline. To do this, the project leader for the GUI team modifies the component list for the GUI project, selecting Baseline 5 (this should be the latest recommended baseline of the core development project) of the core component. This action forces a rebase of the GUI team's integration stream. The GUI team then finishes the implementation and testing of the drop-down dialog box. The team creates a new baseline of the GUI component, and iteration 1 is complete and can be demonstrated to the customer (see Figure 7-10).

In iteration 2, the core team could continue and actually implement the code to determine the right set of colors, while the GUI team made any changes the customer requested. In this way, two architecture-oriented project teams could coordinate their work toward producing a final release of the drawing product.

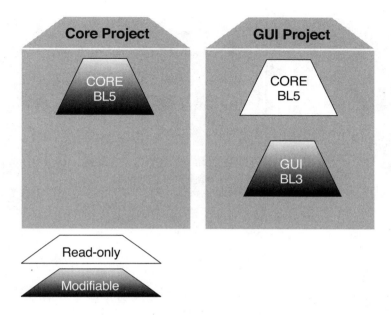

Figure 7-10 Project component lists. (GUI integrates core changes.)

7.4 Coordinating Cooperating Projects: Shared Components

In many circumstances, you might have more than one project team cooperating on producing a final product release. Project teams that are organized around major features (see the section "Feature-Oriented Project Teams," earlier in this chapter) often share components, which leads to the projects modifying the same components in parallel. Creating these projects is easy, but integrating changes is more complicated than in the producer/consumer case discussed in the previous section, "Coordinating Cooperating Projects: Independent Components." It is important to integrate changes early and often. The last thing you want nearing the end of a release cycle is a major integration task among multiple projects.

7.4.1 Project Creation

We'll use the same example as in the previous section. Let's say that you have a product with a core component and a GUI component. You are working on producing Release 2 of a drawing application. Two major features are to be implemented for Release 2: new color-manipulation routines and interfaces, and an online help system.

You decide to organize your teams around features, so you create two projects: Release 2 Color and Release 2 Help. You also create a third project, Release 2 Integration, where changes will be integrated. You now have three projects; their component lists are shown in Figure 7-11.

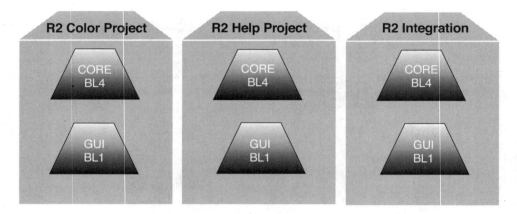

Figure 7-11   Feature-oriented project component lists.

CLEARCASE PRO TIP

If your feature-based teams are relatively small (three developers or less), you can model this development effort as a shared child stream of the integration project and avoid the overhead of creating and maintaining a new project. Also, you can model subintegration streams, useful for large feature integration, through multiple levels of child streams.

7.4.2   Iteration Planning

Let's look at iteration planning. As part of the work on Release 2 in this example, you must define internal iterations or milestones. You would like to demonstrate to a customer a new subfeature of the color-manipulation routines and a piece of the new help system, to make sure both meet the customer's needs. You plan this for the first iteration.

The color team and the help team implement their pieces, and both produce new baselines. Notice that, in this case, both teams produce new baselines for both components. They test their changes independently and decide that they are ready for the first iteration. The three project component lists are shown in Figure 7-12.

7.4.3   Integration

The integrator for the overall Release 2 Integration project must now merge the changes from the Color and Help projects to create new system-integration project baselines. This is done using an interproject delivery (see "Interproject Deliveries" in Chapter 9, "Integration," for more info). ClearCase has the capability to merge nonconflicting changes automatically. Conflicting changes require manual intervention. Any changes made to the same files by both teams are merged at this point, and the combined system can be built, tested, and demonstrated to the customer. The component baseline graph for the core component (see Figure 7-13) illustrates this integration work.

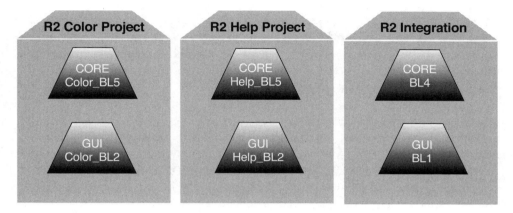

Figure 7-12   Color, help, and integration project component lists.

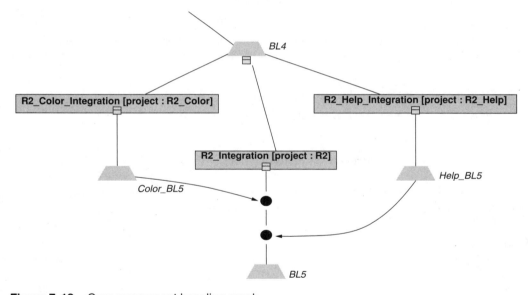

Figure 7-13   Core component baseline graph.

For iteration 2, both teams would continue working on the full implementation of their features. Using this approach, two feature-oriented project teams coordinate their work toward producing a final release of the drawing product.

7.5   Coordinating IS/IT Development Projects

ClearCase UCM is particularly well suited for typical IS/IT development projects, which are often projects being developed by an internal group, where the system being developed is deployed for in-house or internal use. A good example is a trading system for a financial firm. Because the software system is mission-critical for the financial firm, it is developed in-house. It provides a competitive advantage for the company's traders. It is not sold or shipped to other customers. The fact that the system is not sold and that it is deployed to a single internal customer distinguishes these projects from commercial systems. Web sites can also be good examples.

The second thing that is unique about IS/IT projects is that the development group is controlled by the same company that controls the customer group. That means that the customer demands have a stronger influence on the development of the software system than with a commercial system. Commercial systems take in customer input from thousands of customers and must develop products in such a way as to remain profitable. Often in-house systems have only one customer, and the internal software group is held responsible not for making a profit, but for providing the functionality the customer demands as quickly as possible.

The distinctiveness of these projects leads to some unique SCM characteristics, as follows:

- Typically, only one release of a software system is in use at any given time.
- Major release planning and long-term development projects occur with less frequency.
- A procedure for performing emergency fixes is usually employed instead of rolling back to a previous working version.
- An approval process for features is very critical because planning is handled differently from that of commercial projects.
- A feature-oriented rather than architecture-oriented approach is common.

The single release installed and running at any given time is often referred to as the production release. The commercial requirement of maintaining parallel releases in the field is not an issue for these projects.

Parallel development of major releases does not occur as frequently in IS/IT projects. Instead, parallel development occurs on smaller features being added to the production system. There is usually no major release planning; releases occur biweekly, weekly, or, for some organizations, daily. Instead of planning the contents of a release, managers define what goes into the release by what is ready when the release occurs. If a feature misses a release, it just gets put into the next release.

> **NOTE**
>
> These IS/IT systems will undergo some major change at some point, such as a change to of the underlying database, an alteration to the platform the production system is running on, or a major rearchitecting effort. While these major changes occur, parallel development of a planned release is taking place with changes to the current production system. When the new system is ready, a switch-over plan is executed. The new production system is brought online, and the old production system is decommissioned. This is often a major effort for the IS/IT organization because it can involve retraining internal personnel and a Big Bang–style shift. This type of development is the same as that covered in the section "Coordinating Multiple Parallel Releases," earlier in this chapter.

To support critical bug fixes to the production system between releases, often an emergency bug fix procedure allows the production software to be quickly patched. How an organization performs this procedure is often overlooked, introducing many of the same problems described in Chapter 2. When designing an SCM solution, it is important to include this procedure if your projects and systems fall into the IS/IT category.

Finally, the planning of new functionality is usually done differently from that of commercial systems. Planning for each release's content is not usually carried out in as much detail. Instead, releases are performed on a periodic basis, and changes completed at the time of release are approved for that release. Changes are considered complete after defects and requests for enhancement have been collected and reviewed, any changes have been approved (allowing work to commence on that change), and developers have declared that in some way they are done. This declaration prompts an integrator or project manager to approve the change for inclusion in the release. The change then gets incorporated into the project's build and, after being successfully tested, is deployed along with others in the production environment.

Let's look at how to apply ClearCase UCM to this type of project development. First, you create a new project. Instead of naming the project Product X Release Y, you might name the project by referring to the product being developed (as in Product X).

WARNING
Naming a new project after the product being developed is specific to the IS/IT type of project environment. It works only for smaller development efforts when a single project team is working on the entire product.

After the project is created, development members can join the project as usual and work in their stable, consistent, and isolated development streams on their activities.

CLEARCASE PRO TIP
If the team is small enough (three developers or less), it can create a shared stream that is a child stream off the project-integration stream. This allows rapid integration of changes (via check-in) and avoids having to merge to integrate changes among the team. Periodically, a team member would deliver completed activities to the integration area and rebase the stream to pick up new recommended baselines.

7.5.1   Choosing Which Features to Work On

Developers work on activities in their ClearCase view. These activities track the versions of the files they change and allow subsequent operations on those versions to be performed at the activity level (see "The Developer: Joining a Project and Doing Development" in Chapter 3, "An Overview of the Unified Change Management Model," and "Making Changes" in Chapter 8, "Development Using the ClearCase UCM Model"). UCM offers two approaches to managing these activities.

The first approach requires only ClearCase. In this approach, developers receive work assignments through whatever mechanism is available. This could be verbally, by e-mail, or by using a defect-tracking tool. When a work assignment has been approved, a developer goes to ClearCase and creates a new activity in his or her development stream that represents that work assignment.

The second approach requires ClearCase and ClearQuest. In this approach, activities are planned and created in the system before being worked on. These activities can take the form of defects, requests for enhancement, or any other entity your organization tracks. These predefined activities are then assigned to particular projects and particular people. In this approach, developers do not create the activities themselves. Instead, they pick the activity from their to-do list in ClearQuest. This approach is covered in Chapter 12, "Change Request Management and ClearQuest." With either approach, developers work on a particular activity in their development stream. When they have completed their work, they can deliver it to one or more project-integration streams.

7.5.2 Implementing an Approval Process

If you are interested in implementing an approval process, the best approach is to use full UCM, which requires both ClearCase and ClearQuest (see Chapter 12). However, if you are using just ClearCase, you can do one of two things. First, you can lock the integration stream and unlock it only for particular users. In effect, this approach says, "I will grant Joe the ability to deliver any activity." Second, you can use selective baseline creation to include only the activities that have been approved. Using the `cleartool mkbl` command, you can specify a list of activities (the approved ones) to include in the baseline. This method is not recommended because it is hard to manage over time; the default behavior of cleartool is to include all activities in the baseline since the last baseline. Third, you can implement a pull mechanism by which you do not let developers deliver to the integration stream; your integrator performs the deliver of the activities only if they are approved.

CLEARCASE PRO TIP
You can attach ClearCase triggers to UCM objects to implement a wide variety of process and policy on top of your UCM environment. When going down this path, be sure to make it easy to do the right thing and hard to do the wrong thing.

When the activities are in the integration stream, you can lock the integration stream and build, test, and baseline the system, as described in Chapter 9. After QA has verified the resulting system in its testing environment, you can install/deploy it to the production machine and promote the baseline(s) to the appropriate level. If you have not defined your own baseline promotion levels, you should use the default baseline promotion level of Released.

7.5.3 Performing Emergency Bug Fixes

For emergency bug fixes to the production system, you should create a new project for that purpose. This project should come off the mainline project of the released baseline (just like any new project). If there is already a maintenance project created for this release, you can join this existing project to perform your bug fix. If you implement this bug-fix work as a development stream instead of a maintenance project, there is a risk that a developer could rebase the bug-fix stream and pollute it with future activities. When an emergency change is needed, you go to the emergency bug-fix stream/view on the project and create an activity that represents the fix. The fix is then developed, built, and tested. You should then provide a procedure that enables the developer to create/install/deploy the system into the production environment. This is likely to be a set of manual steps or an automated script, or a tool such as Tivoli that packages up and deploys the release. Making sure the fix gets into the next official release is simply a matter of performing an interproject delivery to the integration stream of the next release project.

7.5.4   Planning for a Major Release

If you do need to run another major release in parallel, simply create a new ClearCase project from the mainline project and start work. This is described in the section "Coordinating Multiple Parallel Releases," earlier in this chapter. If you need baselines from another project that is underway but has not yet been released, you can perform an interproject delivery of the baseline to the new project. You might not want to do this if your new project does not desire changes from other active projects.

7.6   Coordinating Documentation Projects or Small Teams

In some cases, the more advanced capabilities in the UCM model are not required. Two examples are projects that are doing documentation and projects that are very small. Projects with two to five developers working on one single software system are considered small (see "Small Project Teams" in Chapter 2 for more details).

This section discusses applying the UCM model to these types of projects. It covers how you use UCM differently than with larger projects and what you give up by using this approach.

First, make sure your project actually falls into this category. The following are the consequences of giving up the UCM features not included in the approach discussed in this section:

- **Developers cannot checkpoint their work.** *Checkpointing* is the ability of developers to check in an intermediate version of a file they have been working on without the changes being made visible to other team members. In the approach described here, the check-in operation makes the change available to other project members. If this presents a problem for your developers, this approach is not for you.

- **Development workspaces are not fully isolated.** In this approach, if developers are using dynamic views, they will see changes made by other developers when those developers check in changes (not when they deliver). This can be desirable for very small teams (fewer than five members) because it encourages early integration. If your developers are using snapshot views, they will still be isolated until they perform a Snapshot

View Update operation. If you want your developers to fully control when they see changes, you should not use the approach described here.

- **Development workspaces might become inconsistent.** UCM ensures that changes are moved around and made visible as a whole. That is, all changes made for a given activity become visible at the same time. The approach described here does not maintain this feature. Instead, files are made visible to the team one at a time as they are checked in, introducing the possibility that another developer will pick up a new version of one file but not the corresponding new version of another. Therefore, if multiple people are working on the same file or files, version skew can occur, creating an inconsistent development workspace. If your development team members frequently work on the same sets of files at the same time, the approach described here is not for you.

- **Deliver and rebase operations are not performed.** The approach described here involves everyone working in the integration stream. Because no development streams are in use, deliver and rebase operations are not performed. This is a side effect of the lack of developer isolation, as just described. You can avoid this situation if, instead of working on the integration stream, you have the team work on a shared development stream. This enables developers to deliver completed changes to the integration to be picked up by QA.

- **The entire system should be contained in one VOB.** If you are considering this approach and you are managing a system that cannot be contained in one single VOB, you should consider using full UCM. However, if you have a system that can be contained in one VOB component, this approach can reduce some overhead (but at a cost, as described in the previous points).

CLEARCASE PRO TIP
The approach described here explains how to use the UCM model to develop on a single branch using the base ClearCase branch/LATEST approach. This enables you to gain some of the advantages of UCM, such as change sets, without using all of the UCM capabilities.

The basic idea behind using just the integration stream is that small teams or teams working serially on documentation require less isolation and so do not need the additional isolation characteristics of development streams and deliver/rebase operations. Simply put, everyone on these projects works in their own integration views attached to the common project-integration stream. The following sections cover how this approach works. If you have a team that is geographically distributed, you should not use this approach, unless remote users use some form of remote client to connect to the project's integration stream. ClearCase MultiSite mastership will prevent other sites from working directly on the integration stream at the remote site.

7.6.1   Project Creation

The project leader creates the project and specifies a single-stream project rather than the traditional parallel-development project (see Figure 7-14). He or she selects the single component that contains

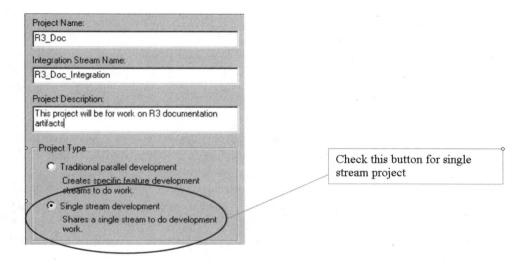

Figure 7-14 The creation of a single-stream project.

all the files needed for the software system being developed or all the documentation needed by a documentation group. Think of this as the system component or the documentation component.

7.6.2 Joining a Project

Developers or writers use the Join Project Wizard as in any project. Because this is a single-stream project, you are prompted only for an integration view to be created.

Developers and writers can now work in their own integration views. They must still create and work on activities even though these activities are not delivered. This allows baselines to be created and ensures that operations such as comparisons between two baselines will report correctly which activities were implemented between baselines.

7.6.3 Delivering Changes

One of the differences in this approach from using the full UCM capabilities is that activities are not delivered. Developers and writers make changes visible to other team members simply by checking in their changes. No delivery operation is performed.

> **NOTE**
> With a single-stream project, you can still deliver and rebase to and from other projects, if needed.

Developers and writers must ensure that they check in all changes they have made at the same time, to avoid introducing inconsistency. This is facilitated from the command line by using the following:

```
prompt> cleartool checkin -cact
```

From the GUI, you can get a list of checked-out elements using the Find Check-Outs Wizard. You can then check in files related to an activity.

7.6.4 Updating the Workspace

Developers or writers using this approach will see each other's changes differently from within the standard UCM model. With standard UCM use, developers use the rebase operation to see changes made by other team members. Because development streams are not used in the approach discussed here, there is no reason for a rebase operation. Instead, standard ClearCase mechanisms are used to make changes visible. The choice of dynamic or snapshot views is, therefore, more significant. In dynamic views, you see other team members' changes the moment they check them in. With snapshot views, you see other team members' changes only when you perform a snapshot view update operation. (The snapshot view update operation is included as a part of the UCM rebase operation for snapshot views.) See "Workspaces: Snapshot and Dynamic Views" in Chapter 4, "A Functional Overview of ClearCase Objects," for more information on how these views work and why you might choose one or the other.

7.6.5 Creating Baselines

The integrator may still create baselines to identify key versions of the source code or documents for use by other groups, or just for historical purposes.

7.7 Summary

This chapter touched on many key organization issues surrounding software development. Your organization should understand where to create a new project, how to finish the project, and how to organize your components and your team of developers to work on those components. One of the most important things you can do as a development organization is to agree on a common usage model for your development project. Different projects might use slightly different usage models, but all the team members should understand how to interact with the SCM system based on the role they are playing and the project they are working on. You should also invest the time to review how the usage model is working with the key stakeholders of the teams. If you cannot achieve this, you will not be an optimized development organization, and you will have to rely on heroic efforts more often at crucial stages in your product's life cycle.

CHAPTER 8

Development Using the ClearCase UCM Model

The goal of any software-development effort is to create high-quality software that is on time and under budget, and that also satisfies the agreed-upon requirements. The last thing you want your SCM tool to do is make it hard for your developers to do the right thing. You want a tool that is easy to use, that integrates seamlessly with your developer's IDE, and that, for the most part, stays out of the way of your developers as they perform their tasks on the project. ClearCase Unified Change Management (UCM) provides the process guidance and bookkeeping to allow your developers to focus on software development, without having to waste time wondering whether they are performing changes against the right code base, whether they are up-to-date with other developer's changes, and where they should integrate their changes. If you are using ClearQuest-enabled UCM, you can streamline your development effort further by assigning activities to your developers to work on. These activities will show up on your developers' to-do list, making it even easier to track progress toward your development goals.

This chapter explores UCM for the developer. After reading this chapter, you should understand how to work on an existing project, make changes to files to accomplish an activity, deliver the changes associated with one or more activities, and rebase your development stream to integrate in your development view changes made by other developers on your project.

8.1   A Developer's Perspective of UCM

As a developer using ClearCase UCM, you must understand what project or projects the activities you are working on are destined for. Figure 8-1 shows the developer's workflow (see "ClearCase UCM Process Overview" in Chapter 3, "An Overview of the Unified Change Management Model," for more details).

Before you can make changes to code, you need to establish your working environment (your development view). ClearCase does this automatically when you join a project. When you have your view created, you can make changes to accomplish a specific activity (or task). This is

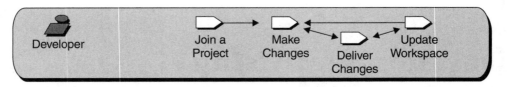

Figure 8-1   Developer process flow.

done by checking out elements, making changes (editing files), and checking the elements back in. As elements are modified and checked in, new versions are created in the VOB and associated with the activity you are working on. These versions are referred to as the activity's change set.

When you have finished implementing and testing the changes you have made, you deliver your changes to your project's integration area. This is done by performing a deliver operation and specifying the activities you want to deliver. The versions of elements that get delivered are dictated by the selected activity's change set. On a periodic basis, you update (rebase) your workspace (your development stream and development view) with changes that have been made by other developers on the same project. Some development projects require you to rebase to the latest recommended baseline from the integration area before performing deliver operations. In the general case, you can also deliver from child streams or other project streams into your stream to integrate changes before delivering them into your project's integration stream. These integration strategies are discussed in detail in Chapter 9, "Integration."

The following sections describe these steps in more detail.

8.2   Working on a Project

ClearCase UCM organizes development teams into projects. For example, a project might be created to develop Release 2 of a software system. You join a project to participate in that project. Joining a project results in the creation of two logical workspaces: one for doing development and one for integrating your changes with other developers' changes. As you read in Chapter 4, "A Functional Overview of ClearCase Objects," a logical workspace is implemented with two ClearCase objects, a view and a stream.

ClearCase UCM provides a Join Project Wizard to walk you through getting started. This GUI wizard is available on both Windows and UNIX platforms. (It is also possible to completely script this step by using the command-line interface and by making all setup decisions.) The Join Project Wizard is available in the ClearCase Project Explorer and the UCM Panel from the ClearCase Explorer, shown in Figure 8-2. It is also available in IDE integrations with ClearCase.

When you join a project, ClearCase creates three new objects: a development stream, a view associated with your development stream (development view), and a view associated with the project's integration stream (integration view). You use your development view for doing development and your integration view for delivering and integrating your changes. Figure 8-3 shows the Join Project Wizard during the creation of your development stream. Figure 8-4 shows the Join Project Wizard during the creation of your views.

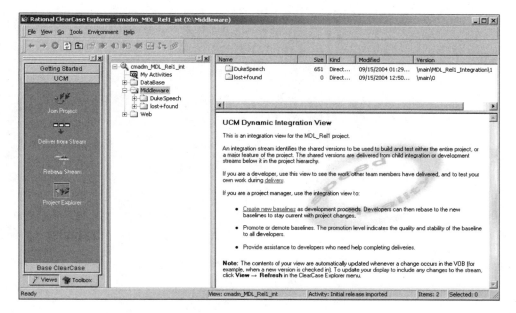

Figure 8-2 ClearCase Explorer: UCM toolbox panel.

You can also begin to work on a project by creating a new development stream from the ClearCase Project Explorer (see Figure 8-5). This also creates a new development view attached to this development stream. You can pick any starting baseline point from the project to use as the foundation for the development stream. Another way to work on a project is to simply create a view that is attached to a stream (see Figure 8-6). This is the easiest way to have a small number of people work together.

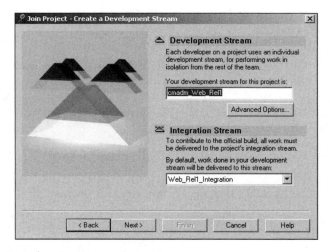

Figure 8-3 Creating your development stream.

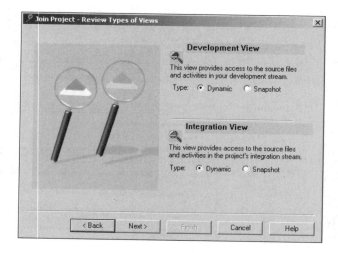

Figure 8-4   Creating a development and integration view.

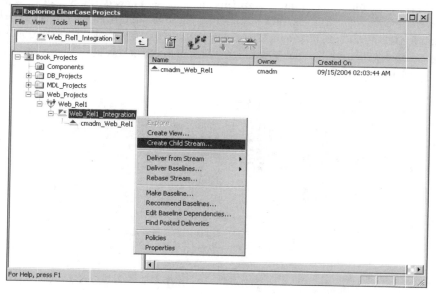

Figure 8-5   Creating a child development stream from ClearCase Project Explorer.

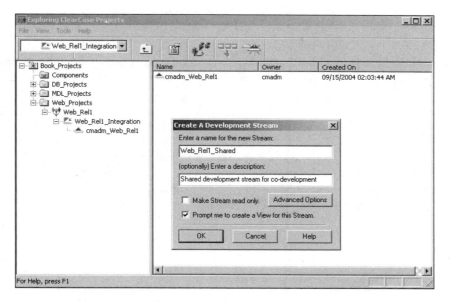

Figure 8-6   Creating a view attached to a development stream.

Your development stream defines a configuration for your development view, which isolates your work from other developers on the project. In your development view, you may check in intermediate changes to the secure storage of the VOB without making them visible to other team members (unless you are sharing the development stream with others, which is discussed more in Chapter 9). The development stream's configuration also isolates you from other developers' changes. You can make changes to a stable baseline of the software without being disrupted by changes going on elsewhere in the project. You are in control of when changes are made visible (by performing a deliver operation) and when you see other developer's changes that they have integrated (by performing a rebase operation).

Your development stream/view selects element versions in this order:

1. The version of an element that you have checked out and are currently modifying

2. If the element is not checked out, the latest version of that element you have checked in to the development stream

3. If you have not modified the element, the version from the baseline in the development stream (this baseline came from your last rebase operation)

The integration view that you create is associated with the project's integration stream and may select different versions of the files than your development view. This view is used during deliver operations, and its primary purpose is to enable you to build and test your delivered changes against the latest project sources. The project's integration stream and your integration view select element versions in this order:

1. The version of an element you have checked out (typically, this is checked out during an ongoing deliver operation)

2. If the element is not checked out, the latest version of that element that has been delivered by any other developer or changes made directly in the integration stream

3. If the element has not been modified, the version selected by the project's foundation baseline

Figure 8-7 shows the relationship between streams in a project with multiple developers. The triangles on the bottom represent development streams; each stream has foundation baselines and a set of activities. The activities are delivered into the common project-integration stream indicated by the triangle at the top of the project. The rebase operation is used to update the foundation baselines of the development stream.

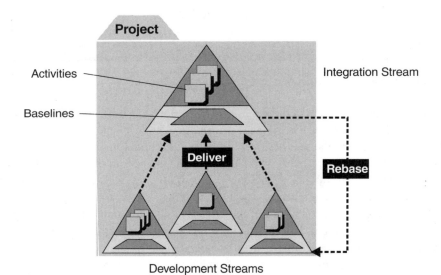

Figure 8-7   Project/view/stream relationship.

8.3   Making Changes

The real work happens when you modify files and directories to implement a specific activity or task. The following sections discuss how changes are made in the context of the UCM model.

8.3.1   Working with Activities

One aspect of the UCM model is that it is activity based (see the "Activities" section in Chapter 4). This means that all the versions you create when modifying elements must be associated with some named activity. You usually do this at check-out time (you can also specify a new activity at check-in time).

If your project is using only ClearCase (that is, you are not working on a ClearQuest-enabled project), you create these activities when you begin working. They identify the purpose for your work. ClearCase activities are designed to be lightweight and involve low overhead. If your project is using ClearCase and ClearQuest, the UCM model uses ClearQuest entities (such as defects and enhancement requests). Therefore, activities will usually already exist, be assigned to you, and be available on your to-do list when you start work. The complexity of an activity when ClearQuest is in use depends on the processes put in place for that activity type. See Chapter 12, "Change Request Management and ClearQuest," for more information on integrating ClearCase UCM with ClearQuest.

Either way, your responsibility is to ensure that the changes you make to a file are recorded against the appropriate activity. If you don't, the real benefits of activity-based CM cannot be realized. You will not be able to deliver complete, consistent changes automatically. You will not be able to see accurately what changes are included in an update to your workspace. Testers will not be able to see easily what changed from one build to the next. Release notes cannot be generated accurately and automatically.

It is up to you, the developer, to ensure that the change set is accurately recorded against the correct activity. ClearCase UCM has made this process straightforward, using either the Check Out dialog box or the command line. In either case, the activity you select is remembered and used as the default for all subsequent check-outs until you change it.

WARNING
The most common mistake made when associating changes with activities is to make two different changes (for example, two different defect fixes) in a file and then check in that file. In that case, you have just included two different changes in one element version. The UCM model does not allow you to associate two activities with one file version, so you would inaccurately record that this version includes changes for only one activity. The appropriate approach is to make one change, check in the change, check out the file again (specifying the second activity as the reason for this change), and make the second change, thereby associating each check-out with the appropriate activity.

(Some SCM systems do allow you to associate two changes with a single version. However, after this is done, these two activities [changes] cannot be separated in an automated fashion. It becomes impossible to automatically include one of the changes in a build without the other. Because of this issue, the UCM model does not support associating multiple changes with one file version.)

8.3.2   Modifying Files and Directories

To make changes, you must be in a ClearCase view. Figure 8-8 shows the ClearCase Explorer, focused in the view cmadm_Web_Rel1, right-clicked on element Logon.java for a check-out operation.

When you check out a file, you must specify which activity you are working on. If your project is using ClearQuest, you will find preassigned activities available to be chosen from a

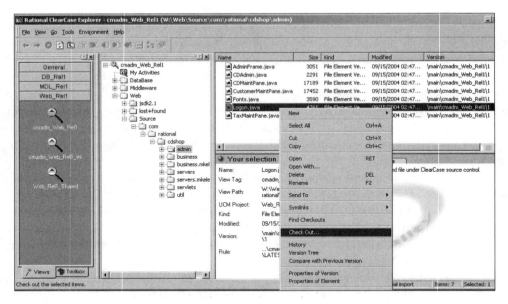

Figure 8-8   Context-sensitive menu from ClearCase Explorer.

pull-down to-do list query (which is part of the Check Out dialog box). If your project is not using ClearQuest, ClearCase asks you to specify what you are working on by providing a brief description (for example, "Fixing missing parameter to the readdata() function call"). Subsequent checkouts in the same development view will present the activity you specify as the default. Figure 8-9 shows the Windows Check Out dialog box. Notice that you have the option of selecting an activity from the drop-down list, creating a new activity, or browsing other activities.

Figure 8-9   Check Out dialog box example.

When you have checked out, you can modify elements using any appropriate tool (such as an editor through your IDE). Elements can be checked in and checked out again as many times as necessary when working on multiple activities, or even when you want to store an intermediate version of the element in the VOB. The check-in operation does not make the changes visible to other developers (unless they are sharing your stream while using a dynamic view). This happens only during a delivery, a baseline, and a subsequent rebase by the other developers to this baseline.

8.3.3 Working from the Command Line

To create a new activity and make changes from the command line, you do the following. (This example is for a UNIX environment on a project that is not using ClearQuest for change request management.)

> **NOTE**
> You can never make a ClearQuest activity from the `cleartool mkactivity` command.

1. Set your development view.
   ```
   prompt> cleartool setview john_hw_rel2
   prompt> cd /vobs/hw_source
   ```

2. Make an activity.
   ```
   prompt> cleartool mkactivity -headline 'fix copyright'
   -instream john_hw_rel2   fixcopy
   Created activity "fixcopy"
   ```
   Here the user specifies the one-line description for the activity with the `-headline` option (this is used when displaying the activity in the GUI). The stream where the user wants to create the activity is specified with the `-instream` option. The activity name (which is used to refer to the activity from the command line) is the final argument `fixcopy`.

3. Set this new activity as the default for the current view.
   ```
   prompt> cleartool setactivity fixcopy
   Set activity "fixcopy" in view john_hw_rel2
   ```

4. Check out.
   ```
   prompt> cleartool checkout -nc example.c
   Checked out "example.c"
   Attached activities:
     activity:fixcopy@/projects "fix copyright"
   ```
   Notice that the activity that was set is remembered and used to associate the new version with the `fixcopy` activity. The `-nc` option stands for "no comment." ClearCase offers a wide variety of comment-handling options, including ways to prevent users from not entering a comment.

5. Edit, compile, and unit-test.

At this point, the files you have checked out are writeable. Using your editor, you make changes to those files, compile them, and perform unit testing. When you are satisfied with the changes, you can check in the files.

6. Check in.

```
prompt> cleartool checkin -cact
Checked in "example.c"
Attached activities:
   activity:fixcopy@/projects "fix copyright"
```

The -cact option is a shortcut that checks in all files that are checked out to the current activity.

At this point, you optionally can pull in other developer's changes by using rebase. It is much easier to integrate changes on a development stream periodically rather than tying up the integration stream.

The final step, delivering the activity, is covered in the next section.

8.4   Delivering Changes to the Project

At some point, you will complete work on one or more activities. Because you are working in isolation, you need to take additional steps to make the changes you have made available to the project integrator. The process of making your changes available is called a delivery.

Delivering a change is a multistep process:

1. Check in any outstanding checked-out elements.

2. Optionally rebase from the project's latest recommended baselines. If you do this, you need to build, test, and debug changes related to this integration effort.

3. Run the ClearCase Deliver command.

4. Build and test the delivery.

5. Complete or cancel the delivery.

After delivery, your changes can be incorporated into the next project baseline and project-level build. The steps that make up a delivery are described in the following sections.

8.4.1   Check In Any Outstanding Checked-Out Elements

When you deliver an activity, only the latest checked-in element versions are delivered. Remember that you can check in multiple times without your changes being seen by other developers. You must check in changes to deliver them. If you deliver an activity and it has outstanding check-outs, the changes in the checked-out files are not delivered.

You can search for outstanding check-outs in a number of ways. First, the deliver operation warns you that you have outstanding check-outs (see Figure 8-10). Second, you can use the Find Check-Out Wizard GUI to list check-outs. Third, you can go to the activities change set either

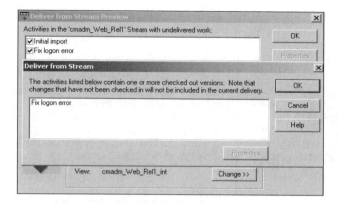

Figure 8-10 Deliver outstanding check-outs warning dialog box.

from the ClearCase Project Explorer or ClearQuest (if your project is using ClearQuest) and check in from the Unified Change Management tab (see Figure 8-11).

From the command line, you can specify a few options to the `checkin` command. The `-cact` option checks in all outstanding check-outs against the default activity set in the view. Alternatively, you can specify a specific activity. In this case, ClearCase checks in all outstanding check-outs that exist for that activity. The following examples show these command-line options.

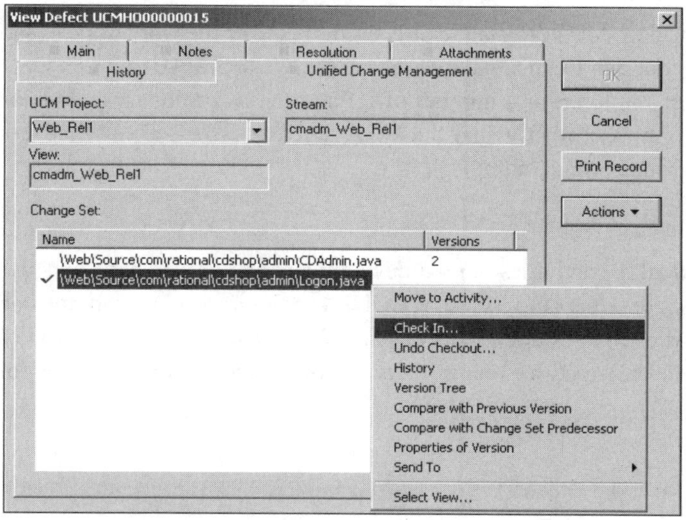

Figure 8-11 Activities properties: showing check-outs.

```
prompt> cleartool checkin -cact
prompt> cleartool checkin <activity selector>
```

> **NOTE**
> It is still possible to deliver an activity that has outstanding check-outs if the project's
> policy allows this (see the "Do Not Allow Deliver to Proceed with Check-Outs in the
> Development Stream" bullet in Chapter 6, "Project Management in ClearCase"). This
> is primarily used when you need to deliver intermediate changes for an activity on
> which you are not yet finished working. The deliver operation delivers the work you
> have checked in, ignoring any change in the checked-out files.

8.4.2   Rebase from the Project's Latest Recommended Baselines

You should always consider whether to rebase your development stream before delivery. Rebase
(described later in this chapter) updates your development stream and view with changes that
have been delivered by other project members and incorporated into baselines. By rebasing
before delivering, you are integrating your changes with other developers' changes in your own
private working environment. This usually makes deliveries go more smoothly and means that
less integration work will need to be performed in the integration stream.

Although it is good practice to rebase before delivery, you might be required to rebase to
the project's latest recommended baseline if your project leader has set this project policy (see the
"Require Development Stream to Be Based on the Project's Recommended Baseline(s) Prior to
Deliver" bullet in Chapter 6).

8.4.3   Run the ClearCase `Deliver` Command

ClearCase has a `Deliver` command that is used to deliver the work done to satisfy one or more
activities. This command can be issued from the ClearCase Explorer (see Figure 8-2), the
ClearCase Project Explorer, or a number of IDEs, such as Rational Application Developer, the
Eclipse Platform, or Microsoft Visual Studio. A delivery can also be started from the command
line via the following command:

```
prompt> cleartool deliver
```

By default, all the activities in your development stream that have undelivered changes are
delivered. You can deselect activities in the GUI (see Figure 8-12). From the command line, you
can specify a particular set of activities as part of the Deliver command. You can also see what
activities would be delivered without actually performing a delivery using the following code:

```
prompt> cleartool deliver -preview
```

> **NOTE**
> As with many ClearCase command-line operations, you can specify the `-graphical`
> switch to the `Deliver` command if you want to use the GUI for this particular operation.

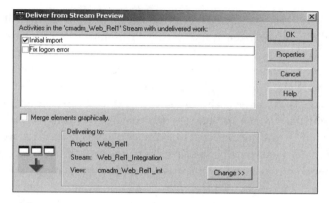

Figure 8-12   Deliver activities: graphical user interface.

> **NOTE**
> When you are working on two or more activities in the same development stream and modifying the same elements for both activities, you might be required to deliver the set of activities together. For example, imagine that you are working on two activities, A and B. You start working on A and check out a file named `system.h`. You make changes to `system.h` and check it in, creating version A1. Without delivering A, you start working on activity B. In the course of working on activity B, you also check out and check in `system.h`, creating version B1. Because you are working on both of these activities in the same development stream, version B1 includes the previously made A1 changes. In this example, you would be allowed to deliver activity A by itself. You would also be allowed to deliver A and B together. However, ClearCase would not allow you to deliver just B because the B1 version of `system.h` also includes a partial piece of the A1 change. This is part of how the UCM model ensures that you deliver a consistent set of changes.

The work performed by the deliver operation occurs in your integration view. In this view, the elements you have modified in your development view will be checked out, and your changes will be merged from your development stream to the project's integration stream.

In most cases, this step happens automatically. In some cases, you might have to resolve conflicts with changes that have been made by other developers on your team. This situation is covered in the section "Dealing with Conflicting Changes," later in this chapter. Delivery is a restartable operation, so large or complex deliveries do not have to be done all at once.

8.4.4   Build and Test the Delivery

After the initial deliver step has finished, you will have elements checked out in your integration view. These will be the same elements that make up the change set for the activities you delivered.

You should now verify your delivery before you commit it. What you do to verify a delivery depends on your organization's policies. In general, you should ensure that your changes build in the integration view. It is also good practice to unit-test your changes.

You might ask, "If I rebase before I deliver, do I need to do any testing?" The answer is, you should. There is a difference between testing in your environment after a rebase and testing in the integration view. Any activities that have been delivered by other developers but have not yet been incorporated into a recommended baseline will be seen in your integration view but will not have been part of the rebase operation (this is because you can rebase only from a baseline, not the tip or latest versions of the project's integration stream). Testing in the integration view is testing your changes with the absolute latest and greatest changes for your project.

In some companies, you are expected to make sure that your changes work with the latest and greatest. In this case, you should build and perform unit testing in the integration view before proceeding. In other companies, an integrator is responsible for making sure everything works together. In this case, simply verifying that your changes build in the integration view is sufficient. It is always a good idea to review automated merges by comparing the checked-out versions with their predecessors; it can be done easily from the activities property sheet.

8.4.5   Complete or Cancel the Delivery

The final step is to either complete or cancel the delivery. Completing the delivery checks in all the changes to the project's integration stream. When completed, a delivery cannot be undone. (However, there is a script that can undo an activity, which is useful for rolling back a deliver operation. This script, `cset.pl`, is described in more detail in Appendix A, "Redoing and Undoing Change Sets with UCM.") If you are not satisfied with the results of the delivery, you can cancel the delivery. Canceling a delivery cancels all check-outs in the integration view and removes any record of the delivery. You can then return to your development stream to resolve any issues, if necessary, and deliver these changes later.

From the GUI, this can be done from the final Deliver dialog box or by restarting the deliver operation if the dialog box has been dismissed. From the command line, use the following code:

```
prompt> cleartool deliver -complete
prompt> cleartool deliver -cancel
```

8.5   Rebasing Your Development Stream

Your development view selects a stable set of element versions. Periodically, you need to update your development stream's configuration, thus updating the versions of the elements displayed in your view. This is done using a command called `Rebase`. Rebase updates your development environment, making changes other developers have made visible to you.

When you rebase, you do not get the latest and greatest element versions. Those versions might be broken or might not even build together (let's hope not, but it is a possibility if other developers are not following good process when delivering their changes). Instead, you receive a stable set of baselines. The project integrator creates new project baselines and builds and tests them. When a set of baselines has reached a known level of stability (generally, this means it has passed some level of testing), the integrator declares the baselines as the recommended baselines (see Chapter 9 for more detail on the integrator's work). The recommended baselines are presented to you as the default when you rebase.

> **NOTE**
> It is possible to override these default baselines, choosing either older or newer baselines. However, it is a good idea to accept the recommended baselines until you get familiar with ClearCase UCM.

Rebasing is a multistep process, as follows:

1. Run the rebase operation.
2. Build and test.
3. Complete or cancel the rebase.

These steps are described in the following sections.

8.5.1   Run the Rebase Operation

The ClearCase `Rebase` command can be issued from the ClearCase Explorer (see Figure 8-2), the ClearCase Project Explorer, or a number of IDEs, such as Rational Application Developer. A rebase can also be started from the command line using this command:

```
prompt> cleartool rebase
```

When you rebase, you are updating the baselines you see in your development view. These baselines, of course, contain new activities delivered by you and other members of your project. You can see this set of activities and explore the changes you are accepting into your development stream by clicking Details on the Rebase dialog box (see Figure 8-13). If you are using Rebase from the command line, you can do this by using the following command:

```
prompt> cleartool rebase -preview
```

> **NOTE**
> As with many ClearCase command-line operations, you can specify the `-graphical` switch to the `Rebase` command if you want to use the GUI for this particular operation.

In most cases, the rebase operation simply updates your development stream's configuration, and you will see new versions in your development view. Rebase also checks to see if there are any conflicts that must be resolved. That is, it checks to see if there are any elements you have modified that someone else also modified. If this is the case, it checks out these elements and performs a merge operation. The section "Dealing with Conflicting Changes," later in this chapter, discusses this in more detail. Figure 8-14 shows a detailed view at the element level of how ClearCase UCM visually represents the project-integration stream, multiple development streams, activities being worked on in parallel, and integration events (deliver and rebase).

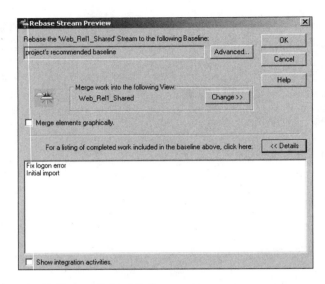

Figure 8-13   Rebase activities: activity details.

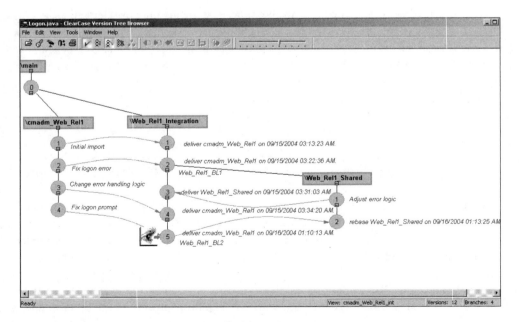

Figure 8-14   Version tree browser: streams, activities, delivers, and rebase.

8.5.2   Build and Test

When the first step of the rebase is finished, but before committing the changes, you have the opportunity to build and test. It is a good idea to test if you can build the software in your development view, particularly if you need to resolve any conflicts.

8.5.3   Complete or Cancel the Rebase

When you are satisfied with the changes that have been made, you can complete the rebase operation. If you ran into problems and do not have the time to resolve them, you can cancel (or back out) the rebase. These operations can be performed from the last page of the rebase GUI or by restarting the rebase operation if you dismissed this page. From the command line, this is done through the following:

```
prompt> cleartool rebase -complete
prompt> cleartool rebase -cancel
```

> **NOTE**
> Some rebase operations might be very large. Large rebase operations usually occur between projects, but if you have not rebased for a while, you might find that you need to incorporate a number of changes. Rebase is a restartable operation, so you do not need to perform a full rebase all at once.

8.6   Dealing With Conflicting Changes

When working in a serial development environment, only one person is allowed to change a file at a time. As discussed in Chapter 2, "Growing into Your SCM Solution," this approach can cause development bottlenecks and make it very difficult to maintain multiple releases. ClearCase UCM supports parallel development, which means that while you are working in your development view, you might be modifying the same files at the same time as another team member in his or her development view. Obviously, these changes must be merged or integrated at some point. With ClearCase UCM, this might happen during deliver and rebase operations. ClearCase provides specific tools to automate as much of this merging work as possible, and tools to assist you in integrating changes when conflicts occur that cannot be automatically resolved.

8.6.1   Delivery Scenario 1 (No Conflicts)

Conflicts occur only when more than one developer works on the same file at the same time. If this never happens, you will never need to resolve conflicts. Figure 8-15 shows a delivery scenario in which no merging is required. You have made a change to example.c, but no other member on your project team has modified the file. When you deliver, ClearCase simply copies the contents from your development stream to the integration stream. In ClearCase terms, this is called a *trivial merge*.

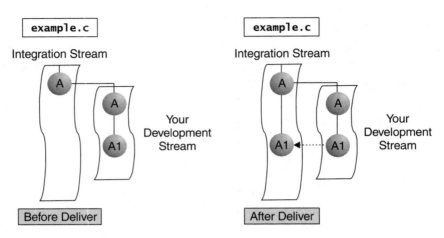

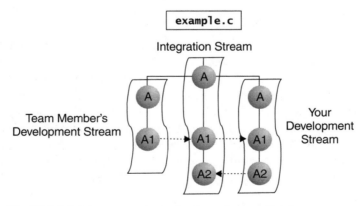

Figure 8-15   Trivial delivery scenario (no conflicts).

8.6.2   Delivery Scenario 2 (No Conflicts)

This case is similar to delivery scenario 1. No conflict resolution is required as part of delivery, and ClearCase performs a trivial merge. However, in this case, another team member did modify the file `example.c` and, in fact, delivered his or her changes before you. The difference from scenario 1 is that you performed a rebase operation before doing your delivery. The arrow shown in Figure 8-16 pointing from the integration stream to your development stream indicates that a rebase operation was performed. This is also a trivial merge for ClearCase.

Figure 8-16   Trivial delivery scenario post-rebase (no conflicts).

8.6.3   Delivery Scenario 3 (With Conflicts)

In some cases, when you deliver, you discover that someone on your project has modified the same element you have, and has already delivered his or her changes. In this case, ClearCase attempts to automatically merge these changes during the deliver process. If it cannot do so, you will be required to merge the changes using the ClearCase merge tool (see the section "ClearCase Merge Tools," later in this chapter, for details). Figure 8-17 illustrates this scenario.

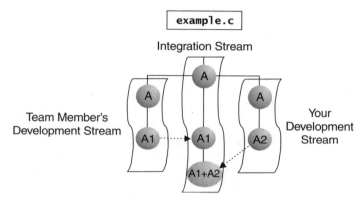

Figure 8-17   Delivery scenario with conflicts.

8.6.4   Rebase Scenario 1 (No Conflicts)

When you rebase, you are essentially updating the baselines in your development stream. In most cases, the changes you accept have not been made to the same elements you are working on, and no merging takes place. Figure 8-18 shows what happens when you have not modified example.c. Your development view simply displays the new version of the file.

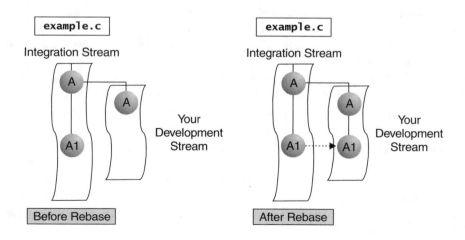

Figure 8-18   Rebase scenario with no conflicts.

8.6.5   Rebase Scenario 2 (With Conflicts)

In some cases, someone on the project will have modified and delivered a change to a file that you are also modifying. Figure 8-19 illustrates this. In this case, ClearCase attempts to automatically merge these files during the rebase. If it cannot do so, you will be required to merge the changes using the ClearCase merge tool (see the next section for details).

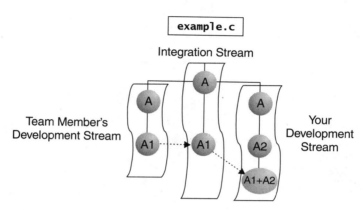

Figure 8-19   Rebase scenario with conflicts.

8.6.6   ClearCase Merge Tools

When a merge during rebase and deliver operations is not trivial—see the sections "Delivery Scenario 3 (with Conflicts)" and "Rebase Scenario 2 (with Conflicts)," earlier in this chapter—ClearCase attempts to merge the changes automatically. ClearCase can do this only for element types for which it understands the content. Out of the box, ClearCase understands how to merge any ASCII text files, HTML files, XML files, Rose models, and Microsoft Word documents. For example, Figure 8-20 shows three text files and the automatically merged output. Original is the initial text file. Contributor 1 is a modification of the original text file. Contributor 2 is another modification of the original. Result is the automatically merged file that ClearCase produces.

Although the merge algorithm supported in ClearCase is smart enough to understand insertions, deletions, and movement of blocks of text, it is important to understand that ClearCase does not know about the syntax of any language when it is merging. ClearCase understands only that it is a text file and performs the merge on this basis. Therefore, it is important to verify the merge after a deliver or rebase even when it has happened in a fully automatic way.

Of course, it is not always possible to fully automate the merge process. Figure 8-21 shows an example in which manual intervention is required. Once again, Original is the initial text file. Contributor 1 is a modification to the original. Contributor 2 is also a modification to the original. You can see that in Contributor 1 and Contributor 2, the same lines have been modified. In this case, you would choose one line or the other. In other conflicting scenarios, the right choice might

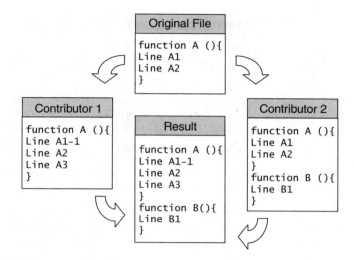

Figure 8-20   Automated merge example.

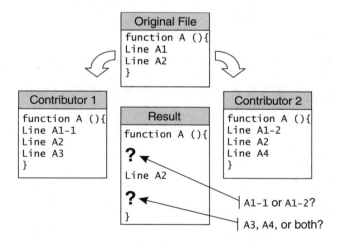

Figure 8-21   Manual merge example.

be to include both lines or neither line. In fact, you might even need to do some additional coding to resolve the conflict.

By default, ClearCase attempts to merge files automatically; however, other developers might have made changes to the same files. For instance, during a UCM deliver operation, ClearCase merges many files. When ClearCase detects that a manual intervention is required, as in Figure 8-22, you can continue merging the rest of the files first or perform the manual merge operation immediately.

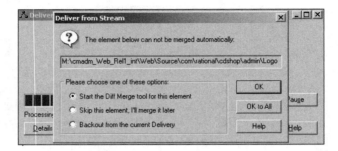

Figure 8-22   Element conflict detection in graphical merge tool—merge needed.

Performing a manual merge can be a difficult process without the right tools. ClearCase provides a graphical merge tool that greatly assists in this process. Figure 8-23 shows a screenshot from this merge tool. The lower panels show the original file, called the common ancestor version. ClearCase computes this version for you. The other panels show the contributor versions. In this case, there are only 2, but ClearCase can handle as many as 16 contributors (32 on UNIX platforms). The top panel shows the results. With the navigation, contributor selection, and editing tools, the ClearCase merge manager makes it much easier to merge conflicting element changes.

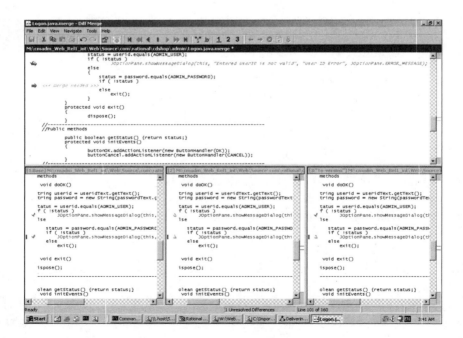

Figure 8-23   Graphical merge tool.

8.7   Seamlessly Integrating with Developer's IDE

You have seen how the UCM development model makes it easy for developers to keep track of their work at a higher level. This gives development managers a better understanding of how their software-development project is progressing. What defects are fixed? Who is working on these defects? Why does this component have so many defects? What has changed between baselines BL2 and BL1? The UCM development model can easily answer these and many more questions. UCM has allowed the developer to focus on development, without having to worry about tedious bookkeeping or maintaining a home-grown layer on top of a CM tool. Another key attribute of ClearCase UCM is its tight integration into the IDEs of choice. This means that developers never have to exit their IDE while performing common ClearCase UCM tasks. Figure 8-24 shows the Eclipse platform's integration to ClearCase. At the top (enclosed in the bold rectangle overlay) is the ClearCase context-sensitive toolbar integration that enables developers to quickly operate on the element that is in focus. In the case of Figure 8-24, it is Logon.java. Another feature of the tight integration to Eclipse is the ClearQuest perspective. The ClearQuest Navigator on the right hand side is showing ClearQuest's query workspace. From here you can run ClearQuest queries, charts, and reports. The ClearQuest Query Results view (in the lower middle window) is presenting the resulting records from the "all defects" query. You can perform many ClearQuest actions and query executions without having to go outside your Eclipse environment.

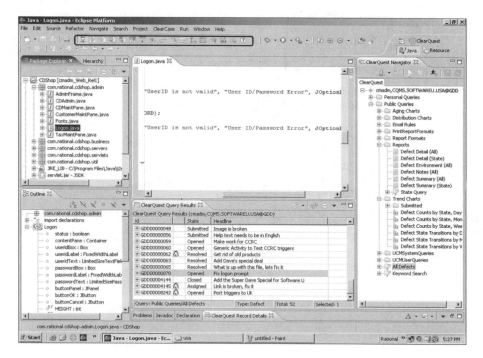

Figure 8-24   Eclipse Platform: ClearCase toolbar.

Another ClearCase integration point to Eclipse is through the standard right-click action on the element in the Package Explorer in the left window. This context-sensitive integration is exposed through the Team menu, as shown in Figure 8-25 (showing the check-in operation because `Logon.java` is in the checked-out state, indicated by the green check mark on the element).

ClearCase also provides a ClearCase menu integration to Eclipse. This integration point provides access to ClearCase operations that affect the workspace rather than the element. Some of these operations are also available from the ClearCase toolbar. Figure 8-26 shows the Eclipse Platform ClearCase menu integration with the Deliver option highlighted.

ClearCase and ClearQuest provide integrations at various levels with many IDEs, including a very tight integration with Microsoft's .NET Framework. ClearCase also supports IDE integrations through Microsoft's Source Code Control (SCC) interface on the Windows platform.

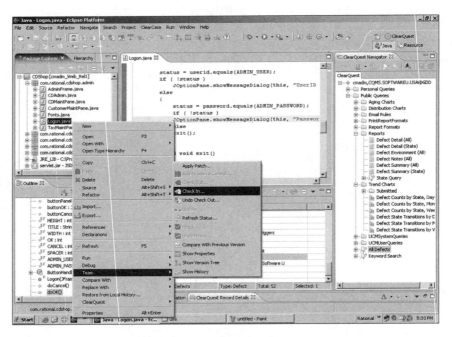

Figure 8-25   Eclipse Platform: ClearCase team integration.

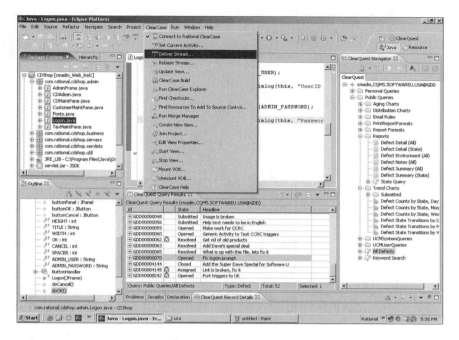

Figure 8-26 Eclipse Platform: ClearCase menu.

8.8 Summary

This chapter presented the basic developer workflow with ClearCase UCM. It highlighted how ClearCase UCM keeps track of activities and manages streams, and how a developer interacts with those objects on a daily basis. It also showed how easily these powerful features are exposed to developers in various ways: through command-line, GUI, and IDE integrations. ClearCase UCM has made it very easy for the developer to do the right thing while working on the daily tasks of modifying software-development artifacts. ClearCase UCM not only makes this development experience easy to use and understand, but it also makes it easy for project managers to track progress of their development projects by providing insight into the activities that are under development. By integrating ClearCase UCM with ClearQuest, you get even more power to model your software-development process by enriching activities to be defects, enhancement requests, or any other type of development entity you want to model. This chapter also touched lightly upon integration issues by showing how ClearCase UCM handles merging of activities to project-integration areas. It showed merge algorithms and logical concepts of how changes move between streams during deliver and rebase operations. This is the foundation for understanding how to model more complex and larger software-development efforts because, at some level, the developers will act in this fashion within their development streams. Chapter 9 introduces more complex integration strategies that arise in software development across the team and across the organization.

CHAPTER 9

Integration

To integrate means to form, coordinate, or blend into a functioning or unified whole. Integration within software development is the act of bringing together separate efforts into one. During software development, there are many forms of integration, and they can occur at different places within the software development life cycle and at different times. For instance, before you can expose your software-development effort to another group for testing and verification, you need to make sure that you have all your features and defects together in a place where they can be built and assembled into whatever form your application or product needs to exist in before it can be tested. It is critical to define within your software life cycle when these events will take place. Before integration, you have many different changes developed in some sort of isolation. After successful integration, you have a system that contains these different changes, and the system functions against the desired requirements at some quality level. If you were forced to deliver something to your customer, it would usually be the most recent highest-level quality configuration you had, depending on the particular customer milestone you were meeting. Integration is the first step toward the validation of your system.

Many people participate in the integration activities. However, there is usually a role for the individual who performs the integration activity that will bring together the changes from the individual efforts into a functioning whole. It is the job of the integrator to use the work of the team to construct a single version of a software system or set of software components. It is also the integrator's job to assemble the work of the many teams into a single version of a software system that can be tested against a set of requirements and ultimately deployed or released.

This chapter discusses merge and assembly, two types of software integration, and their application to the categories of software teams (see the section "Five Project Team Categories" in Chapter 2, "Growing into Your SCM Solution"). It also discusses how ClearCase branches are used for isolation and integration, using either your own branching strategy or ClearCase UCM.

Build, staging, release, and deployment processes are covered in Chapter 10, "Building, Baselining, and Release Deployment."

9.1   Software Integration

Software integration is the process of bringing together independently developed changes to form a testable piece of a software system. It can occur at many levels, eventually culminating in a complete software system. The larger the software system is and the larger the teams working on that system are, the more levels of integration are required to manage the software-development effort.

It is always cheaper to find problems as early as you can in the software development life cycle. If you find problems at the customer site, it is more expensive to fix. If a developer finds an issue during integration activities, he or she can fix it much more cheaply because fewer people, systems, and processes are involved. Another reason to perform integration activities sooner is that usually the problems found during integration are harder to solve (because they might involve many pieces of the system). If you delay integration, you could be delaying the hardest-to-fix problems, which might end up delaying your product release.

Basically two types of integration are relevant to SCM: merge and assembly integration.

9.1.1   Merge Integration

Merge integration involves the resolution of parallel changes made by different team members to common files or components. In this case, multiple people have modified the same set of system artifacts in parallel. Therefore, it is necessary to combine—or, in ClearCase terms, merge—these changes. In some cases, this can be automated with tools that understand the structure of the files. In other cases, the merge must be performed manually (for example, if there are conflicting changes). It should be clear that merge integration requires some knowledge of the changes being made to the software system. In addition, more changes might be introduced to the software as part of performing merge integration (for example, changes required to resolve merge conflicts).

9.1.2   Assembly Integration

Assembly integration involves combining baselines of software components into a larger piece of the overall system. The Rational Unified Process defines integration as "the software development activity in which separate software components are combined into an executable whole" [RUP 5.5 1999]. Unlike merge integration, assembly integration does not modify the source code; it puts together the puzzle pieces of the software system (hopefully, they all fit).

Assembly integration can occur at build time or runtime or both. With build-time assembly, you bring together two sets of source components, build them, and then link them together to form a testable executable. With runtime assembly, you copy a set of prebuilt objects into a runtime environment, which can then be executed. A set of dynamic link libraries (DLLs) from two different software components is a good example of runtime assembly integration.

The type of integration and the number of integration levels used are largely determined by the size of the software system and the size of the team. Integration choices also depend on whether the teams are organized around architecture or around features (see "Organizing Large Multiproject Development Efforts" in Chapter 7, "Managing and Organizing Your ClearCase Projects"). At some level, a system that has well-defined software architecture uses assembly integration. A monolithic system is more likely to use merge integration all the way to the top.

9.1.3 Integration Scenarios for Teams of Differing Sizes

Let's take a look at some integration scenarios based on the team sizes defined in the section "Five Project Team Categories" in Chapter 2.

Individual Integration

Three integration scenarios exist for the individual: No integration is required, integration for the individual happens all the time, and individuals develop separate pieces of the system independently and then perform their own assembly integration. In any case, integration for the individual is the easiest, usually just happens in the course of that person's work, and is relatively uninteresting.

Small and Modest Team Integration

Most small and modest-size teams have one level of integration. Individuals work on their pieces of the software system, and, at some point, those pieces are integrated and tested as a whole (see Figure 9-1).

With monolithic systems and feature-oriented teams, each team member is allowed to make changes to any part of the software system that is required for the task they are trying to accomplish. This means that merge integration is usually used.

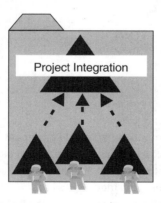

Figure 9-1 Merge integration for small and modest teams.

Major Team Integration

Major teams have two levels of integration. The first is done by each project team and is largely the same as that performed by small and modest-size teams. The second level brings together the work of the teams.

Whether the team is architecture oriented or feature oriented usually dictates what type of integration is performed at the second level (see "Organizing Large Multiproject Development Efforts" in Chapter 7 for information on team orientation). For architecture-oriented teams, the second level of integration is typically assembly integration. For feature-oriented teams, the second level is typically merge integration.

Although terminology in this area is still rather varied, the first level of integration is often referred to as subsystem or feature integration. The second level is often called system integration (see Figure 9-2).

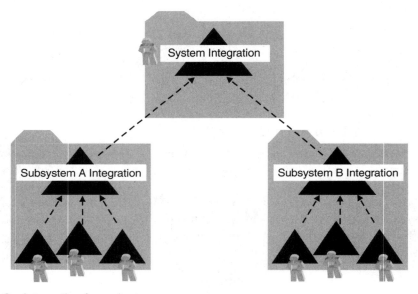

Figure 9-2   Integration for major teams.

Extensive Team Integration

Extensive teams often require more than two levels of integration because of the size and complexity of the systems being developed. It is important to avoid monolithic systems for projects of this size and to have an architecture that will allow the use of assembly integration at the higher levels. If you allow more than 150 individuals to make modifications to all the source code in parallel, the advantages of parallel development will be lost in the complexity of trying to perform merge integration. Even if you are using feature-oriented teams, you should try to define the features in such a way as to isolate the changes to individual subsystems.

The way a system gets integrated and the number of levels of integration used can sometimes depend on the system architecture itself. Figure 9-3 shows an example of a system divided into six subsystems. Figure 9-4 shows how the teams and projects could be laid out for this example system and how integration could occur.

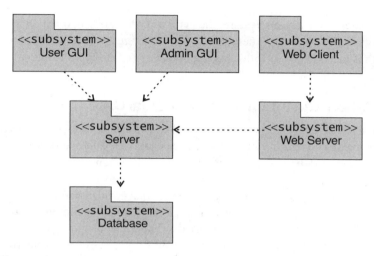

Figure 9-3 System hierarchy example.

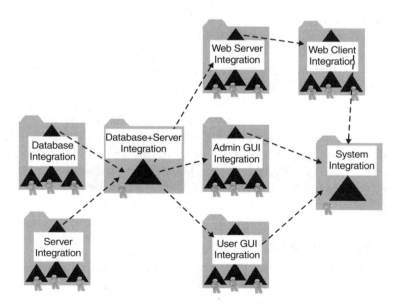

Figure 9-4 Integration for extensive teams.

Even if extensive teams are feature oriented, major features are often divided into a hierarchy of subfeatures. Teams independently develop subfeatures, which are integrated into a larger feature, which is then integrated with other major features of the overall system.

9.2   Isolation and Integration with ClearCase

Developer isolation occurs when developers are working in stable workspaces where changes other developers are making do not affect them and where changes they make do not affect other developers. Similarly, teams can be isolated from other teams. Isolation is used to manage complexity. Problems or new features are divided up across teams and individuals. To work efficiently, teams and individuals isolate themselves from others' changes that could destabilize their workspace.

For example, Developer A might be making a change that requires alterations to a common interface as well as underlying code. If you tried to build and test the system after Developer A changed the interface but before Developer A changed any calls to that interface, the system would be broken. So, if Developer B was not isolated from Developer A's changes, Developer B might be blocked from proceeding even if Developer B was working on a completely separate part of the system.

When you isolate work, at some point, you must integrate. The difficulty is deciding when and how often this should take place: the developer isolation versus project integration dilemma. You are balancing a stable development environment against a better understanding of whether the pieces of the system being developed independently really work together. Infrequent integration means that you discover integration issues late in the project, causing significant and unplanned redesign work, which often results in a missed project deadline. Integrating too often causes unnecessary lost productivity. A destabilizing change that is integrated too early can cause an entire team to be unable to complete its work on time. Changes likely to cause destabilization should be isolated and unit-tested before being integrated. Deciding when and how often to integrate is how you tune the performance of your SCM process.

An improper approach to isolation and integration is probably the no. 1 cause of SCM-related problems on a software project. How you apply your SCM tool does have a serious impact on how well your development organization performs. ClearCase supports a number of integration approaches, which are described in the next few sections. Only you can pick the right approach for your projects. This section covers the topic of using branching and merging to implement your own integration strategy and how the ClearCase UCM model supports integration. We begin by discussing two interesting integration approaches: no isolation and branch/LATEST development.

9.2.1   The Shared View: No Isolation

This section on shared views is included only for completeness; it is not recommended that you use shared views for development. The only place I've seen them used is for browsing purposes only (such as a build or release view that might contain derived objects). A view is typically used by one individual. However, when you desire no isolation between team members, multiple individuals can share a single ClearCase view. The best way to think about this is as a single copy of your source tree in which everyone works at the same time.

Everyone working in a shared view is isolated from each other's changes only while a change is being made in an editor. Any commitment of a change to disk (such as a save) makes the change visible to others working in the shared view. Basically, this means that you have almost no isolation between team members and that integration occurs automatically and constantly. When a file is checked out, it becomes writeable by anyone working in that view. ClearCase checks out files to a view rather than an individual. Because the view is shared, anyone has access to it. Thus, developers cannot work on the same file in parallel.

If you use shared views as a general-purpose solution, you will experience many of the problems encountered in early SCM systems, as described in Chapter 2.

9.2.2 Branch/LATEST Development: Maximizing Integration

ClearCase supports a style of integration called *branch/LATEST development*, which is unique to ClearCase and offers some distinct advantages. For small and modest-size teams, the branch/LATEST approach attempts to replicate the ease of integration enjoyed by an individual. Branch/LATEST development minimizes isolation and maximizes integration. Team members work on the same set of source files, but each individual on the team is isolated in his or her own view. Changes become visible to other team members at check-in time rather than file save time, as in the shared-view approach.

Team members can work on the same files in parallel by using the reserved/unreserved check-out mechanisms described in "Concurrent Changes to the Same Project Files" in Chapter 2. Conflicting changes are integrated/resolved at check-in time.

Branch/LATEST development supports rapid integration because no explicit integrate or merge action is required for team members to share each other's changes. A team using branch/LATEST development integrates "on the fly," similarly to the way an individual would. Branch/LATEST development has different isolation and integration characteristics, depending on the type of view being used (see "Workspaces: Snapshot and Dynamic Views" in Chapter 4, "A Functional Overview of ClearCase Objects").

Let's take a look at an example using both dynamic and snapshot views. Let's say that a team has three developers: Xena, Hercules, and Godzilla. Xena and Hercules are using dynamic views, and Godzilla is using a snapshot view. Figure 9-5 shows what each individual sees in his or her view. Notice how the dynamic views access file.c, version 1, directly out of the VOB, while the snapshot view must load (copy) file.c, version 1, into local file storage.

Hercules checks out file.c to make a change, using a reserved check-out. In Figure 9-6, notice that the reserved check-out is seen only by him. Xena and Godzilla will not see the changes Hercules is making even when he saves them. The changes become visible only at check-in time.

In branch/LATEST development, using the check-in operation is the way to declare that a change is ready to be seen by other developers on your team. Hercules checks in and creates version 2 of file.c. Automatically, through the ClearCase dynamic view mechanism, Xena will see

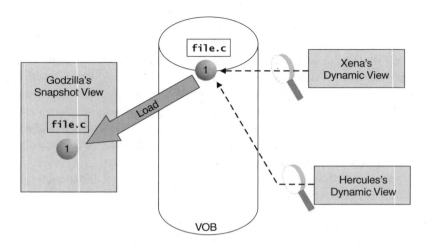

Figure 9-5   Branch/LATEST view: initial situation.

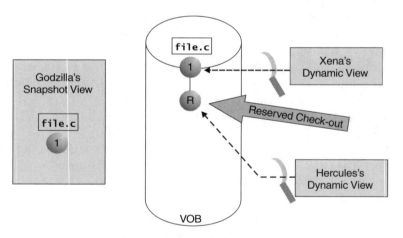

Figure 9-6   Change isolation using branch/LATEST.

this change in her view. Godzilla, on the other hand, is working in a snapshot view and does not see the change (see Figure 9-7).

With snapshot views, Godzilla has an additional level of isolation. To see changes made by Hercules, Godzilla must use the snapshot view Update command. A snapshot view update looks at the view's configuration and copies (or updates) any files that have changed. After the update operation, all team members now see the changes that Hercules checked in (see Figure 9-8).

The advantage to branch/LATEST should be clear. It provides some level of isolation, but integration occurs without explicit integration operations or merge actions. This approach works well for teams of up to eight developers. When the team size grows much beyond this, problems

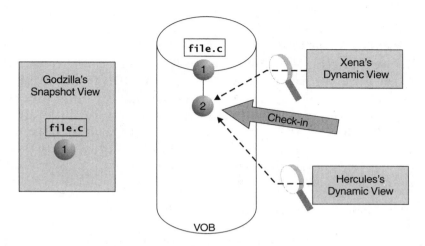

Figure 9-7   Check-in under branch/LATEST.

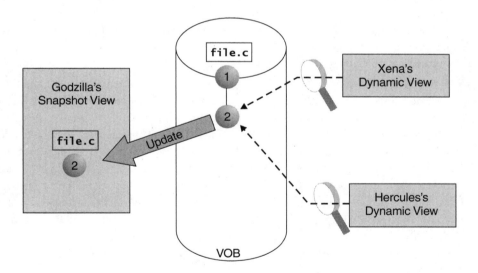

Figure 9-8   Final branch/LATEST view situation.

can occur, caused largely by the fact that developers need more isolation from each other than this approach provides. The drawbacks of branch/LATEST development are as follows:

- **No ability to checkpoint**—One of the disadvantages of branch/LATEST development is that developers cannot checkpoint their work. Checkpointing is checking in a file before a change is complete, to securely save an intermediate version. This is similar to creating a backup file but is more secure because the version is stored in the SCM repository. In the branch/LATEST approach, check-in makes changes visible to other developers, so checkpointing an intermediate change is not desirable.

- **Unexpected integration at check-in time**—Because integration of parallel changes to common files occurs at check-in time with branch/LATEST development, developers might be required to do extra integration work when they finish their tasks. This can cause problems in certain circumstances. For example, imagine that you are working on a critical bug fix that you want to finish by the end of the day, and it is already 5:55 p.m. When you go to check in, you find that someone has modified and checked in some of the same files that you changed during the day. You must resolve any conflicts between your changes and that person's before you are allowed to check in.

- **Version skew**—Version skew occurs when your view selects file versions that are not compatible. An extreme case of this involves seeing files from Release 1 and some from Release 2. A more common example of version skew might occur when using branch/LATEST development. You make changes to two files—an interface and its implementation—but forget to check in both files. Although everything builds fine in your view, the partial change in another developer's view could cause the build to break or cause unexplained runtime errors. This is because that developer's view selects the interface change you made and checked in, but not the implementation change you made but forgot to check in.

- **Decreased productivity**—You might see a decrease in productivity using branch/LATEST development for a number of reasons. First, individual build times might increase. For example, if a developer checks in a change to a low-level header file, this change becomes visible to all dynamic view users immediately. This can cause each developer to rebuild the entire system. Second, developer builds might fail more frequently if developers are undisciplined about checking in changes (for example, checking in changes that were never compiled). Finally, the rate at which new changes are being introduced by a development team might be too much for each individual developer to integrate automatically. For example, if 50 developers are using branch/LATEST development, the frequency of change would cause most developers to spend a lot of time getting their code to work with everyone's changes throughout the day instead of focusing on the problems they are solving or the features they are implementing.

Branch/LATEST development is a clear advantage for smaller teams that require some level of isolation but also want to integrate as frequently as possible with the least amount of effort. However, for larger teams, more isolation is required, and branch/LATEST development cannot be recommended. The additional isolation needed by larger teams is achieved using ClearCase's branch and merge capabilities or through the use of the ClearCase UCM model.

9.2.3   Using Branches for Isolation and Integration

ClearCase provides rich branching and merging facilities, which have been used to implement a wide range of approaches to isolation and integration. Branches are used to isolate a change or class of changes for any given element. The ClearCase merge tools are used to find and integrate these isolated changes by moving changes from one branch to another and by helping the integrator resolve conflicting changes that might have occurred on individual branches.

The types of branches you use, how these branches relate to one another, and how you merge changes between branches are referred to as your *branching strategy*. When you define a branching strategy, you are really defining the isolation/integration strategy for your project. ClearCase UCM has its own branching strategy, described in the section "Integration with UCM," later in this chapter. This section provides a brief introduction to branching strategies outside the context of UCM. Most of these strategies (and many others) have been previously documented as SCM patterns by the collaborative efforts of Brad Appleton and Stephen Berczuk (see [Appleton, 1998] and [Berczuk, 2002]).

For the purposes of this discussion, branches are classified into two types: development and integration. This is the same as the UCM classification of streams. Development branches are those used to perform new development. Integration branches are those used to manage lines of development, typically serving as the starting point and the integration point for development branches.

The following are some typical uses of the development and the integration branches:

- **Development branch per activity/task**—Each development task is performed in isolation on its own task branch and then merged/integrated into an integration branch, which usually represents a release. That is, each developer is isolated for each task he or she performs. This approach is similar to the ClearCase UCM activity-based approach (see the section "Integration with UCM," later in this chapter). It differs from UCM in that it uses the branch to capture the change set. If you really wanted to, you could implement this strategy with ClearCase UCM and restrict the development streams to be limited to contain only one activity.

- **Development branch per developer**—Each developer works in isolation on a private development branch. When a developer is finished with a task, he or she merges the changes into an integration branch. The developer reuses the development branch for the next task he or she will perform. The advantage of this approach over the task-branching model is that fewer branches need to be created. The disadvantage is that the branch does not capture the change set for the task; the change set must be captured by some other means. This approach is similar to the use of ClearCase UCM development streams within the traditional parallel project. The difference is that UCM provides the built-in activity object to capture the headline and the change set of the task, separately from the branch upon which the task was performed.

- **Development branch per major feature/subproject**—Each major feature or subproject is developed on its own branch. This case differs from the branch-per-activity approach in that there is a small team of developers working on the feature or set of related features using the branch/LATEST approach for the development of the major feature. As in the branch-per-activity approach, there is an integration branch usually representing a release into which the feature is merged/integrated. ClearCase UCM, with

its flexible stream hierarchy, can model this strategy by having subintegration development streams that contain feature work. These streams eventually get delivered to the
UCM project's integration stream.

- **Integration branch per promotion level**—In this approach, there is a branch-per-promo-
  tion level. For example, for a release with three levels of promotion, there might be a development branch, an integration branch, and a production branch. The advantage of this
  approach is that controls can be placed on the branches, allowing different organizational
  groups to control the different branches. For example, a test group could control the integration branch and allow only approved changes to be merged from the development branch.

This approach to branching models one of the original ways SCM was performed—by
having different copies of the software system and moving files from one copy of the system to the next. This approach to branching is also the way many companies implement a
promotion model for the source code.

Another advantage of this approach is that the graphical version tree browser for any
given element makes it very easy to determine code quality levels. The disadvantage of
this approach is that file contents must be merged from one promotion branch to another
even when the contents of the file didn't change between promotion levels. Such copy-
merging can be time-consuming and inefficient, and can cause unnecessary recompila-
tion for new versions of unchanged files. ClearCase UCM provides baselines to
implement promotion levels. It also supports a slightly different variant of this strategy
through the notion of read-only streams. These types of streams are useful for modeling
production, staging, and other quality levels used during release deployment. By rebasing these streams to the appropriate baseline, the appropriate configuration is presented
to views attached to the streams without the file copy-merging, as explained earlier. This
strategy is explored more in Chapter 10.

- **Integration branch per release**—This approach is the classic reason branching is used.
  It supports parallel development of multiple releases simultaneously by isolating in its
  own branch changes for any given release. The most common example is maintenance
  work continuing on an existing release while development work proceeds on a future
  release. This allows a company to produce a minor or point release while still working on
  the major release. This approach provides isolation between the teams.

The disadvantage to this approach is that integration between the maintenance release
and the development release must be planned in advance, or it is likely to take place near
the end of the major release's development cycle. This "Big Bang" approach to integration can cause significant delays to the release because integration problems are uncovered late. To avoid this, plan early integration points while the major release is ongoing.
For example, plan an alpha release of the software and integrate the existing maintenance
work at that point. Do this again for beta. By the time you reach the final release, the
major integration issues will already be resolved.

- **Active-development integration branch per release**—This approach is one way to resolve a typical conflict between a development team and an SCM team: Development often wants to use the most recently checked-in contents that successfully builds as the basis for subsequent development activities, whereas the SCM team often wants only stable, baselined builds to be used as the basis for change. Splitting the release integration branch (one for SCM, the other for development) lets SCM use the release integration branch for its less frequent and more stable integration and baselining activities while allowing development to build and integrate at its own more frequent and fast-paced active-development "rhythm."

  The advantage of this approach is that SCM gets to choose which development baselines are suitable for acceptance into the release integration branch. Development must be responsible for ensuring the integrity and consistency of its active-development integration branch. The disadvantage of this approach is the same as for promotion branches: It becomes necessary to copy-merge files from the active-development integration branch to the release integration branch. With its flexible stream hierarchy, ClearCase UCM can model this strategy by allowing development to work as needed on the integration stream. Periodically, the SCM team can rebase the build stream to the appropriate development baseline on the UCM project's integration stream.

- **Mainline integration branch**—A common branching pitfall is for every release integration branch to branch off from its predecessor release in a continually cascading staircase structure. This can quickly lead to very deep and wide branching hierarchy requiring additional merging effort to propagate the same initial change set across multiple releases. It can also create very long branch-path names that eventually need to be "cleaned up" later.

  A mainline integration branch is a top-level branch in a hierarchy that helps coordinate and synchronize work across parallel/concurrent releases and minimizes the complexity of merging efforts for change propagation. Instead of branching a subsequent release from its predecessor release branch, the predecessor release branch is merged to the mainline (a process often called mainlining) if it isn't there already, and a new branch is created off the mainline for maintenance and support of the previous release.

  The advantage of this approach is that it allows development of the "latest under development" release to stay on the same integration branch, thereby maintaining fewer parallel release branches, with a smaller evolutionary distance between existing release branches. It also avoids drawbacks of the continual cascading problem. UCM has its own equivalent strategy utilizing a mainline project, which is discussed in Chapter 7.

- **Development branch per patch**—Another common reason for branching is to support a patch process. A patch is a single fix to a defect in a release that can be applied independently to that release, creating a variant of a given release. Thus, it is similar to the development branch-per-activity/task approach.

By developing a patch on its own branch, you can integrate the patch into multiple releases at different times by using merge integration from a patch branch to a release branch. This allows these changes to be applied without the developer having to physically make the changes over and over again by hand.

- **Development or integration branch per patch bundle**—A "patch bundle" is a grouping of individual patches that are applied as a whole. Service Packs from Microsoft for its operating systems are good examples of patch bundles. If all the patches were developed together by a single team, the patch bundle branch would be a development branch and would behave similarly to the development-branch-per-major-feature strategy. If all the patches are developed on independent branches (using the development-branch-per-patch strategy) and then merged onto a single patch bundle branch, the patch bundle branch would be an integration branch. These patch bundles, just like patch branches, should be merged into release branches at the appropriate time in the development cycle.

- **Integration branch per system variant**—Sometimes branching is used to maintain different variants of a system. A variant is a slightly modified version of a specific release of a software system. For example, porting a system to a new operating system would create an OS-specific variant of the system (for example, Release 1.0 of a software system could have a Windows variant and a UNIX variant). Variant branches can also be used to support customer-special versions of the software. A customer-special variant of a software system is one in which the system has been modified, built, and released for a specific customer. (Care must be taken when doing customer specials because they are very resource intensive and must be maintained independently.)

  The primary disadvantage of the branch-per-variant approach is that it is hard to reliably merge changes from one variant to another. In general, only some of the changes in the branch for one variant should be applied to another variant, which means that every merge from one variant branch to another must be carefully inspected for whether a particular change should be merged, ignored, or handled in a different way in the destination variant. The longer the variant branches exist, the further they diverge from each other and the harder it is to successfully merge between them. A superior approach is to divide the system into variant-independent and variant-dependent components, and then to control variant selection at build time.

Typically, a combination of the branching approaches described here is used to implement a branching strategy, and much more detail on these approaches is necessary for a complete discussion of branching strategies. Although ClearCase can be used to define your own branching strategy, the ClearCase UCM model offers an out-of-the-box approach described in the following section.

9.2.4   Integration with UCM

As you've seen, the issues of isolation and integration are critical to the efficiency of a software-development project. ClearCase UCM provides a very flexible model for how a project performs isolation and integration. UCM provides the capability to model any isolation and integration characteristics your project team desires. It is always best for your project team to decide how it wants to operate and then look into the facilities within UCM to map the desired development paradigm to the appropriate UCM project, stream, and baseline mix. For instance, you can have a traditional parallel project that also has some of its streams shared by more than one developer. You can also model a read-only project by creating a project and making all its components non-modifiable. Again, it is critical to create the "rules of the road" for your development organization before unleashing any SCM tool on them.

The following subsections explore these development models in more detail, as well as some other integration techniques that might be useful in your development process.

The Assembly Project

This type of project is used during assembly integration. Integration with this UCM model forgoes the use of writeable components. That is, a project is configured to have only read-only access to all of its components. This project simply consumes baselines from existing components. This type of project is used if you want complete flexibility on which baselines you pull from whatever components you have in your project (there are no UCM restrictions using a read-only project because no changes are ever made). When you are ready to verify a new configuration, you can pick up the new changes in this project by simply changing the project's foundation baseline to point to the new desired baseline set (you need to know what component baselines to point to). The advantage of this approach is that you can pick whatever baseline you want for assembly. The drawback is that after you change the project's foundation baseline to bring in a new component baseline mix, you can't easily get back to the component/baseline mix where you were, unless you keep track of this mix somewhere over time. This is where projects that consume composite baselines have an advantage; the composite baseline keeps track of the configuration over time. So, your project that is consuming a composite baseline can simply rebase to the new composite baseline for testing. If this does not work out and you want to revert, you simply can rebase back to the old composite. You want your highest-level system baseline to be a composite of the underlying subsystem baselines developed by the individual subsystem teams. In the major team example in the previous sections, one composite baseline links the two subsystem component baselines. So, when you create a project to assemble these, you can simply start your project from composite baselines in the rootless component. Figure 9-9 shows the configuration in UCM that supports Figure 9-2 in the previous section.

This saves all the bookwork of keeping track of what configuration of baselines go together to form a given release version. This is really simple when you are integrating only two subsystems. However, let's look at how UCM would implement the other example from Figure 9-4 of extensive teams. In this example, there are many more subsystems to assemble from, with a hierarchy imposed. ClearCase UCM can support a hierarchy of composite baselines to assemble and keep track of different architectures. Figure 9-10 shows the creation of a project to assemble artifacts from a very top-level WebSystem composite baseline. As you can see, it assembles from multiple subsystems, which, in turn, assemble from lower-level architectural subsystems (platform, in this case).

Figure 9-9   Composite baselines used to assemble subsystems of major teams.

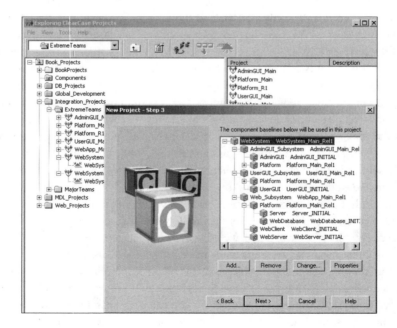

Figure 9-10   Composite baselines used to assemble subsystems of extensive teams.

Setting up a hierarchy like this takes some thought and should be done with the help of the lead architects of your system. If you can model your development environment to use component development teams that integrate through assembly of baselines, your software-development organization will be much more productive.

The rest of the sections within this chapter focus more on the individual teams within a subsystem development effort.

The Single Stream Project

Integration with this UCM model forgoes the use of development streams altogether. In this case, each developer works in his or her own view, and all views are attached to the same integration stream. In effect, developers are working in the UCM model with isolation characteristics that are identical to those described in the section "Branch/LATEST Development: Maximizing Integration," earlier in this chapter. In short, they would see each other's changes at check-in time for dynamic views and at update time for snapshot views.

The advantage of this approach is that you still gain the benefits of UCM activities, components, and baselines without the overhead of deliver and rebase operations. The disadvantage is that developers do not have a stable working environment. This approach is recommended for smaller teams (fewer than four people) that want to integrate as early as possible and are willing to deal with changes occurring to their workspaces while they are developing. It is also recommended for technical-writing teams primarily doing documentation in a format that does not support merging. See the section "Coordinating Documentation Projects or Small Teams" in Chapter 7 for more information on this type of project.

The pros and cons of the multiple developers/one integration stream approach are described in the section "Branch/LATEST Development: Maximizing Integration," earlier in this chapter. Even though this model uses a single stream, your development team can deliver baselines from this project to other projects (if allowed by the other project). Also, you can deliver from other projects to this project.

Some drawbacks are associated with the single-stream project. After you have created a single-stream project, you can't change it to be a traditional parallel project. If remote development is needed on the single-stream project, you must use the ClearCase Remote Client or the ClearCase Web interface to make changes on this project. So, if you simply want your developers to share a stream, you might still want to consider the traditional parallel project and simply create a shared stream off the integration stream for developers to work on together. This is explored further in the next section.

The Traditional Parallel Project

Integration within the traditional parallel project in UCM can occur in many ways, depending upon the "rules of the road" of the development organization. This section describes various ways you can operate within this type of project.

Developer Streams

This form of using the UCM traditional parallel project was how most organizations adopted UCM in the early days (circa ClearCase 4.0). For one, it was the "out-of-the-box" process. That is, most organizations simply started using UCM and used this model as a starting point because it required no thought or effort to get started. This model has some basic tenets that impose some structure on how isolation and integration are handled:

- Each developer is isolated from other developers' changes because each developer has one or more of his or her own streams.
- Developers are responsible for integrating their changes with those of other team members.
- Developers control when they see changes made by other developers.
- Changes integrated into any stream are consistent.

First, in this model, each developer is isolated from other developers. Unlike in branch/LATEST development or shared views, developers do not see each other's changes at save or check-in time. Each developer works in his or her own development view attached to his or her development stream. Branching is used to ensure that each development stream is isolated from changes going on in other development streams. The branching model can be described as "per stream, per project," where "project" can be defined in any way necessary to achieve the right isolation characteristics. For example, a project could be a release or the implementation of a patch bundle. And "stream" can be defined as a set of related activities that a developer must implement. Developers can work in one single stream for the life of a project, create a new stream if they need to work on two unrelated or conflicting tasks in parallel, or create a new stream when they have finished a major set of work and want to start fresh.

The reason for isolating developers is so that they can focus on the task at hand without being disrupted by changes going on elsewhere in the project. This is the most efficient way for an individual to work because it avoids all the problems associated with the branch/LATEST model.

One developer might have multiple streams for any given project if he or she needs to isolate pieces of his or her own work. Developers make their changes available to other project members using a UCM operation called deliver (see "Delivering Changes to the Project" in Chapter 8, "Development Using the ClearCase UCM Model"). They update their development environment using a UCM operation called rebase (see "Rebasing Your Development Stream" in Chapter 8).

Second, developers are responsible for integrating their changes with those of other team members. They explicitly make their changes available to other project members by issuing a UCM command called `Deliver`. The deliver process copies development-stream changes to the project's integration stream. This is done on a per-activity basis and is a merge integration operation. That is, if there are conflicting changes made by two developers, resolution/integration is done during the deliver by the developer. Usually, UCM delivers can be called push delivery because the developer "pushes" the changes into the project's integration stream. See "Delivering Changes to the Project" in Chapter 8 for more details on delivery.

Third, developers control when they see changes made by other developers. Developers make changes available to other team members by delivering those changes to the project's integration stream. The basic UCM model gives each developer control over when he or she will see the changes made by other members of the project team.

As discussed, when developers want to see changes made by other team members, they perform a rebase. Rebase also causes a merge integration (for elements that you and others have changed), but this time from the integration stream to the development stream. Rebase uses assembly integration for read-only or unmodified components. See "Rebasing Your Development Stream" in Chapter 8 for more details.

This model then gives control of the developer's working environment to the developer. This is different from the branch/LATEST approach in which the developer's environment is dynamically updated as changes are checked in by other developers (see the section "Branch/LATEST Development: Maximizing Integration," earlier in this chapter).

The advantage to this UCM approach is that developers are often more productive because their environment is stable. The disadvantage is that it can become easy for a developer to remain isolated forever. By never rebasing the development stream, a developer could choose to never see changes made by other team members. In effect, this developer would drift further out of date with the latest source code changes. The result of this behavior on the integrator would be that changes being delivered by that developer would often not work with the latest software. This might mean that it wouldn't build or would have problems in a runtime environment. When this happens, the integrator spends more time getting things to work, basically integrating this developer's changes for him or her.

To combat this problem while still providing the developer control of the working environment, UCM provides a project policy that can be set. This policy is described in the "Require Development Stream to Be Based on the Project's Recommended Baseline(s) Prior to Deliver" bullet in Chapter 6, "Project Management in ClearCase." The purpose of this policy is to require the developer to rebase (update) to the project's recommended baselines before delivering any changes. In this way, developers can choose to remain isolated until they need to deliver a change. At that point, they are required to rebase their development stream to the latest baselines recommended by the integrator. The UCM approach provides an effective compromise between developer isolation and project integration.

Finally, changes that are integrated into a stream are consistent. UCM reduces the problem of version skew (see the discussion of version skew in the section "Branch/LATEST Development: Maximizing Integration," earlier in this chapter) by using automation to ensure that changes moving between streams are consistent (either deliver, or out-bound changes, and rebase, or in-bound changes). Various deliver policies can be set in the UCM project. Chapter 6 covers the details of setting policies of a UCM project. See Figure 6-3 for the default settings.

Deliver operates on an implicit set of versions that are consistent in terms of the activity or activities being delivered. That is, when you issue a `Deliver` command, you specify one or more activities, not a set of versions. The primary purpose here is to make sure that the new versions created to perform a logical activity are made visible in the integration stream as a whole.

Rebase operations operate on baselines and, therefore, on a consistent set of versions that have been included in the baseline by the integrator. See the section "Baselining Software Components" in Chapter 10 for more on the steps the integrator performs to incorporate developer deliveries into new baselines.

Shared Streams

One alternative to the basic UCM model is to have multiple developers working in one development stream, with each developer using his or her own view. This is good for a small group (fewer than five) of developers who must cooperate closely on some pieces of work. In that case, the developers are isolated from each other by means of the view. Each developer sees other developers' changes at check-in time for dynamic views and update time for snapshot views. Having multiple developers use a single development stream is how you get the same characteristics of the branch/LATEST development approach while using UCM (see the section "Branch/LATEST Development: Maximizing Integration," earlier in this chapter).

UCM has a few restrictions because of the activity-oriented nature of the model. First, each developer must be working on his or her own activity. This might require that a single logical activity be decomposed into smaller activities and assigned to each developer. (If members of this small group *must* collaborate on one activity, they would all use one view attached to one development stream. This essentially simulates the no isolation characteristics described in the section "The Shared View: No Isolation," earlier in this chapter.) Second, if two developers make changes to the same files while working on two different activities, they introduce a deliver dependency between these activities, causing the activities to be delivered together or in a specific order to ensure consistency.

The approach of multiple developers/one development stream should be used in a UCM project when specific circumstances require close cooperation between a small group of developers. It is also a good transition for those teams migrating from other SCM tools where managing multiple variants through branching is hard and is often avoided. The team could periodically deliver to the integration stream when it was ready to expose others to their work. It could also rebase this stream at a point when the team was ready to accept changes from other efforts.

Hierarchy of Streams

ClearCase UCM supports configuring a hierarchy of streams in the form of what is usually called parent/child streams. Your project team can now model any form of stream hierarchy that you desire. Usually, it is a good idea to not get too far removed from the integration stream. A UCM project still has only one UCM integration stream. However, you can configure streams that default their deliver operations to a different stream. This is useful when dealing with longer-lived feature streams or architectural change streams. Instead of having a team work on a shared feature stream, you can create a feature stream that is a child of the UCM project's integration stream. Developers can then join the project, or create streams, and default their delivery operations on these streams to the feature stream rather than the project's integration stream. This feature stream can collect deliveries from the developers working on the feature and periodically deliver to the project. So, a hierarchy of delivers can occur, with the child streams delivering to their parent streams and ultimately delivering the integration stream. The same can be done with rebase in the opposite direction. The parent stream can rebase from the integration stream, and the child streams can rebase from their parent (assuming that baselines are being used on the parent stream). Figure 9-11 shows the initial step in creating a child stream.

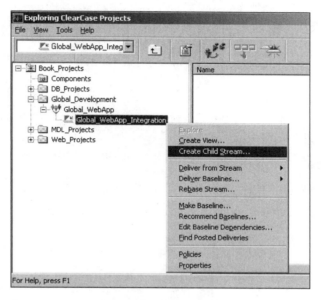

Figure 9-11   Creating a child stream from ClearCase Project Explorer.

You can also use this technique to model iteration streams. Developers work off an iteration stream, which collects the features and defects geared for that iteration. You can then stabilize that iteration stream before delivering to the project's integration stream. Many iteration streams can be active at any given point. Activities planned for different iterations can be worked on in the appropriate iteration stream. If an activity or feature is not going to make it into a particular iteration stream, it can be reparented to the next iteration stream simply by delivering the appropriate activities to the next iteration stream's context rather than the current stream. Figure 9-12 shows joining a project and setting the default integration stream to be something different than the project's integration stream.

Another application for having multiple levels of logical integration streams is to support localized integration streams for remote teams participating in development on a multisite UCM project. This allows each site to have its own local integration stream where developers can deliver to and rebase from. This prevents developers from having to post their deliveries to a remote site. The posting of deliveries can then occur periodically by the integrator to the remote site. Figure 9-13 shows local integration streams in a multisite project. Geographically distributed development is discussed in more detail in Chapter 11, "Geographically Distributed Development."

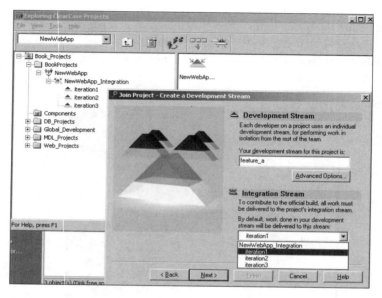

Figure 9-12   Joining a project and setting up an alternate stream for delivery operations.

Figure 9-13   Site-specific integration streams.

Mixing Streams and Projects to Meet Your Needs

You might find that you end up using all types of streams and projects in your organization's development model. Your project might have a 2-month feature stream that has developers working on child streams that deliver to the feature stream. You might also have a documentation effort be a single-stream project. And your overall release project simply collects baselines of the various subsystems in play. You might also let each subsystem development team control how it develops its deliverable. You want to know only which baseline to pull from. The more you can architect your product or application to consist of components that are worked on by small component-development teams, the easier time you will have with integration. Your integration effort will mostly be assembly of baselines instead of merging of features to release streams.

Common Variations with Deliver

Even though UCM is an "out-of-the-box" process, it has evolved over the years to allow for variations in the normal UCM usage model flow. Most of these variations are enabled via click-button options via the UCM project properties sheet. Other variations can be accomplished through the use of ClearCase triggers on UCM objects. UCM is flexible enough to support any type of development paradigm your organization follows. This section takes a look at some common variations around the UCM deliver operation.

Push Deliver Versus Pull Deliver

Deliver has two forms: push delivery and pull delivery. With *push delivery,* a developer is responsible for integrating his or her changes into the project's integration stream where the integrator can create baselines and perform project builds. The developer "pushes" in the changes. With *pull delivery,* developers indicate that their changes are ready for integration, but the integrator is responsible for integrating the developer's changes into the project's integration stream. The integrator "pulls" in the changes. After being notified that an activity is ready to be delivered, the integrator can simply go to the development stream and deliver the activities. This process could also be automated to some extent, with the automation kicking back the delivery if the merge is not a trivial merge.

A pull deliver can also be performed by a developer working on a new release. An example of this is when a defect fix was completed and merged into a patch release stream. If that fix also needs to be incorporated into the latest release, the developer responsible for integrating that fix can simply deliver the defect fix from the patch stream into a development stream off the latest release. To accomplish this, the developer needs to deliver to an alternate target and select his or her local development stream, as shown in Figures 9-14 through Figure 9-17.

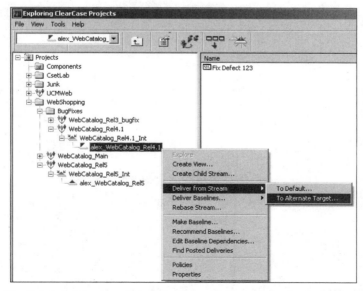

Figure 9-14 Starting to integrate a defect fix from a Rel4.1 stream into a current release.

Figure 9-15   Selecting the Rel5 stream as the target stream to deliver to.

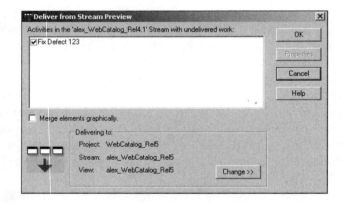

Figure 9-16   Selecting Defect Fix 123 to deliver.

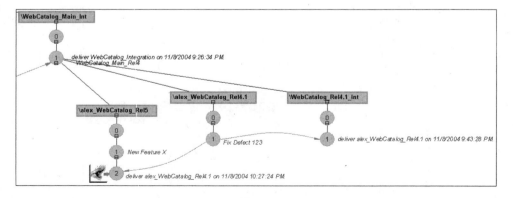

Figure 9-17   Version tree showing result of integration.

Posting a Deliver

When a developer is working on a remotely mastered project, a developer deliver to the project's integration stream is called a *posted delivery*. That is, an integrator at the remote site needs to complete the posted delivery (see Chapter 11 for more details on mastership and working with remote projects).

Gating Deliveries with Process

In some cases, you might want deliver to behave differently than "out of the box." One way to customize the process is through the use of ClearCase triggers, which are supported on all UCM operations. For example, by default, deliver allows multiple people to merge their changes into the integration stream, as long as the change set of the delivering activities is unique (no namespace collision). If you want to enforce a serial deliver, regardless of namespace, you can install a ClearCase trigger on deliver to have a process fire to control concurrent access to the target stream. Some organizations desire this control.

If for your project you want more control over who can deliver and what got delivered, you can install a trigger to allow only the integrator to make changes on the integration stream. You would then have to create a submit process to notify the integrator that activities were ready for delivery. If you were using a ClearQuest-enabled UCM project, this submit notification could be modeled in ClearQuest. After being notified, the integrator could then go to the developer's stream (via the Project Explorer) and execute the delivery himself. Most development teams, however, simply trust their developers to integrate their activities according to a scheduled, agreed-upon timeframe.

Interproject Deliveries

ClearCase UCM supports interproject deliveries. You can deliver from a stream to any other stream in another project. If you are delivering from a stream used for integration, you can deliver baselines instead of the individual activities that went into the baseline. Before you can perform interproject deliveries, you need to enable the correct deliver policies on the target stream (not the source stream) to enable interproject delivery and to control some of the behavior. See Figure 9-11 for the UCM project deliver policies. For a typical project, you would set these policies to the values shown in Table 9-1. See Chapter 6 for more details.

Table 9-1   Policies and Settings

Policy Name	Recommended Settings
Allow Deliveries from Streams with Pending Check-Outs	Disabled
Require Rebase Before Deliver	Enabled (This helps make sure that development streams are caught up with the project's latest recommended baseline before attempting to deliver.)
	(Table 9-1 Continued)

(Table 9-1 Continued)	
Allow Deliveries That Contain Changes in Foundation Baselines	Disabled (within the project) Disabled (outside the project)
Allow Deliveries That Contain Changes Made to Components Not in Target Stream	Disabled (within the project) Disabled (outside the project) You don't want to accidentally get half a change.
Allow Deliveries from Streams in Other Projects	Enabled (unless, of course, you don't want other projects to deliver to this project)
Require That All Components Are Visible in the Target Stream	Enabled You don't want to accidentally get half a change.

Other Integration Scenarios

You should be aware of a couple other integration scenarios because they can be very useful when using UCM in certain situations. You might run into some conditions in which UCM does not supply an out-of-the-box solution. One of these conditions arises when you find a problem with an activity in a stream and want to back out the activity. There is no "undo" UCM operation. Another condition that might arise during UCM development that you want to reapply an activity's change set from another stream to your current stream (a redo operation). A UCM deliver operation or even a `cleartool findmerge -cset` operation might introduce more activities to your stream than what is desired.

Fortunately, Base ClearCase provides mechanisms to perform these operations, through the subtractive and additive merge utilities. More good news: A script named `cset.pl` has already been developed that implements these two operations. Refer to Appendix A, "Redoing and Undoing Change Sets with UCM," for more details on these two scenarios, the location of where to get the script, and examples of how to use it.

9.3   Summary

This chapter showed many ways to integrate software with ClearCase and ClearCase UCM. No matter what strategy you end up using, you should plan for regularly scheduled integration activities during your software development life cycle. During integration of the system, you tend to find problems that affect the entire system, which are harder to resolve. The sooner you can find these problems, the sooner (and cheaper) they can be fixed. Some companies continuously integrate and build; they want to find integration issues as soon as they can. If you delay integration, integration activities will take longer and require heroics from your development organization to not let the schedule slip because of integration issues found late in the development life cycle. You can use streams to model iterative development, which promotes integration more frequently, or use them for feature, bug fix, patching, and so on.

You should architect your system so that it can be worked on by component development teams, which produce baselines that are assembled by a system-level assembly project. This allows for teams of people to easily consume new changes from other components and perform integration activities sooner, verifying new functionality. This also makes integration much easier and more scalable to larger systems. After integrating or assembling changes from various subsystems, the fastest way to get a warm, fuzzy feeling on how well this new configuration will work is to build and test the system. The next chapter focuses on building, testing, and release/deployment.

CHAPTER 10

Building, Baselining, and Release Deployment

In the last chapter, you saw how to integrate the changes produced from the various development teams. To make sure your system still works, you need to build and verify your software. If there is a problem during this stage, you can reject this build attempt, triage the problem, and work at resolving the issue. No other external organization will have been exposed to the problem because it would have still been using the previous configuration from your team. This verification step is needed before you can expose others to your software.

It's not just your customers you need to protect from these release candidates that do not achieve a certain quality level. Time is critical in the software development life cycle. If you allow your development organization to haphazardly throw release candidates over the wall for the testing organization to test, you might find that your testing group is spending time setting up its testing environment, securing resources to perform the testing (both hardware and people). When it finally performs the tests, it fails because of issues that could have easily been discovered during a testing effort within the development organization. Now, not only has this testing effort been wasted, but the resources that performed the effort also have been wasted by not allowing them to be available to test other products. As you can see, a small oversight in this process has a major impact on the development organization.

Mistakes happen. You can limit and reduce the chances of mistakes occurring in your development process if you have a documented and repeatable build and release process. In today's world, where audits of development practices are becoming more the norm, your development organization needs to establish best practices within the development, testing, and deployment processes. Every release needs to be tracked back to the configuration that built it. From that configuration, you should easily know which features and defect fixes went into the release. And from those features and defect fixes, you should know what customer, marketing, or government requirements you are trying to address. Haphazard development and release processes will only get you into trouble. You should spend the time and money up front to address these issues within your organization before they become major problems.

This chapter explores baselining, building, and release-deployment strategies and how ClearCase and UCM fit into those strategies.

10.1   Baselining and Building with UCM

In your development organization, developers perform a build to verify their changes. They might perform another build after they integrate their changes with the rest of the team (see Chapter 9, "Integration," for more details on integration). However, the build process that is performed in the integration area for the product is usually performed by an integrator, project lead, or release administrator. This person is responsible for building, baselining, and smoke-testing the software. This could be a part-time job for a development lead on a small project or a full-time job on a much larger project, or it might be performed by several individuals. To get a stable configuration in place, you want your release area baselining and build process to be documented and, ideally, automated so that you can have it run unattended and at times when the local development team is not working (if possible). During this time, changes to the integration area will not be allowed. Developers can still perform changes against the next iteration or the next release while the current release candidate is being built.

With ClearCase UCM, the integrator needs to perform the following steps in the product-integration area to ensure a reproducible configuration.

1. Lock the integration stream.
2. Baseline the components.
3. Build.
4. Execute any smoke tests available.
5. Promote the software component baselines to the desired state.
6. Optionally recommend the baselines for use by the project.
7. Unlock the integration stream.

The following subsections discuss each of these steps and the variants of this sequence, including how to automate it.

10.1.1   Locking the Integration Stream

The first step is to lock the integration stream. This can be carried out most easily from the ClearCase Project Explorer (although, when automating a build system, this step and all steps that follow will most likely be scripted through the use of cleartool commands; automating the build system is discussed later). Figure 10-1 shows how to bring up the properties sheet for the integration stream. Figure 10-2 shows the properties sheet of the integration stream for the Web_Rel1 project. The Lock tab is displayed. Make sure that you exclude yourself from the lock. As shown, the user cmadm is still allowed to make changes in the integration stream. Locking the

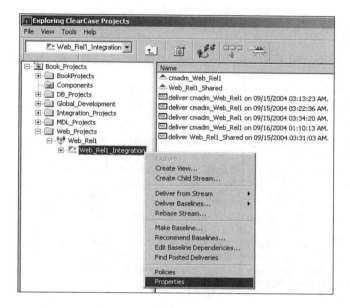

Figure 10-1 Bringing up the properties sheet from the ClearCase Project Explorer.

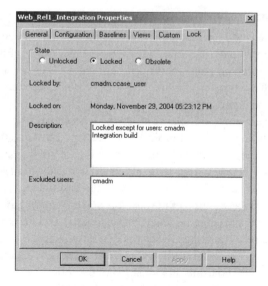

Figure 10-2 Locking the integration stream from the properties sheet.

integration stream stops deliveries from occurring so that you can baseline and build against a stable code base.

You could also perform the same step through the command line, as follows:

```
prompt> cleartool lock -nusers cmadm >>
stream:Web_Rel1_Integration@\Book_Projects
```

CLEARCASE PRO TIP

A decision when implementing your build system is whether to build and then baseline, or baseline and then build. Both approaches offer advantages and disadvantages. The easiest approach with UCM is to build first and baseline second.

Many times build problems arise that can be fixed easily by a quick change to a file. These fixes are so minor that it is desirable to slip them into the baseline. This was traditionally accomplished in ClearCase by sliding a label down to the new versions on some files. However, component baselines do not allow you to tweak their content. After they are created, they cannot be changed. To fix a build problem within UCM, you must create a new baseline.

If your build times are short and you want to allow for minor fixes before you create a baseline, simply build first and then baseline afterward. If your build times are long, you will have to baseline, unlock the integration stream, and set up a build-stabilization stream founded at the baseline to resolve any build issues. This will free up the integration stream for deliveries bound for the next build attempt.

10.1.2   Baselining Software Components

Baselining is a ClearCase UCM operation that creates new versions of components (see "Component Management: Components and Baselines" in Chapter 4, "A Functional Overview of ClearCase Objects," for more on components and baselines). To create a new baseline, the integrator goes to the ClearCase Project Explorer and selects Make Baseline on the context menu of the integration stream (see Figure 10-3).

The Make Baseline operation looks at all the activities that have been delivered. It determines which components on a particular project have been modified and then offers to create new component baselines for each of these components. In Figure 10-4, you see the Make Baseline dialog box, which includes a few options to manipulate. First is the name of the baseline, entered in the Base Name field. By default, ClearCase names the baseline by appending the date to the project name. Second is the description of the baseline you are creating. Third, you have the baseline type: full or incremental. An incremental baseline is a baseline that ClearCase creates by recording the last full baseline and those versions that have changed since the last full baseline was created. A full baseline is a baseline that ClearCase creates by recording all versions below the component root directory. Fourth is an indication of the project and stream in which the baseline is being created. The final entry indicates the view that will be used to create the baseline. By default, all activities modified since the last baseline was made are included in the new baseline.

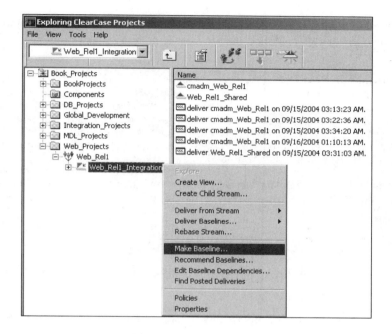

Figure 10-3 Make Baseline operation from the ClearCase Project Explorer.

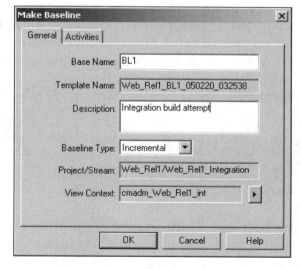

Figure 10-4 Make Baseline dialog box with baseline-naming template.

Occasionally, you might want to create a baseline that includes only a subset of activities. To do so, click on the Activities tab and select the activities to go into the new baseline.

CLEARCASE PRO TIP
Instead of using the default baseline name (baseline identifiers are made up of two parts: a user-specifiable root name, known as the basename, and a generated, unique numeric extension), you can create a baseline-naming template to allow the integrator to easily supply an identifier into a project-specific baseline format. Some of the variables you can use to create a template are basename, project, stream, component, date, time, user, and host. You need to set up this template from the command line using the `blname_template` option of the `cleartool chproj` command. For example, to set a template name based on the project name, an identifier you enter, the date, and the time, you would execute this command on the project object:

```
prompt> cleartool chproj -blname project,basename,date,time
project:Web_Rel1@\Book_Projects
```

Baseline creation can also be scripted or performed from the command line with the following:

```
prompt> cleartool mkbl
```

The two types of baselines supported by ClearCase UCM, incremental and full, have different performance characteristics. A baseline identifies a single version of elements contained in a ClearCase component either directly or indirectly. A *full baseline* is a baseline that directly records a version of every element contained in the ClearCase component. An *incremental baseline* is a baseline that directly records a version of elements that have changed since the last full baseline and indirectly records versions of elements by recording the last full baseline.

Initially, incremental baselines are faster to create. However, over time, they begin to take as much time as a full baseline. At this point or before, you should convert an incremental baseline to a full baseline, and then subsequent incremental baselines will be faster. It is highly recommended that you convert important incremental baselines to full baselines. The conversion from incremental to full can be done as a background operation.

CLEARCASE PRO TIP
Using base ClearCase, you relate a set of versions by creating a label type and then attaching instances of that label to each element version (see "Labels" in Chapter 4). To better understand incremental and full baselines, think in terms of labels. A full baseline is then a baseline in which every single element of the component has had an instance of a label type attached. An incremental baseline is a baseline in which only those elements that have changed (since the last fully labeled baseline) have a label attached.

10.1.3   Building Software Components

Building is the first level of testing performed by the integrator. The purpose is to ensure that all the new changes made to the system will actually build together. The idea here is that one person (the integrator) debugs any build problems first, rather than allowing a build problem to cause all the developers' builds to break, as it could using the branch/LATEST development model.

Builds can be done using clearmake, make, Ant, or any other build utility. The UCM model does not provide any specific support for building, nor does it hinder any approach to building the software.

If the system builds correctly, you can move on to running smoke tests or promoting the baselines to a higher level. However, builds often fail. For example, problems can occur when project builds have happened on multiple platforms but the developer has built and verified their changes only on one platform. Some build problems are easy to diagnose. Sometimes it is clear that the problem is specifically build related, and it can be easily fixed. For these problems, the integrator usually makes the changes and continues to try to get a successful build. With UCM, the easiest way to do this is for the integrator to create an activity in the integration stream and make these changes. No delivery is required because the changes are made directly in the integration stream (remember, the integration stream is locked to all users except for the integrator).

Build problems that are harder to solve are often the result of changes delivered by multiple developers and usually require some knowledge of the software internals to determine what needs to be done. In these cases, the integrator can engage one or more developers to help diagnose the problem. It might be necessary for a developer to make further changes to an activity that has already been delivered and redeliver the activity.

UCM supports the capability to deliver an activity multiple times (although when an activity is logically contained within a baseline, we would rather see a new activity be created to fix the mistake rather than to work on the original activity that had the mistake in it). To allow the developer to redeliver a change, the integrator can modify the lock on the integration stream to grant this developer access while keeping other developer deliveries from occurring.

If you can isolate the problem to a particular deliver operation, you could "undo" this deliver activity, as indicated in the utility described in Appendix A, "Redoing and Undoing Change Sets with UCM," and try again. However, this would depend on the problem space and the dependencies on the particular deliver activity to be undone.

10.1.4   Executing Smoke Tests

Smoke tests are usually subsets of a system's full-regression test suite that can be executed automatically. Smoke tests verify the basic functionality of a software system. The purpose of running them is to increase the level of confidence in the software system by ensuring that a basic runtime system works. If the smoke tests are successful, an integrator can conclude that the changes that have been delivered and integrated are stable enough to be used by developers to rebase their development streams, and so will promote the new baselines to the appropriate level.

10.1.5   Using Build Stabilization Streams

In some cases, the smoke tests fail and you don't know how long it will take to find the solution to the problems. You can try to fix the build on the integration stream and leave it locked until fixed. This action typically causes developers to stack their changes on their development streams and wait until the build is "fixed," and immediately follow that success criterion with a flurry of deliver activities that again could break the build because their changes were allowed to go on without frequent integration. You could also just "reject" the baseline, unlock the stream, and try again at the next planned integration build time. This usually delays finding problems with the system and creates risk with your project's delivery schedule. Another approach is to create a build-stabilization stream. With this approach, you can unlock the integration stream so developers can continue to deliver activities. You then create a new stream founded at the baseline you just created. Developers can then attach views to that stream to fix any problems that were uncovered during smoke tests. This approach can also be used to address problems found in later testing cycles. After this stream has fixed the problems associated with the failing smoke tests, there are a couple of options for how you can proceed. One is to simply deliver the activities on this stream into the integration area and wait for the next integration build attempt to verify that these changes work with any other changes that have been delivered since this stream was created. The other choice is to put a new baseline down on this stream and promote it to the desired level to allow for consumption by other projects. If the team you are working on needs to produce a stable baseline for consumption for higher-level subsystems, you need to draw the line somewhere to allow for integration to occur at higher levels. You can then deliver this baseline into the integration stream to be included in the next build attempt. Other projects can consume the baseline from the stabilization stream until the next integration build cycle. Figure 10-5 shows an example of a build-stabilization stream that was used to fix some smoke-test problems while allowing developers to continue to deliver changes for the next iteration.

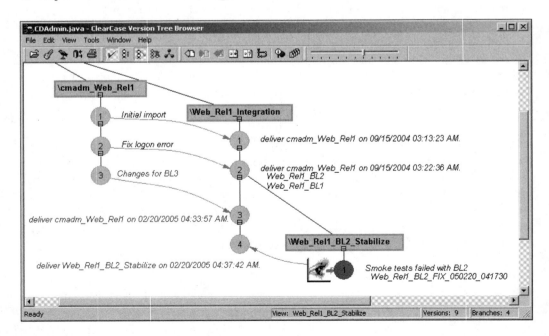

Figure 10-5 Example of a build-stabilization stream.

10.1.6   Promoting and Recommending Software Component Baselines

Promoting baselines to an indicated level and recommending them for consumption by a project involve two different steps. Baselines are assigned a promotion level. Within a UCM PVOB, you can define a promotion level for all projects within that PVOB. The end of Chapter 5, "Establishing the Initial SCM Environment," outlines more about baseline levels and how to set them— specifically, see Figure 5-22, which shows the default promotion levels for a baseline. Your organization can define a set of promotion levels that fit the software-development and deployment process you desire.

You can set these levels in your UCM PVOB by using the GUI or by using the `setplevel cleartool` command. For example, to set the promotion levels to Rejected, Initial, Dev_Test, Sys_Test, Prod_Test, Prod, Last_Prod in the PVOB `\Book_Projects`, you would use the following command:

```
prompt> cleartool setplevel -nc -invob \Book_Projects -default
INITIAL >>
REJECTED INITIAL DEV_TEST SYS_TEST PROD_TEST PROD LAST_PROD
```

CLEARCASE PRO TIP
ClearCase UCM does not allow a definition within the tool of which user can perform certain promotion transitions. However, through the use of ClearCase triggers, you can accomplish a very flexible promotion level transition model. This can be accomplished through preoperation and post-operation triggers on the `chbl` (change baseline) command. This is very useful in implementing promotion-level authorization and deployment strategies.

As your baselines become more stable, they will transition to higher promotion levels. This will indicate they have a higher level of quality because they have passed more testing cycles. From the ClearCase Project Explorer, the easiest way to promote and recommend baselines is through the Recommended Baselines dialog box, which is brought up by right-clicking on the project's integration stream, as shown in Figure 10-6.

The Recommended Baselines dialog box then shows you the stream's current baselines that it recommends (see Figure 10-7). For every project, one promotion level is defined as the Recommended level (see "Recommended Baseline Promotion Level" in Chapter 6, "Project Management in ClearCase," for how this is set). The latest baselines in the project's integration stream that are promoted to that level and recommended will become the default set of baselines offered during developer rebase operations.

To view the recommended baselines of a stream using the command-line interface, you use the `describe` command. In this example, we are looking at the recommended baselines of the Web_Rel1_Integration stream:

```
prompt> cleartool describe -fmt "%[rec_bls]p" >>
stream:Web_Rel1_Integration@\Book_Projects
```

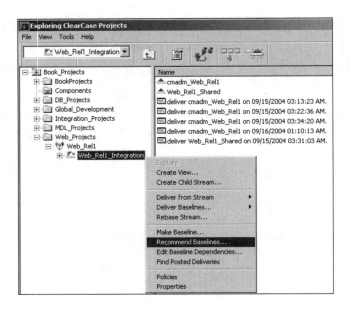

Figure 10-6   Using ClearCase Project Explorer to recommend baselines.

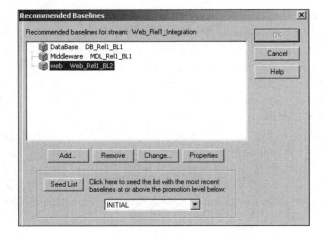

Figure 10-7   Recommended baselines of a project's integration stream.

Integrators have a choice at this point. The easiest approach is to use the Seed List button to get the latest baselines at or above the listed level. Alternatively, the integrator can select each baseline individually and manipulate it.

Before recommending the list of baselines, make sure they are at the desired promotion level. Select the appropriate baseline and click the Properties button. From here, you can promote the baseline to a new level. Figure 10-8 shows the baseline property sheet. After the baseline has been promoted, you can click the OK button on the Recommended Baselines dialog box to recommend the list of baselines for this project to use.

From the command-line interface, you can change the level of a baseline with the `chbl` cleartool command. For example, to promote the Web_Rel1_BL2 baseline to TESTED, you would use the following cleartool command:

```
prompt> cleartool chbl -nc -level TESTED baseline:Web_Rel1_BL2@ >>
\Book_Projects
```

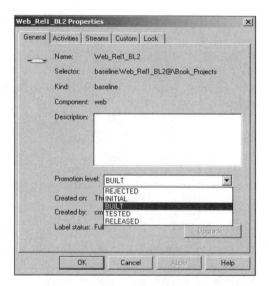

Figure 10-8 Baseline property sheet used to change promotion level.

From the command-line interface, you can recommend a set of baselines for a stream with the `chstream` cleartool command. For example, to recommend the latest set of baselines in the stream at or above the project's recommended level, you would use the following cleartool command:

```
prompt> cleartool chstream -nc -rec -default >>
stream:Web_Rel1_Integration@\Book_Projects
```

Another view in which the integrator can see a list of baselines and which baseline is recommended is through the Baselines tab on the properties sheet of the project's integration stream. Figure 10-1 shows how to bring up the stream's property sheet from the ClearCase Project Explorer. Figure 10-9 shows the Baselines tab. Click on a component in the list to see a history of baselines for that component. The recommended baseline is indicated by the star next to it.

Integrators should demote baselines that have known problems. If a baseline fails to build, it should be moved to the Rejected or other appropriate promotion level. This avoids the accidental use of bad baselines.

Figure 10-9 Baselines tab of integration stream properties dialog box.

10.1.7   Unlocking the Integration Stream

When the baselines are laid down and the build process and smoke tests are complete, the integration stream is unlocked. New activities can be delivered, and developers can rebase to the new recommended baselines. You can unlock the integration stream by selecting the Lock tab on the stream's property sheet and clicking the Unlock button. From the command-line interface, you perform this command:

```
prompt> cleartool unlock
stream:Web_Rel1_Integration@\Book_Projects
```

10.1.8   Automating the Nightly Build Process

If you perform automated nightly builds, the entire process just described could be scripted using the ClearCase command-line interface (or the ClearCase Automation Library on Windows). Some things to consider before automating your build process are the time it takes to build your system and any deployment considerations. Before automating any build or release system, make sure you have performed it manually to a degree of satisfaction to work out any issues. It is easy to automate something that works. If you have an automated test suite that can programmatically determine whether the tests succeeded or failed, you can automate the smoke-testing portion of this process as well.

This approach is good for larger teams because it does not block deliveries during the day and allows developers to rebase in the morning to pick up the previous day's changes. Automating this process is particularly important near the end of a software-development project when you want developers to regularly stay up-to-date with project changes.

10.2 Staging, Deployment, and Release

Up until now, we have talked mainly about versioning of source code. Two other very important processes with respect to SCM are staging and release. *Staging* is the process of putting derived object files (executables, libraries, data files, generated header files, and so on) under version control. *Release* is the process of putting the runtime software into its final form and making it available to its intended users. These staged artifacts typically get *deployed* to various systems for further testing. They also get deployed to the production environment. In this case, the system gets released when it has been deployed to production. So, for some development shops, a release might be deploying the artifacts to manufacturing where CDs get burned and shipped out to customers, or are available for download. In other shops, a release is deployed to production, where it is brought online and is serving the needs of its customers. In general, the UCM development and deployment process is shown in Figure 10-10.

The primary purpose of staging is to store copies of the executable or runtime parts of the system so that they are secure and can be reliably recalled. The reasons behind staging and how staging is performed can be very different, depending on the type of software system you are developing. In fact, it is very hard to generalize the process of staging.

Most companies model their UCM baseline-promotion levels to reflect how the software artifacts move through their development and deployment life cycle. By integrating ClearCase UCM with deployment tools, you can have the promotion of a baseline trigger a deployment of the software artifacts from the UCM staging components to the desired test or production environment.

The primary purpose of release is to make the software available to its end users. The act of deployment moves the staged software to the various systems for further testing. Deployment is also the act of moving the software to its end users in some shops. Whereas staging is very hard to generalize, the processes surrounding a release are almost impossible to generalize. Every company has its own release processes that are almost always dependent on a number of factors, including but not limited to the following:

- The way the software will be delivered
- How the software is built

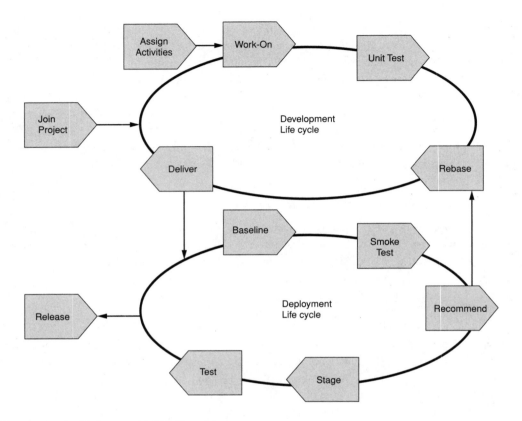

Figure 10-10   The general UCM life cycle. Source: [Brown, 2004]

- How the software is staged
- How the company is organized
- How manufacturing occurs
- How many end users or customers exist
- How many releases are produced per year/month/week/day
- Whether the customers are internal or external to the company

To be clear, you can stage a number of builds over the course of a software project, and you can produce a number of release candidates for deployment for installation-testing purposes, but there will be only one "official" build that was both staged and released (of course, in some shops, this one official build might last only a day until the next release gets deployed).

10.2.1   The Staging Component

In UCM, you use components to contain the artifacts of your software-development effort. It is best to have your UCM components hold specific types of artifacts. You will have separate components that contain requirements, tests, models, source and deployment artifacts. The deployment artifacts will be stored in the staging component. This staging component will be writeable by the Assembly project and not by the development project. Developers are never allowed to update this component. Only the release build team has access to the Assembly project that has write access to the staging component. What should go in your staging component? Everything that is needed as input by your deployment tools should be versioned within this component. Remember, deployment will be performed by another team that has no knowledge of how to build and assemble these deployment artifacts. These staging components could potentially get quite large (if your deployment artifacts are large), so be prepared to have a large amount of disk space handy for the VOBs that will contain these components. There are many factors to consider when planning for the mechanisms to manage the staging components as they grow. Many of these decisions depend on how large the deployment artifacts are, how frequently you intend to perform release builds that populate the staging component, how many recent versions of the deployment artifacts you need to keep active, and how long you want to keep these components active on your system.

10.2.2 Using the Assembly Project for Deployment of Releases

During software development life cycles, (at least) two types of builds and baselines deal with software deployments (typically seen more frequently in Web service applications). We can refer to these as developer builds and release builds. A developer build is the nightly or more frequent build that verifies some feature set of the application for development and integration purposes. This build is done with no intent of pushing it into system testing or production. Its baseline is meant for developers to rebase to periodically, to stay up-to-date with the latest development activities. When a configuration is meant to have its output versioned into the staging component and bound for consumption by some other organization, the Assembly project is used. This project has read-only access to the source components but read-write access to the staging component (see Figure 10-11). This Assembly project is rebased to pick up the new development baseline(s) ready to be considered as the next release candidate. This is the project where you perform the release build. This project might also have a relationship to other components not in the normal development project, such as a release tools component. This depends on the requirements for building and releasing the application.

The release build rebuilds the source selected by the Assembly project and versions the output into the staging component. So, in this sense, the development build is different from the release build. The release build knows how to version and package the output into the staging component. When this step is successful, a new release candidate baseline is created through the Assembly project that links the source components with the staging component. This release candidate baseline will get promoted into testing, staging, and production.

10.2.3 Modeling the Deployment Stages of a Release with Streams

One nice feature of read-only UCM streams is that they can be rebased forward, backward, and sideways without worry because no changes are allowed to occur within them. This feature is useful when modelling deployment needs with UCM. The Assembly project can have read-only

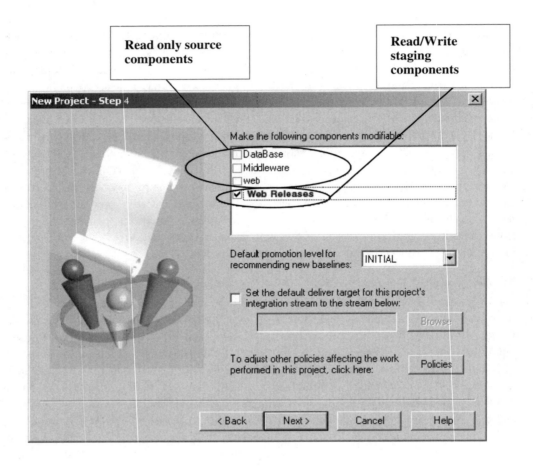

Figure 10-11   Assembly project with writeable staging component.

child streams defined to mimic the configuration deployed to the different testing and production environments (see Figure 10-12). These stream names would match the deployment stages of your environment (as in System Test, Production Acceptance Test, Production, and so on). For instance, when an Assembly project release candidate baseline gets promoted from System Test to Production Acceptance Test, you would rebase the Production Acceptance Test stream to pick up this release candidate baseline. Next, you can attach a view to the Production Acceptance Test stream and have your deployment tool move the staging artifacts selected by this stream to the Production Acceptance Test server. If there is an error with this process, you can fail the promotion attempt by changing the baseline back to the original state and then rebase the stream to the previous baseline.

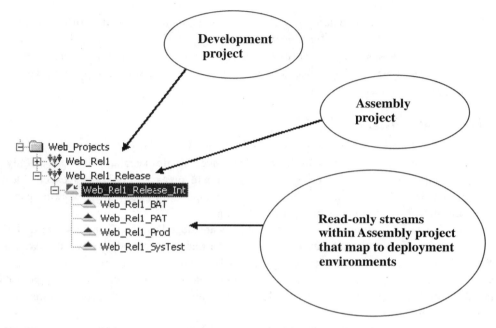

Figure 10-12   Assembly project and read-only deployment streams.

10.2.4   ClearQuest's Role in Deployment

Quality assurance logs defects during the testing phase of deployment in ClearQuest. At a minimum, this is what you can use ClearQuest for, especially in environments where you are not using ClearQuest-enabled UCM. However, you can use ClearQuest for so much more in the deployment scenario. Most companies create a deployment record in ClearQuest and track the approval process to gate the transition through the various levels in the testing life cycle. For instance, a process is created to send e-mail notifications when a release candidate baseline is ready for transition from one state to the next. As all of these approvals are processed, the last approval kicks off a process that performs the actual baseline promotion. This then fires the ClearCase triggers, which perform the automated deployment operations.

Another way ClearQuest is used in this process is to keep track of baseline configurations in ClearQuest where more detailed reporting and charting is available. This is accomplished by synchronizing the baseline records into ClearQuest via a ClearCase trigger. Usually, only the release candidate baselines are tracked in ClearQuest, not the development baselines. You can then use this strategy to submit defects against baselines in ClearQuest and to verify that certain conditions are met at the defect record level (for example, don't allow a defect that has not been verified to be deployed to System Test).

Even though it is extremely difficult to generalize about the specifics of the staging and release processes, looking at a few examples should help clarify the concepts. Four broad categories have been chosen to highlight the differences in the staging and release processes: commercial software, embedded systems, Web sites, and internal software components. This is not intended to be an exhaustive list.

Commercial Software

Commercial software release is probably familiar to everyone involved in the software industry. For extremely small systems (such as those that produce a single executable that runs on only one platform), software can be tested easily, and installation involves just copying the executable onto a target machine. Most software systems are more complex; they have many working parts and must be installed on a target machine for final testing.

When a build is complete, the derived objects are staged (in the ClearCase world, derived objects are specific outputs of a build script using clearmake. In general, the output of your build process is staged in components for deployment to the various test environments). These version-controlled objects are then used to create an install area on the network, which can be used to install the software on a target machine and perform the testing. This testing is often referred to as software system testing.

Near the end of the development cycle, a test CD-ROM is created from the staged derived objects, and the installation and testing is performed from the CD-ROM instead of over the network. Usually, there is a bit-for-bit comparison between the files and directories on the CD-ROM and those in the install area used for the system testing. If the CD-ROM is good, the software is ready to enter the release cycle. The CD-ROM becomes the master and is sent to manufacturing, where it is mass-produced, packaged with documentation, shrink-wrapped, and shipped to the customer.

> **NOTE**
> Many commercial software systems today are distributed from a Web site. No physical media is produced; the software is downloaded from a Web site and installed on the target machine. The final testing is done by performing this download/install/test process. Release is performed by making the downloadable software available for customers on a Web site. No manufacturing takes place.

Embedded Systems

Staging and release for embedded systems are different because the software resides in a hardware device. There is no CD-ROM produced and no installation performed. A good example is staging and release for a cellphone.

As for a commercial system, the software is built and staged. For most complex embedded systems, there is some level of software-only system testing. This is done using hardware emulators or test harnesses. After this software-only testing, the staged software is downloaded to the target machine (this time an embedded device) for final system testing.

When testing is complete, one of the staged builds is used by manufacturing to load the hardware. This can be done directly by downloading the software to the hardware device or, in other cases, by creating a hardware chip (just like producing a CD-ROM). This chip can then be mass-produced and used in the manufacturing of the final hardware device.

Some embedded systems have only one version of software. For example, a microwave has one version of the software for its lifetime. If you want some new features, you get a new microwave. Many embedded systems have ways of upgrading the embedded software through any number of methods: CD-ROM, download through a serial port, download over the airwaves, or chip replacement.

> **NOTE**
> For embedded systems that allow software upgrades, it is particularly important to establish traceability from the hardware device to the software source code. That is, given a hardware device (such as a cellphone), you can find out what release of the system is being used. From this release, you can identify the staged derived object files, and from those files, you can identify the right versions of the source code. Traceability from hardware to software source is often where some CM processes are lacking.

Web Sites

Staging and release of Web sites is entirely different from that of embedded and commercial software systems. You might not even think about a Web site in terms of "release," but in terms of "deployment" or "publishing." For basic Web sites with very little dynamic content, all the files that make up the site will already be under version control (at least, they should be). Generally, the directory structure these files are stored in mirrors that of the live Web site. Typically, with these simple, static sites, there are really no build or staging processes. However, this is changing on even simple sites with more dynamic content (such as Java applets).

For more complex sites, build processes are involved. This is particularly true for e-commerce sites that have back-end database systems and for internal corporate sites that provide a Web front end to legacy systems. In these cases, staging is similar to that of commercial software systems: The built pieces of the system are placed under version control and managed along with the source code.

Whether you stage or not, there is still a specific release process. In the case of a Web site, releasing involves copying the files from where they are managed to the live Web site.

The release process for a static, content-only site is easy. Sites with only a few scripts and gizmos also have few problems. However, today many sites have a requirement to remain live 24 hours a day, 7 days a week. These sites are often very complex and have back-end databases, front-end content, and many scripts. One of the interesting release challenges is to figure out how to update these 24×7 sites with no downtime. It is like updating a software system database or user interface while the software is running.

The telecommunications industry has a somewhat similar problem with telephone switches. Phone switches must remain live constantly, just like Web sites; you can't turn them off and upgrade the software. So with many switching systems, the new software is installed while the switch is running. This is an incredibly complex process that is specific to each switching system.

For Web sites, the general solution used today is to provide multiple Web servers to handle the Web site load. Servers are taken down one at a time, upgraded, and brought back online. However, as Web sites get more complex, this might not always be possible: for example, when changes occur to a centralized database back end, making the front end or middleware incompatible.

Let's take a look at this process in more detail with an example promotion life cycle, shown in Figure 10-13. In this example, the software-development and deployment processes occur as follows (note that most of the following processes can be automated):

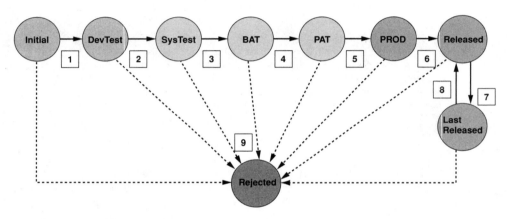

Figure 10-13 Sample release process promotion model.

1. **Initial to DevTest**—The integrator has locked the integration stream of the project and performed a build. Smoke tests have been passed. A new development baseline has been laid down on the development components. This baseline starts at the Initial state. At this point, if the integrator wants this baseline to be used only for development integration, he or she can proceed with unlocking the stream and notifying the team that the baseline is ready to rebase to. If this baseline is in need of further testing by the development testing team (or is deployed to a development test server), the integrator copies the build artifacts from the view onto the development test system, unlocks the stream, and promotes the development baseline to DevTest. At this time, the development QA team gets notified and can proceed to test the build artifacts installed on its test system. This deployment from the build view can simply be a build task to copy the artifacts to the test system. They are not versioned at this time in a staging component. As the testing proceeds in the development area, defects are logged in ClearQuest, triaged, and assigned to developers to be worked on. The process continues as the next build attempt occurs and defects are verified.

2. **DevTest to SysTest**—Eventually, a milestone needs to be met or the development effort is good enough for integration testing with other subsystems. The release build person is

notified that the development baseline in DevTest is ready for SysTest. That person uses the Assembly project of this product for the release build. This Assembly project is rebased to pick up the desired development baseline in the DevTest state. A release build is performed in the Assembly project, and smoke tests are run. If successful, the build output is versioned and packaged into the staging component. A new release candidate baseline is created from within the Assembly project that links the source components with the staging component. The release candidate baseline starts at the Initial state (just like any other baseline). This baseline is then promoted to SysTest. Triggers fire on the change baseline operation that process this request and rebase the SysTest stream of the Assembly project to this new baseline. These triggers also execute a deployment task to physically move the artifacts from the staging component, through a view attached to the SysTest stream, onto the desired system test server. Deployment tools such as Tivoli can be used to manage the deployment process better. ClearCase simply serves up the correct versions of the artifacts through the view to whatever deployment mechanism you have in place.

3. **SysTest to business acceptance test (BAT)**—After the system testing has been performed, defects again can be found and logged in ClearQuest to be worked on. At some point, though, the release candidate will be good enough to pass the system tests. At that point, there could be other testing hurdles in place within your organization. The sample flow shows that the baseline gets promoted to BAT. At this point, the release candidate baseline also gets promoted to BAT. Again, the trigger fires and processes the request, rebases the BAT stream to this baseline, attaches a view, and deploys to the BAT environment. The ClearCase view provides the window into the staging components so that the deployment tasks can pull out the correct artifacts for this test environment. This testing effort verifies the business requirements, legal requirements, and other issues that the release is dealing with. Again, problems could be found and logged. But once the release passes BAT, the baseline gets promoted to PAT.

4. **BAT to production acceptance test (PAT)**—When the baseline has been promoted to PAT, the trigger processes the request, rebases the PAT stream, attaches a view to the stream, deploys to the PAT environment, and notifies the PAT team that a new release is ready for production acceptance testing. In some cases, it might take some time for this team to set up the production test environment or schedule the next slot for testing this release. In that case, the PAT team would perform the promotion when the environment is ready to accept it. This environment mimics the production environment. If issues arise, the baseline can be rejected. Once passed, the baseline is promoted to PROD.

5. **PAT to PROD**—This transition puts the release candidate baseline into production. The PROD state is used to signal the production team that it should deploy the artifacts into production. Again, the production system needs to be readied to accept the new release. The production release team rebases its PROD stream to pick up the release candidate

baseline at the PROD level. It executes the same deployment task to move the artifacts through the production view onto the desired systems using its deployment tool.

6. **PROD to Released**—When the deployment to the production environment is successful and the production environment is running the new release, the release candidate baseline is promoted to Released. There should be only one baseline at the Released level at any given time, so you can always know what baseline is currently in production. Plus, the production stream of the Assembly project selects the configuration that was used to deploy to production.

7. **Released to Last Released**—To facilitate a rollback operation, you want to keep track of the staged artifacts that were in production before you move a new set into production. So, in actuality, the baseline in the Release state gets moved to Last Released before the new release candidate baseline gets moved into production. That is, before you allow the PROD to Released transition to complete, you need to move the Released baseline to Last Released and rebase the last_released stream to this baseline. This way, if there is a problem, you can always use the configuration selected by the last_released stream and redeploy to production, and move the baseline back to Released.

8. **Last Released to Released**—In case something drastic happens in the production environment that your testing did not catch, you need the capability to roll back to the previous release. You don't want to think about what to do; you just want to push the Rollback button. This process rebases the production stream to the Last Released baseline; the triggers fire to execute the deployment task, and the production environment is back to the way it was.

9. **Rejected**—From any state, you can reject a baseline. This prevents it from being used by a project during a rebase operation.

Internal Software Components

In this discussion, "internal software components" refer to components in very large software systems being developed by multiple project teams. Such organizations that arrange themselves along architectural lines might have, for example, a platform group, a core group, or a database group that provides the basic services other development teams reuse. Whatever it is called, that group must stage and release its components for internal development customers. A good example of what gets staged and released is a library file and a set of header files that describe the public interfaces to the library. Other groups do not rebuild these components; they link against them. In fact, in many cases, it might be desirable that other groups not be capable of seeing or modifying the source code for these reusable components.

Staging is exactly the same as in a commercial software system. The build objects are placed under version control. Release is somewhat different, however: The other groups access the released software components directly from the ClearCase VOB. Internally, most teams working on a single software system will be using the same SCM tools. So, copying files to uncontrolled directories or shipping around a set of tarred/zipped archive files does not make sense. Different development teams can simply select the baseline of the staged components they are interested in, and these files will become visible in their working environments.

This approach works well for managing complexity in a large software system. It is also effective for groups that are geographically distributed. See "Architecture-Oriented Project Teams" in Chapter 7, "Managing and Organizing Your ClearCase Projects," and also Chapter 11, "Geographically Distributed Development," for more information.

10.3 Summary

In this chapter, you have seen how typical build and release systems can be put together with ClearCase UCM. A lot of what your organization will do in this area depends upon the type of software you are developing and the frequency of the releases. You also need to consider the time it takes to build your system and any deployment considerations.

By defining a release model and implementing it within ClearCase UCM, you can explicitly understand the requirements and checks and balances in the process. You will understand what it means to promote a baseline from one state to another. And if you understand this, you can explain it to any auditing agency that will want to know in detail about your development and release practices. When you have your integration build, release build, and baselining process documented and working, you can look to automate it to schedule it more frequently or perhaps during off-hours. Hopefully, by putting time and energy into this area of your software development, you will be able to release higher-quality software to your people testing it and, eventually, your customers using it. In the end, this will allow you to either decrease your software-development costs or be able to deliver more releases in the same time frame.

Geographically Distributed Development

Geographically distributed development is the development of software systems by team members who are not located in the same geographic region. This could mean teams distributed at different sites in the same city or in different countries around the world. Although this presents a number of challenges, many companies are finding sound business reasons to do it, including the global nature of their own company, use of third-party components, coordination with third-party software houses, and mergers and acquisitions.

A whole book could be dedicated to this topic. This chapter briefly discusses the organizational, communication, and technical challenges that need to be overcome for success in distributed or geographically dispersed development. This chapter also covers the support for distributed development provided by ClearCase and an add-on product, called ClearCase MultiSite.

This chapter then explores how best to apply ClearCase to three common distributed development scenarios:

- **Multiple teams: producer/consumer**—Multiple project teams are located at different sites that share software components in a producer/consumer relationship. The consumer does not modify the components delivered by the producer.

- **Multiple teams: shared source code**—Multiple project teams at different sites are modifying the same shared software.

- **Single team: distributed members**—A single project exists with team members at different sites working on shared software components. This differs from the previous two scenarios in that the distributed members are not organized into a remote team. Instead, there are many individuals working remotely (perhaps from home).

The chapter finishes with a brief discussion of other uses for ClearCase MultiSite.

11.1   Distributed Development Challenges

Developing a single software system with distributed teams is no easy task. Organizational, communication, and technological issues must all be addressed to succeed. This section covers these issues in general. Later sections cover specific approaches to doing distributed development and discuss how each approach relates to these three challenges.

11.1.1   Organization

Organization deals with how team members are grouped into projects, who is responsible for leading the team, how multiple teams are interrelated, who is responsible for making project-wide decisions, and, who ultimately, is responsible for the success or failure of the project. There are probably an infinite number of ways to organize development efforts into projects—an infinite number of ways to assign team members to these projects, to distribute those team members around the globe, and to divide the work among team members. Interestingly, the managerial structure within an organization might not reflect the project team organization. The first issue a project manager faces is how to organize the available members of the development staff into projects.

In distributed development environments, often there are different cultures and different development styles. This is easily seen between sites located in two different countries, but it is also true within a country. These cultural differences introduce additional and sometimes subtle obstacles to attaining success.

These key facts need to be determined and understood by all team members:

- Who is responsible for the overall success of the project?
- Who is responsible for the managerial issues the project encounters?
- Who is responsible for the overall system architecture?
- Who are the team members on this project?

Distributed development efforts tend to be large in scope. So, in general, there will be many smaller projects, with the teams from each collaborating on an overall project, which we'll refer to as the "superproject." All members of the collaborating teams should be able to answer the questions just listed about the superproject.

In our experience, many distributed development projects fail because they do not establish this superproject organizational structure between teams working at two or more sites. Without this infrastructure, the tendency for the project teams is to make independent architectural and technological decisions. Ultimately, this makes the system more difficult or impossible to integrate. Even if integration can be done, the lack of overall direction could make project boundaries visible to the end users through the look and feel and other subtle behavior of the resulting system.

Smaller projects that have team members that are geographically dispersed might be able to get away without the superproject organizational structure, but the requirement for rapid and robust communication among team members remains.

11.1.2 Communication

The second challenge of distributed development is communication. Because the teams are geographically separated, communication is impaired. Even today, with e-mail, instant messaging, fax, voice mail, and videoconferencing, two teams that are not at the same location have far fewer communication channels. The value of the community environment established by people working in one site cannot be underestimated. Therefore, it is important to maximize the teams' ability to communicate while minimizing the amount of day-to-day communication necessary for teams to have with each other to succeed.

To do this, the teams must have a common vision of how the system will work, expressed in an agreed-upon system architecture. Randomly dividing the features to be developed between separate teams at different sites is rarely successful.

Establish a system architecture up front. Then divide that architecture into components that can be separately developed, and assign each component to one co-located team. In this way, the communication channels must be strong during architectural definition and system integration, but during the development of each individual component, the only time the teams must communicate is when the component interfaces require clarification or modification.

Beyond establishing and communicating a system architecture, each project team must have a formal distributed mechanism for reporting and tracking change requests and defects. Such a mechanism allows teams to internally track change requests and defects that apply to their products and allows consumer teams to submit change requests and defects to their respective producer teams.

11.1.3 Technology

Distributed development involves two technological tools: implementation technologies and development technologies. Implementation technologies are those used in the creation of the system being developed (for example, the operating system, GUI components, languages used, and database). Development technologies are those used to establish an effective distributed software-development environment (such as the SCM tool, the defect-tracking tool, the compiler, and the IDE).

Implementation Technologies

The technology used in the software system should be clearly specified as part of the system architecture. It is certainly possible for different teams to use widely differing technologies to develop their component pieces of the system, but this could significantly affect many aspects of the resulting system, such as usability, ease of installation, ease of administration, and look and feel. It is important to establish some agreement between teams on what technologies and standards will be used. When these technologies differ, there should be sound business reasons for these differences and an understanding of how these technological decisions might impact the final system.

For example, let's say that two teams are developing a Web-based application. When it comes to choosing the language, one team wants to use Java and the other wants to use Visual Basic (VB). They might each have sound reasons for their choices. One team might have significant experience in Visual Basic and has developed a set of core components used to develop similar applications. The Java team might think that VB won't meet the functional demands it believes the system is likely to require. Left to their own devices, both teams could develop separate components that communicate through an agreed-upon interface. However, the look and feel and the portability of the overall system would be jeopardized.

So, within the system architecture definition, you should nail down the technologies used to implement the system early on and demand commonality, unless there are sound business reasons for deviating from this approach. The following are some things to consider:

- Target operating system and version
- GUI presentation and GUI toolkit
- Database and database version
- User-exposed application interfaces (such as COM and CORBA)
- Communications (such as TCP/IP, HTTP, WebDAV, and SOAP)
- Data interchange format (such as XML)

Development Technologies

The second technological decision facing distributed development teams is what technology will be used to build and manage the development of the software system. This is often referred to as the software-development environment. You must determine the tools and processes your software teams will use and also ensure that the tools you employ can support distributed development.

Although it is possible and sometimes necessary to use different software-development environments, the number of issues your distributed teams must face will be greatly reduced if you can choose one set of tools and processes. Arriving at consensus between distributed teams is almost always a painful process, but achieving this will minimize the number of issues the project will face otherwise.

For example, if you use two different defect-tracking tools, it becomes more difficult for the project manager to determine defect closure rates for the overall superproject. Even worse, if each team is using a different process for resolving defects, you must figure out how these processes relate. Communicating defects between teams requires knowledge of two defect-tracking tools and processes. Decisions such as what compiler (and what version of the compiler) to use can impact how easy it is to integrate, build, and release a system developed by multiple teams.

Try to achieve a common set of development technologies early on and demand commonality unless there are sound business reasons for deviating from the homogenous approach. The following are some things to consider:

- SCM tools and processes
- Defect and change-request tracking/reporting (tools and processes)
- Build technology (such as compiler and make)
- Project-management tools

Finally, you must ensure that the tools you choose are capable of supporting distributed development. Many tools claim that they can, but you need to carefully explore what capabilities they really provide: You cannot afford to discover deficiencies in your development tools near the end of a release cycle as you try to integrate the efforts of multiple teams. (Note that if you are waiting until the end of the development cycle to integrate, you are probably already in trouble.)

In terms of software configuration management, here are a few things to look for:

- The tools should be capable of supporting a few geographically dispersed developers as well as larger co-located teams of developers.
- For larger co-located teams of developers, there should be an automated, secure means of replicating and synchronizing development and defect/change-request data between sites.
- The tools should make the fact that the team is distributed as transparent as possible. The more teams feel as if they are working at the same site, the better the communication and coordination will be.
- There must be a clear distinction between which site currently owns which parts of the shared data.
- Flexibility, flexibility, flexibility. Distributed development between two teams is great, but how about three teams? How about five teams worldwide that work in a round-robin fashion as the sun rises and sets?

11.2   How ClearCase Supports Distributed Development

ClearCase supports five technological solutions for remote developers. Each approach has its own characteristics that make it the right choice in different scenarios. The five options are as follows:

- **Remote terminal or desktop access**—Logging into the primary site from a remote location (for example, home)
- **Remote client access**—Using client software to access the primary site from a remote location
- **Web access**—Using the Web and HTTP protocol to access the primary site
- **Disconnected use**—Working disconnected from the network with a local view
- **Local access**—Copying VOBs and keeping changes in sync so that all work is done locally, regardless of site

11.2.1   Remote Terminal or Desktop Access

Remote terminal or desktop use is simple and can be accomplished in one of two ways. The remote developer logs into the primary site using a terminal or terminal emulator and works remotely. In this scenario, all aspects of ClearCase are readily available for use because the developer is technically working at the primary site. The drawbacks to this approach are that if a terminal interface is being used, only the command-line interface to the SCM tool can be used, with no GUI support. The primary advantage is that little or no additional infrastructure is needed.

The remote developer uses a remote desktop or windowing tool and works remotely. Again, in this scenario, all aspects of ClearCase are readily available for use because the developer is again technically working at the primary site. The drawback of this approach is that the network connection between the remote developer and the primary site must be fast enough to allow for a quick transport of the GUI data inherent in desktop and windowed environments. This approach usually requires some additional infrastructure to support a remote desktop or windowed environment. This can become even more complex if the remote connection must work through corporate firewalls.

Each scenario relies on establishing secure, reliable, and reasonably fast connections between the remote developer and the primary site.

Remote terminal or desktop use is illustrated in Figure 11-1.

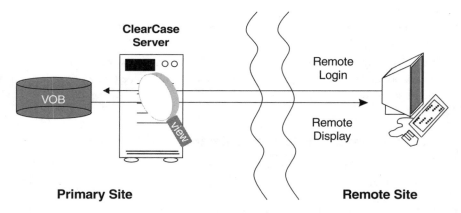

Figure 11-1   Remote access.

11.2.2   Remote Client Access

In this approach, the ClearCase Remote Client is used to perform SCM operations and access versioned elements at the remote, primary site. Because the ClearCase Remote Client (CCRC) is a client application, it must be installed on a machine before it can be used. After being installed, it communicates with a ClearCase Web Server at the primary site to access versioned data and perform SCM actions. The CCRC also enables you to access SCM actions from within the popular Eclipse IDE and eventually from within other IDEs, such as Visual Studio .NET.

ClearCase Remote Client access is illustrated in Figure 11-2.

11.2.3   Web Access

Similar to Remote Client Access, the ClearCase Web client is used to access versioned elements and perform SCM operations on data located at a remote, primary site. Because the ClearCase

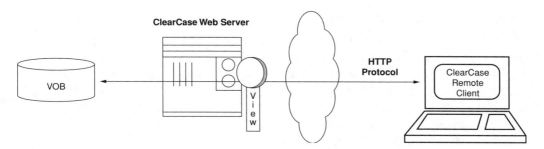

Figure 11-2   ClearCase Remote Client.

Web client doesn't require installation of a separate client application, it can be used in an emergency, allowing a developer to access files from home or from another office even though no ClearCase client software is installed.

The primary drawback to this approach is that the ClearCase Web client does not allow integration with popular IDEs. Although you can still use the IDEs for development, whenever you want to perform an SCM action, you need to interact with a Web browser to accomplish that action. An additional drawback to the ClearCase Remote Client is that it doesn't provide you with access to all the ClearCase features that are available. Only the most common SCM operations can be used.

Web access is illustrated in Figure 11-3.

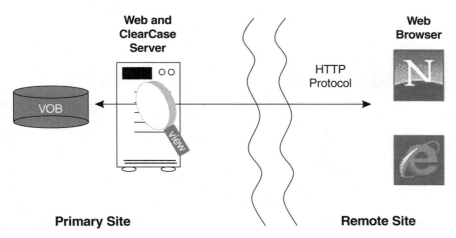

Figure 11-3   Web access.

Web access also works very well for occasional ClearCase users even when located at the same site. For example, if you have a number of users who need to browse design documents stored in ClearCase, rather than installing ClearCase on each machine, they can simply use a Web browser to access the files.

11.2.4   Disconnected Use

With the disconnected use approach, a user connects to the network from a remote site, loads a snapshot view, disconnects from the network, and then works on the downloaded files. Disconnected use is similar to Web access use, in that the files are downloaded to a local machine. However, in this case, a full ClearCase client is installed on the user's machine. While connected, the user has full access to ClearCase features. This approach could also be described as remote use while the network connection is down. It works only with snapshot views (see "Workspaces: Snapshot and Dynamic Views" in Chapter 4, "A Functional Overview of ClearCase Objects"). Disconnected use can be problematic for large systems with a large number of elements. Download/update time might discourage updates and cause developers to drift out of sync with project sources. However, the advantage of disconnected use is that it clearly supports the laptop user who is often away from the office. Disconnected use is illustrated in Figure 11-4.

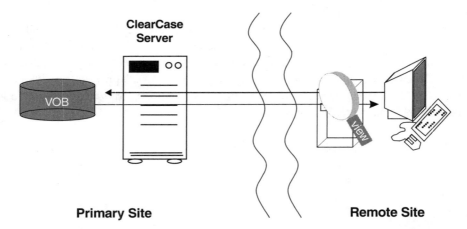

Figure 11-4   Disconnected use.

11.2.5   Local Access

Local access removes barriers for the remote developer while adding some administrative requirements. In local access, the repositories are replicated and synchronized exactly as in the multiteam scenarios. The setup and administration of the replicas are the additional administrative cost. The benefits are that developers no longer need to think about whether they are working locally or remotely, connected or not. They work locally all the time, and performance is not reliant on network bandwidth. The data they produce and operations they perform are then replayed automatically and asynchronously back at the primary site. Similarly, actions and changes happening at the primary site are replayed at the remote site. In this way, developers do not need to consider where they are located. Local use is illustrated in Figure 11-5. Local use is supported by a ClearCase add-on product called ClearCase MultiSite.

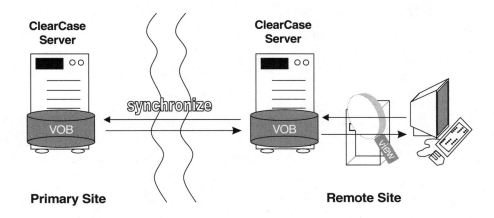

Figure 11-5 Local access.

11.2.6 What Is the ClearCase Remote Client (CCRC)?

The ClearCase Remote Client (CCRC) is based on the Eclipse platform, which is an IDE that is an open platform for tool integration. As noted earlier, the CCRC is a ClearCase client application that must be installed on a computer before it can be used. The CCRC uses the HTTP protocol to communicate with a ClearCase Web server located at the primary site to access versioned data and to perform SCM actions. This is advantageous because the HTTP protocol is often available outside a company's firewall, whereas arbitrary TCP/IP connections generally are not.

Two manifestations of the CCRC exist. The first manifestation is as a standalone client, based on the Eclipse Rich Client Platform. This standalone client is suitable for people who need only remote SCM functionality and have no need for the full Eclipse IDE.

Figure 11-6 illustrates the standalone version of the ClearCase Remote Client.

The other manifestation of CCRC is as an SCM adapter for Eclipse that "plugs into" an existing Eclipse IDE installation. This is suitable for people who are already using an Eclipse-based tool, such as the Rational Application Developer, for development and want access to ClearCase SCM functions from within that pre-existing Eclipse environment.

Figure 11-7 illustrates the Eclipse SCM adapter version of the ClearCase Remote Client.

Both the standalone and SCM adapter versions of the CCRC are optimized to support those ClearCase functions commonly used by developers. These functions include base ClearCase and UCM functions such as view management, UCM project joins, check-in, check-out, un-check-out, compare, merge, deliver, and rebase. More advanced functions such as renaming, removing (actually, rmname) ClearCase elements and interactive triggers, and support for the ClearQuest integrations with base ClearCase and UCM are also supported by the CCRC. These advanced functions set the ClearCase remote client apart from the ClearCase Web client.

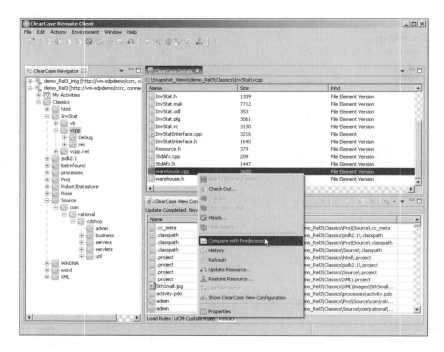

Figure 11-6   Standalone version of the ClearCase Remote Client.

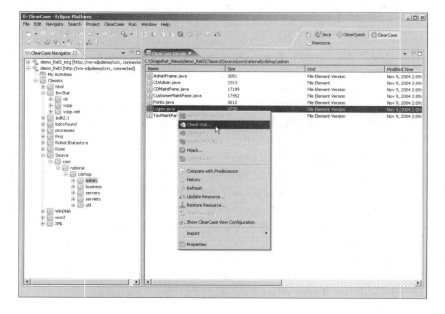

Figure 11-7   The Eclipse SCM adapter version of the ClearCase Remote Client.

11.2.7   What Is ClearCase MultiSite?

This overview of ClearCase MultiSite is brief and intended to familiarize readers with the additional capabilities required to support MultiSite development. Setup and administration of ClearCase MultiSite is covered in the ClearCase documentation set.

In ClearCase, repositories are called *versioned object bases*, or VOBs, as discussed in Chapter 4. In a MultiSite scenario, VOBs are replicated or copied so that a copy of the VOB lives at each site. These copies are called *replicas*. The CM administrator creates replicas and then sets up the synchronization pattern and schedule. Changes made to one VOB are sent to the other, and vice versa, on a regular schedule. This could be nightly, hourly, or even every 5 minutes. MultiSite sends only the changes made between synchronizations, thus reducing network traffic and minimizing performance impact.

As in networking, the set of replicas and how they are synchronized is extremely flexible. The most common patterns are one-way read-only, two-way peer-to-peer, star, and circular (see Figure 11-8).

To avoid contention problems and ensure that synchronization can be completely automatic, MultiSite supports a notion called *mastership*. Each object in a VOB is mastered at a particular site. If you have mastership, you can modify the object. If not, you cannot modify it. So, for example, for a branch type mastered at site A, only people at site A can create branches of this type and check out elements on these branches. Developers at site B can check out only on site B

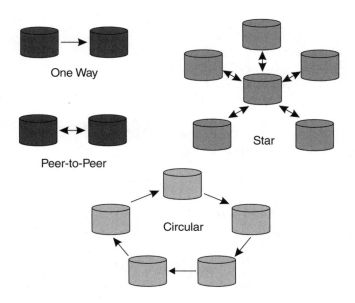

One Way

Peer-to-Peer

Star

Circular

Figure 11-8   Common MultiSite replication patterns.

branches, which are mastered at site B. Alternatively, you can set up schemes that hand off mastership of objects after a specific time or after specific operations. Changes between sites are integrated by merging changes from one branch to another (see Figure 11-9).

ClearCase UCM provides explicit support for MultiSite by removing the need for developers to understand the underlying branching structure. The following sections discuss three approaches to geographically distributed development and how ClearCase and ClearCase MultiSite can be used to support them. These are the producer/consumer, shared source code, and distributed members scenarios.

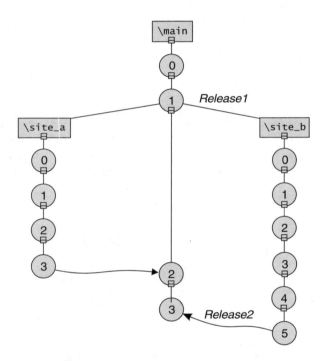

Figure 11-9   Branch mastership and integrating changes.

11.2.8   What Is ClearQuest MultiSite?

As in the overview of ClearCase MultiSite, this discussion of ClearQuest MultiSite is brief and meant to familiarize readers with the fundamental concepts associated with the use of replicated databases containing change-request information. Setup and administration of ClearQuest MultiSite is covered in the ClearQuest documentation set. See Chapter 12, "Change Request Management and ClearQuest," for a discussion of the ClearQuest Change Request management tool itself.

Just as ClearCase has repositories (VOBs) that contain data associated with version-controlled elements, ClearQuest has repositories that contain data that corresponds to change requests. These are called user databases. Beyond that, however, ClearQuest has repositories that contain information about the structure and behaviors (schemas) that are to be applied to the data contained in the user databases. These are called schema databases. For ClearQuest to work, both the ClearQuest user database and its associated schema must be present. It follows, then, that any mechanism to replicate the change-request information that is managed by ClearQuest must be capable of replicating both the appropriate schema databases and their associated user databases, as illustrated in Figure 11-10.

Note that in Figure 11-10 not all user databases associated with a schema database need to be replicated. But all schema databases associated with replicated user databases must be replicated.

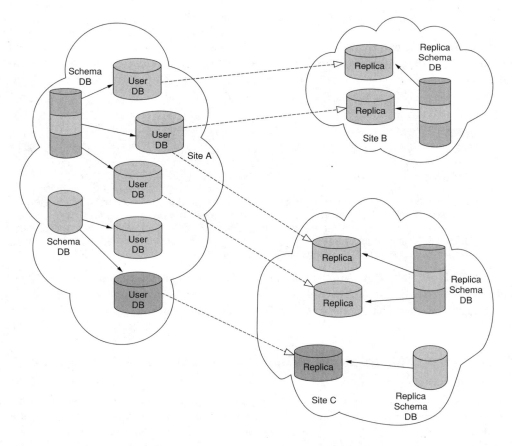

Figure 11-10   ClearQuest MultiSite replicates the ClearQuest schema databases and their associated user databases.

The ClearQuest MultiSite Administration manual provides detailed guidance on how to organize and replicate ClearQuest schema and user databases.

Also as in ClearCase MultiSite, ClearQuest MultiSite makes use of the notion of object mastership to prevent contention when changes are made to individual change request records. In particular, only one replica at a time can modify a given change-request record. Mastership of records can be manipulated manually by interacting with a ClearQuest native or Web client, or automatically with ClearQuest hooks that are executed when, say, a record changes state. This mastership scheme allows teams with non-co-located groups or individuals to work together with a controlled mechanism for governing the flow of work in the project. Object mastership in Clear-Quest is not limited to change-request records; it extends also to other objects, such as queries and the schema database itself. The mastership of an object is initially set to be the site where it was created. Object mastership is visible to users in the case of those ClearQuest objects with which a user interacts, such as change-request records or queries.

For example, consider a change-request record created at site A. If a user at site B tries to change that record, he will be unable to do so until the mastership of that record is changed from site A to site B. A user from site B could use the ClearQuest Web interface to log into site A to change the mastership of the affected change request record. Then after sites A and B are synchronized, the user at site B will be able to make desired changes to the record.

> **NOTE**
>
> As noted earlier, if a ClearQuest user database is replicated, its associated ClearQuest schema database must also be replicated. Because of the tight linkage between a ClearQuest schema database and its associated user databases, care must be taken to maintain the integrity of that linkage when the schema database is replicated. A best practice is to limit schema changes to one site that is the "master" of the schema database. In addition, you should rigorously adhere to the procedures for introducing a new schema version to a ClearQuest MulitSite environment, as described in the Clear-Quest MultiSite documentation.

Figure 11-11 illustrates a simple example of how a distributed team can use ClearQuest MultiSite.

Note that, in this example, the development team is at one site and the QA team is at a different site. In practice, these sites could be in adjacent buildings or in different parts of the world.

11.2.9   Using ClearCase MultiSite and ClearQuest MultiSite Together

The integration between ClearCase and ClearQuest involves linking the ClearCase VOB and the ClearQuest user databases. This linkage is done automatically by the integration, and that linkage is preserved when ClearCase MultiSite and ClearQuest MultiSite are used to replicate those databases. It is important that this linkage be consistent in all the MultiSite database replicas. The best way to make sure that these databases remain linked consistently is to establish a synchronization schedule that causes the ClearCase VOB database replicas and the ClearQuest database replicas to be synchronized at the same time.

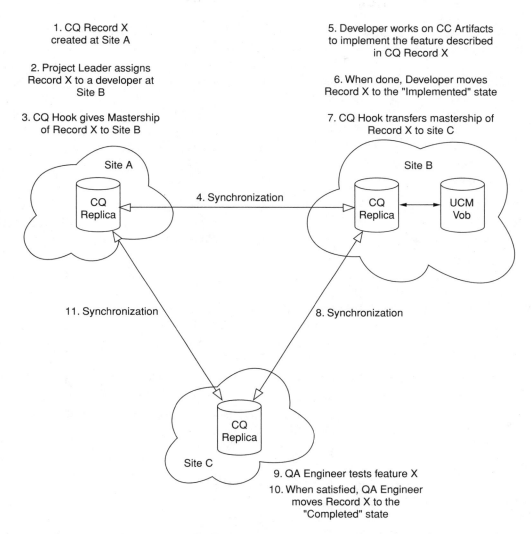

1. CQ Record X
created at Site A

2. Project Leader assigns
Record X to a developer at
Site B

3. CQ Hook gives Mastership
of Record X to Site B

5. Developer works on CC Artifacts
to implement the feature described
in CQ Record X

6. When done, Developer moves
Record X to the "Implemented" state

7. CQ Hook transfers mastership of
Record X to site C

Site A

CQ
Replica

4. Synchronization

Site B

CQ
Replica

UCM
Vob

11. Synchronization

8. Synchronization

CQ
Replica

Site C

9. QA Engineer tests feature X

10. When satisfied, QA Engineer
moves Record X to the
"Completed" state

Figure 11-11   An illustration of how a distributed team can use ClearQuest MultiSite.

UCM and ClearQuest MultiSite

The tight UCM integration between ClearCase and ClearQuest is also affected by the mastership status of ClearQuest records, as described next.

Working on Activities

When a developer checks out a ClearCase-controlled artifact, he or she is required to denote what activity is being worked on. This list is generated from a preinstalled ClearQuest query called UCMCustomQuery1. In a ClearQuest-enabled project in which ClearQuest MultiSite is being used, this query does not filter out nonlocally mastered ClearQuest records from this list; instead, it annotates the list to show ClearQuest record mastership status for that activity.

In this scenario, if a developer selects a ClearQuest activity record that is mastered at a site other than the one at which the developer is performing the check-out operation, the UCM integration displays an error message because the ClearQuest record cannot be modified unless it is mastered at the site where the check-out operation is occurring. A common way to change mastership of the ClearQuest record to allow such a check-out is to use the ClearQuest Web client to log into the ClearQuest site where the desired record is mastered and transfer mastership of that record to the desired site. After that is done and the ClearQuest replicas are synchronized, the check-out can be performed.

Delivering Activities

Recall the discussion of UCM project policies in Chapter 6, "Project Management in ClearCase"; two UCM project polices relate directly to the use of ClearQuest MultiSite:

- **Transfer ClearQuest Mastership Before Delivery**—When enabled, this UCM project policy causes UCM to examine the target stream of the UCM delivery and to transfer mastership of the ClearQuest activity records that are being delivered to the site that is master of the target stream of the delivery. This policy works in conjunction with the Transition to Complete After Delivery project policy, to allow it to work correctly if the target stream of the deliver operation is mastered by a remote site.

- **Transfer ClearQuest Mastership After Delivery**—When this policy is enabled, mastership of ClearQuest activity records is transferred back to the site that mastered them before the delivery operation was started. This policy is a convenient way to "undo" the Transfer ClearQuest Mastership Before Delivery policy after the deliver operation completes.

Use of these policies allow ClearQuest-enabled UCM deliver operations to work correctly when the target stream of the delivery is mastered by a site that is not the same as where the deliver operation is initiated. In the case of such a "remote" or "posted" delivery, the ClearCase and ClearQuest replicas at the local and remote sites must be synchronized before the delivery can be completed.

11.3   Multiple Teams: Producer/Consumer Scenario

In the producer/consumer model, the geographically distributed project teams produce or consume components of the overall system. Only the producer team can modify a component. Projects that consume components do not make any modifications to the components they consume.

Sharing is accomplished by first defining the architecture of the system. When the architecture is defined, you then assign each component of the system to a single, locally situated project team.

> **NOTE**
>
> If projects at a site develop more then one component, the components chosen for that site should be cohesive, if possible. They should also have very little coupling (particularly build dependencies) with components being developed at other sites.

The simplest producer/consumer model is based on a system composed of two software components with two project teams located at different sites. One project produces a software component; the second project consumes that software component, incorporating it into the final system. For example, let's say that one project team is in Sydney and another is in San Francisco. The Sydney team is producing a software component that provides all the database services and isolates the application from any specific database technology. The San Francisco team builds the final application on top of this database component (see Figure 11-12).

Of course, most software systems are much more complex. A simple but more realistic example might be a multitier architecture in which there are one or two commercially available databases, a database abstraction layer, a middle tier that captures the business logic, and a client layer that provides the user interfaces (see Figure 11-13).

Figure 11-12   Producer/consumer model.

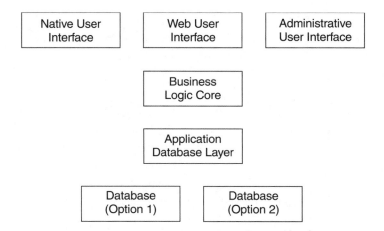

Figure 11-13   A simple architecture.

A very large software system might have hundreds of components, all being provided by different third-party suppliers or other groups internal to the company. Each of these groups might be working at different sites. It is also possible to have a producer/consumer supply chain in which project B consumes a component produced by project A, and project C consumes the component produced by project B (see Figure 11-14).

The producer/consumer approach to distributed development is very productive and has the least integration-related problems associated with it. Organizationally, each project team has a project leader, and the entire team is located at a single site. This makes management of the project more efficient and effective.

The basic idea here is to minimize the number of dependencies between project teams. The key is to break these dependencies along architectural lines. To do this, there must be a well-defined system architecture, and the system must be decomposed into components. The architecture describes these components and their interfaces. These components are then assigned to project teams, who produce their components and consume components produced by other teams. Ultimately, one team holds the responsibility for consuming all other components and integrating them into the final software system.

The key management and organization challenge inherent in the producer/consumer approach is establishing an effective means of defining and evolving the architecture and component interfaces. This is best done by establishing a cross–project/site architecture team. But—and this is a big *but*—there should be a clearly defined chief architect who has the authority to make the final decisions on all debated architectural issues. Likewise, it is usually necessary to establish a single program manager who has responsibility for overall management of all projects and who can resolve personnel, organizational, process, and cultural issues that might come up

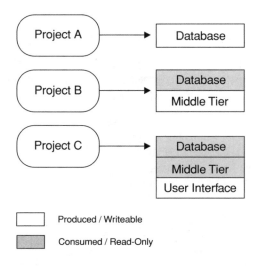

Figure 11-14   A producer/consumer supply chain.

between project teams. The big benefit of this approach is that after the architecture has been defined and the interfaces between major components have been clearly articulated, the various project teams can work in relative isolation to produce their components.

Technically, three issues are involved from a software-configuration management standpoint. First, you must be able to identify a version of a component. Because a component is made up of many elements, you must select one version of each element and identify it. ClearCase refers to this version of a component as a component baseline. Second, you must have a means to reliably and efficiently deliver the components from one project team to another over a potentially low-bandwidth or unreliable network. Third, you must ensure early and regular integration between components to eliminate the risk that a major design error exists in the architecture. This means that each project team should plan first to produce an early baseline of a component that stubs out the external interfaces. This baseline implements the interface without implementing the full functionality behind the interface. Consuming teams can use this to begin testing the interface and early functionality.

This third point leads to the final aspect of managing a distributed development project: iteration or integration planning. The overall program manager must establish an integration plan for all project teams. This plan must identify key project iterations (milestones), what component baselines must be delivered at each iteration, project dependencies, and what functionality will be demonstrable. This enables each team's project leader to plan his or her development accordingly. It also enables the overall project manager to encourage early integration, assess overall project status, and facilitate communication between the teams.

11.3.1   Supporting Producer/Consumer Teams

Supporting the producer/consumer model comes almost for free after you pay the cost of Multi-Site administration. That is, after you have set up the VOBs, created the replicas, and established the automated synchronization, it all just works (he says with a smile). To implement a secure producer/consumer relationship, you should do one of two things: adopt the UCM model for both teams, or use the correct configuration specifications and VOB layout.

11.3.2   How UCM Supports the Producer/Consumer Model

UCM provides direct support for the producer/consumer model. Let's take the simple example just described to explain how it works (see Figure 11-7). We have the Sydney team producing the database and the San Francisco team producing the rest of the application while consuming the database from the Sydney team.

The CM administrator configures the replication environment. First, he creates a replica of the project VOB containing the project and component information. Second, he creates a replica of the VOB that contains the database deliverables. (This could be the database source's VOB or a separate database deliverable VOB, depending on the staging strategy, the build strategy, and the relationship between the teams [see "Staging, Deployment, and Release " in Chapter 10, "Building, Baselining, and Release Deployment"].) In this case, there are two projects: the database project and the system project. Both physically reside in a single, replicated project VOB. A database component would also be created.

When the system project was created in San Francisco, the project manager would see the database component and its available baselines on the pick list when declaring components for the system project (see Chapter 6 for more details). When a component was selected, the project leader would indicate that this is a read-only component for the San Francisco–based system project team. ClearCase UCM handles the details from there, making the file versions visible and ensuring that they cannot be modified.

11.3.3   How Base ClearCase Supports the Producer/Consumer Model

If you are not using UCM, there are a variety of ways to accomplish a producer/consumer model on your own. The two things you need to ensure are that the right versions of the files and directories are available and that they cannot be modified. As with UCM, the CM administrator must set up and replicate the VOBs containing the database files.

After this is done, the administrator must ensure that the configuration specification (config spec) used by all San Francisco–based developers is set appropriately. This can be done by telling developers what config rules to set, providing a template for them to use, or writing some scripts to set it for them. Either way, the correct configuration specification rule would be as follows:

```
element    <VOB root path>/...   LABEL -nocheckout
```

Here, `<VOB root path>` lists the path to the root directory containing all the database elements, and `LABEL` is the label type that has been applied to the appropriate versions of all the elements. The `-nocheckout` part of this rule declares that any versions of files selected by this rule should not allow check-outs, for example:

```
element    /vobs/database/...   RELEASE3 -nocheckout
```

You may list multiple rules to cover files not all stored in the same place or under the same root directory. You may also list subdirectories of a VOB. (Detailed configuration-specification rule syntax can be found in the ClearCase product documentation.)

Three notes of caution are warranted when setting up your own config specs to support this scenario. First, if you ever plan to adopt UCM, all elements in a component should exist under one root directory. Second, although you can specify a directory that is not at the VOB root, it will take a bit longer for ClearCase to search for and find the right versions. If you have too many of these rules in a configuration specification, it can affect dynamic view performance. Third, if you are working in a heterogeneous environment and use VOB-rooted paths in your config specs, the configuration specifications must be written differently for UNIX and Windows. For example, the database VOB might be mounted under `/vobs/db` on UNIX. For Windows access, it is under `\db`, so dynamic views might access the VOB from `z:\db`. When a VOB is specified in a config spec, the UNIX version would look like the following:

```
element    /vobs/db/...        RELEASE2
```

the equivalent Windows config spec would look like the following:

```
element      \db\...                RELEASE2
```

CLEARCASE PRO TIP

An alternative to following strict tag conventions or maintaining two config specs is to use VOB tag-neutral format. Instead of specifying the VOB tag in the config spec, you specify the VOB family ID number. This can be found by using the following:

```
prompt> cleartool lsvob -l <vobtag>
```

The VOB family ID number is found under the `Vob` family `uuid`: heading. It is a long string of digits.

```
prompt> cleartool lsvob -l /vobs/example
Tag: /vobs/example
...
Vob   family   uuid:    0c53996a.8faa11ce.a28f.00:01:72:33:a3:f6
...
```

VOB tag format:

```
element   /vobs/database/...RELEASE2
```

VOB tag-neutral format:

```
element  [0c53996a.8faa11ce.a28f.00:01:72:33:a3:f6]/...RELEASE2
```

11.3.4   Producer/Consumer Summary

The producer/consumer model is easy to establish and manage, and has a strong likelihood of success, given a common system architecture. You should do the following:

- Define a system architecture and assign architectural components to co-located teams.
- Assign a common architect, who is responsible for developing the architecture and making the final decisions on architectural issues.
- Assign a common overall program manager, who is responsible for defining an overall project-integration plan and tracking the progress of each project iteration.

Each individual project team is responsible for producing the assigned component functionality for each project iteration. One system project is responsible for consuming, integrating, and testing the final deliverable system.

11.4   Multiple Teams: Shared Source Code Scenario

In the producer/consumer model, the consumer does not modify the components that are produced. Now let's examine the case in which multiple teams are working on components that may be modified by any team at any site. When two or more teams are modifying the same set of source code in parallel, the development and integration processes are more complicated if your objective is to maintain a common code base and not diverge from it. Doing this when the teams are located at the same site is difficult. Geographically distributed teams make it even more complicated.

Because of this complexity, it is best to avoid the shared source code scenario, if at all possible, and use the producer/consumer scenario. In the real world, this is not always possible or practical. Therefore, optimally, some combination of the producer/consumer model and the shared source code model would be employed.

In a number of legitimate situations, you need to support shared source code. A number of legacy problems also can lead to the shared source code model as the only solution. Many of these problems are avoidable if detected early. A number of situations that could cause you to support shared source code with distributed teams are listed here. Some of these are similar, and often you will find more than one of these in play at any given site.

- The system architecture is monolithic or brittle. If the system architecture is monolithic or brittle, it becomes impossible to define components on any functional boundary. Because the system cannot be decomposed, the development teams cannot be assigned pieces of the system that do not have a high degree of coupling.

- The system is in maintenance mode. If the system is fairly old and most work being performed is maintenance work, it is often easier to think in terms of adding features even if those features span architectural boundaries. Sometimes maintenance team sizes are smaller, as compared to new development, so dividing the work by components is not always practical.

- The organization favors a feature-based approach. A feature-based approach is often applied during system maintenance. It assigns features to individuals or teams even if those features cross architectural boundaries. The individual or team is responsible for implementing the feature, regardless of what code is touched. Organizations that favor this approach require developers to have a broad knowledge of the entire system.

- It just happened that way. In many cases, shared code just happens. One team needs some of the code from another team and just takes a copy. In this case, each team modifies all parts of the code, but there are essentially multiple variants of the same code evolving in different groups. Inevitably, this leads to costly project delays during integration or when the receiving teams want to incorporate further changes made by the original team.

- There are remote porting/platform teams. This case is slightly different, and it is a very legitimate and unavoidable scenario for shared source code. In this case, both teams work on the shared source code. One team produces new functionality, and the second makes secondary changes. Typically, the second team is porting the product to a new platform, making changes to support a different language, or both.

This case comes close to a producer/consumer relationship because it is largely one-way. However, to optimize future porting efforts, it is often a good idea to incorporate changes made by the porting/platform team into the primary team's source code base.

- You deliver source code to your customer. In this case, "you" may be a software house that delivers components to an outside party, which incorporates or modifies the components for use in its own products. In this case, your only concern is that you know your customer will need to integrate future changes from you with its own changes. Using a common SCM tool with a replicated repository will significantly reduce problems in the future instead of following a throw-it-over-the-wall approach.

- A third party delivers source code to you. This is similar to the previous point, but in this case, you are on the receiving end of third-party source code that you will modify. Again, it is to your benefit to encourage the third-party vendor to use the same SCM tool as you do. If not, you need a way to capture and componentize the source code you are receiving so that you can treat the third party as a remote development team.

- There is no common core team. Ideally, when there is common core code used to build different products, there should be a separate team that develops and internally releases this core code. In many cases, there is no such team, so multiple product teams make modifications to the shared code. This case is easier to eliminate if the architecture is such that the interfaces to this common piece can be easily identified and the build dependencies can be reduced (for example, a common library can be constructed).

Organizationally, in a shared source scenario, you can say that there is no relationship between system architecture and the teams developing the system. However, the farther the feature view of the system, the team organization, and the system architecture are from being aligned, the more likely it is that your system and its architecture will become brittle and monolithic. This increases the cost of maintenance and reduces your capability to add new features to the system.

Look closely for the shared source code scenario in hiding. For one large customer one of the authors worked with, the project teams were organized architecturally. There was a core team, a database team, a server team, and several application teams. However, any team was allowed to modify any source. This meant that the application teams could modify the source in the core. Basically, this was a shared source code scenario in hiding.

Supporting shared source code scenarios provides a great deal of flexibility for your organization, at the cost of requiring significant tooling and additional integration work. It is vital that the overall project leader do integration planning, defining points in time when the shared source is to be integrated. In shared source development, this integration is likely to take longer than it does in a producer/consumer model. Additionally, if it is not planned, the code streams can often diverge for a long time. The longer they diverge, the more difficult integration becomes.

For example, at a large telecommunications firm, two project teams produced two different products starting from a common core set of source code. When each team had a separate copy of the original source code, it quickly diverged. At one point, one team needed new functionality in the core that had been developed by the other team. It took three months for the entire development team to merge the core to a common code base and establish the necessary tooling and processes to ensure that it did not diverge again. This was a full three of development time lost, which could mean missing a critical market window in this industry.

The shared source code scenario need not conform to any specific architecture. That is, if you have a monolithic system or a system in maintenance, you can simply divide the work by feature/fix among the teams. This is at the cost of lost architectural integrity and a more complex integration cycle. Architectural integrity can be compromised unknowingly because all source code can be changed. Integration is more complex because of feature-level integration. Generally, how each feature of a release is to work with other features is not well specified; therefore, problems are often caught only at integration time.

The shared source code scenario cannot be easily established without the right technical infrastructure. ClearCase MultiSite provides the support to make shared source development possible. The key technological aspects are replication and synchronization of the repository (VOB), explicit mastership of data and elements, and the means to diverge and merge the code base in a practical way. Of course, you need these capabilities regardless of whether your teams are located at the same site.

ClearCase MultiSite supports multiple distributed teams working on the same source through mastership. Mastership, as discussed earlier in this chapter, means that certain pieces of data are owned by certain sites. When it comes to version control, this means that one site might own a branch of an element, and another site might own another branch of the same element. Parallel changes at the sites get integrated through the merge process.

The following sections discuss setting up this scenario for two different projects: one using ClearCase UCM and one using base ClearCase. If you have only a few developers at your remote site and they are not organized into a separately managed project, see the section "Single Team: Distributed Members Scenario," later in this chapter.

11.4.1   How UCM Supports Shared Source Code

With ClearCase UCM, developers can deliver changes to the project-integration stream and rebase their development stream with changes made by others on the project. This is described in the section "Single Team: Distributed Members Scenario," later in this chapter. This section discusses two collaborating projects when one team is remote but both teams are working on the same source.

Using ClearCase UCM, it is possible for two or more projects to modify shared source code at the same time. Each UCM project is isolated from other projects' changes in the same way developers are isolated from each other's changes within a project. UCM uses a per-project/per-stream branching strategy. So, when you have local and remote projects, both projects will have their own project-integration branch. To integrate changes between projects, you would merge changes between projects' integration streams using base ClearCase merge functionality or rebase between integration streams, where it is supported.

11.4.2   How Base ClearCase Supports Shared Source Code

If you are using UCM, you can still use base ClearCase to support the shared source code scenario. This is done using branches.

With ClearCase MultiSite, a branch can be mastered by only one replica at any time. This means that each site must have mastership of at least one branch, to check in changes for elements in the replica. The temptation is to create a site-wide branch. This approach can be limiting, as you will see shortly.

Let's explore an example. Imagine that 10 developers work at a remote site in the United Kingdom and 20 developers work at the primary site in Washington. The overall project everyone is working on is code-named teatime, and you are working on Release 3. The U.K. team is responsible for adding some new GUIs, which will require database work; the Washington team is responsible for implementing support for a new database, which will also require database work. You divide these teams into two projects.

You could create two branches, washington and uk. However, when you have more projects underway and more releases to support, this approach will break down. A per-project, per-release, per-site approach is recommended. So, the two branches would be teatime_rel3_washington and teatime_rel3_uk. You should establish one branch as the primary branch where final integration will take place or have a third branch that is used for integration and stabilization. This could be the main branch or a project-only branch, such as teatime (see Figure 11-15).

Integration between project teams is done in a pull fashion. The project that masters the main project branch can periodically integrate changes from the other project branches using the `FindMerge` operation or the ClearCase merge manager.

This branch per-project, per-release, per-site approach allows each team to work in isolation with a coordinated, planned integration schedule that ClearCase MultiSite can automate and support.

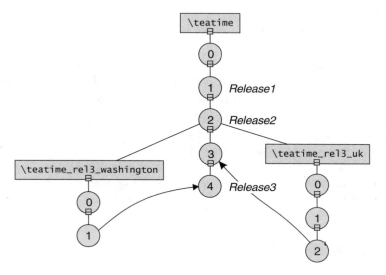

Figure 11-15   Branching for shared-source, distributed, collaborating projects.

11.4.3   Shared Source Code Summary

In the shared source code scenario, multiple teams modify the same shared sources. This approach to distributed development is more difficult and has significant integration issues. In some cases, it must be supported (as with monolithic systems and remote porting teams, for example). The organizational and architectural constraints for success are relaxed, but this is at the cost of integration time and architectural integrity. Robust technological support and a focus on multiteam integration planning are essential to success.

11.5   Single Team: Distributed Members Scenario

This scenario is a bit different from either of the other scenarios. It deals with a single project team that has distributed team members. Typically, fewer developers are involved and less remote management structure is in place than with either of the multiple-team scenarios. For example, if you have 20 developers at one site and 50 developers at another site, you are likely to have project management at each site. However, if you have 20 developers at one site and 3 developers at a remote site, you might have project management only at one site (that is, the 3 remote developers report into the same management structure as the others).

So, in this scenario, you will have a shared architecture and project management located at one site. The site you pick should contain the majority of your development team members. The remote site should contain only a small group of developers. (It is difficult to give concrete guidelines on how many developers can be at a remote site before you need to establish a remote team and adopt one of the preceding scenarios. If pressed, I would say that when a remote site has more than five developers, you should consider establishing a technical lead to handle coordination and day-to-day interactions. With more than 10 developers, I would move to a multiteam approach.) Another variant of this approach is to have multiple remote sites with only one or two developers at each site. For example, you might be running a project in which each developer is working from home.

Architecturally, things are not much different from the previous two scenarios. You must define a system architecture, divide it into components, and assign components to individuals rather than teams. This approach reduces contention among different individuals for the same source files. However, completely dividing components among individuals is rarely possible in practice. Some code must be shared, so the shared source scenario on an individual level can be applied to these pieces. This approach is best implemented by assigning specific features to individual team members; it works well on projects in a maintenance phase (see "Organizing Large Multiproject Development Efforts" in Chapter 7, "Managing and Organizing Your ClearCase Projects," for a discussion on architectural versus feature orientation).

Whether or not code is shared, you will want to integrate changes much earlier and much more often. In fact, you want to treat each remote developer as if he or she is not remote at all. That is, he or she should deliver changes in the same way as other team members, and those changes should be incorporated into the nightly build.

It is inefficient to establish a producer/consumer–style relationship at the individual developer level. You want the development team to be cooperating closely and integrating early and often. This means that the technology you choose must facilitate this kind of support. In particular, the ClearCase Remote Client lends itself to this kind of development model.

You can use any of the four approaches described in the section "How ClearCase Supports Distributed Development," earlier in this chapter, to support distributed team members. If you are using local access and ClearCase MultiSite, other interesting aspects are discussed next.

11.5.1   How the UCM Model Supports Local Access

ClearCase UCM provides support for local use. After the project VOB and source VOBs have been replicated to the remote site, the remote developer can join a project exactly as if he or she were working at the primary site. ClearCase UCM handles the details. The remote developer's development stream is mastered at the remote site, and the remote developer can create activities and make changes as necessary.

After changes have been made, the remote user performs a deliver operation. The delivery process is slightly different for remote users. The deliver is performed using the pull model instead of the default push model used by developers at the primary site. In pull deliveries, the remote developer marks a set of activities as ready for delivery. The project integrator at the primary site then pulls the changes into the project-integration stream. This approach removes the SCM details of branching and merging from the developer and automates the merge step as part of the delivery operation.

11.5.2   How Base ClearCase Supports Local Use

Just as for multiple teams, the remote user can create branches that are mastered at the remote site. These are usually referred to as private branches and can be either per user, per site, per activity (or task), per project, or a combination of those, depending on the integration approach you choose to take (see "Using Branches for Isolation and Integration" in Chapter 9). The ClearCase UCM model basically uses a per-project, per-stream branching scheme. These four branching styles are discussed later, after we set up an example scenario.

Let's say that you have 3 developers in Boston and 20 developers at the primary site in San Jose. The project everyone is working on is code-named fuji, and you are working on Release 2. In San Jose, the primary site, you have a project branch fuji_rel2, which will be used to integrate all the project changes. You replicate the VOBs to Boston, and now you want to set up the right branches and configuration specifications for the remote users.

Branch by Project or by Site

In this scheme, you could set up a remote project branch or a remote site branch. So, for example, you could set up a site-specific branch called boston. However, using a site-specific branch isn't recommended. It works fairly well if there are developers working on one project and you are supporting only one release of the product being developed. However, when you have multiple projects underway and you are maintaining earlier releases while developing newer releases (classic parallel development), this approach breaks down.

As described earlier, if you have multiple projects, you might use just a project branch, such as projectA_rel2. However, in this case, we have one project in which we want all the developers to participate. So, you should set up a per-project, per-site, per-release branch, such as fuji_boston_rel2. In this example, the Boston developers start from a specific project baseline identified by a label created on the fuji_rel2 branch and do their work on the fuji_boston_rel2 branch (see Figure 11-16).

This approach requires integration steps. The San Jose integrator needs to merge changes from only one remote branch, fuji_boston_rel2, into the project branch fuji_rel2. Similarly, the remote developers need only merge out from one branch to update their work with work that has gone on at the primary site.

The disadvantage of this approach is that the remote users will need to work closely together to coordinate their changes because any checked-in changes will be visible to all remote

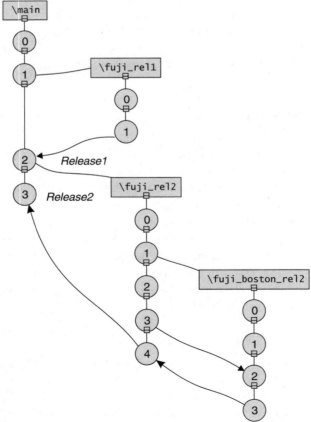

Figure 11-16   Branching by project and by site.

users. Because there is a small group of remote users, this is usually acceptable and desirable. However, sometimes this is not a workable solution, depending on the type and frequency of the changes being made. The other approach is to use a per-user or per-task branching scheme. (Additionally, you could use a per-user or per-task branching scheme off a per-project, per-site branch. But generally, the additional level of branching is too complicated for only a handful of remote developers. It is more applicable and beneficial for the remote teams of 10 or more.)

Branching by User

In this approach, there is no single remote branch for your three Boston developers. If you use a per-user branching scheme, there would be three branches. For example, if one of the remote users was Lorie, the branch for Lorie's development could be lorie_dev. However, again, just a per-user branch is probably not a good idea unless there is only one project and one release in your team's future (let's hope this is not the case). A better approach is per project, per user. So, the user branch would be fuji_rel2_lorie.

Using branch by user, each remote user (and maybe even each user at the primary site) would work on his or her own branch. At certain points in time (usually new project baselines), users would merge out from the project branch fuji_rel2 to their development branches. When they had completed some work, the integrator would merge from the development branches into the project branch (see Figure 11-17).

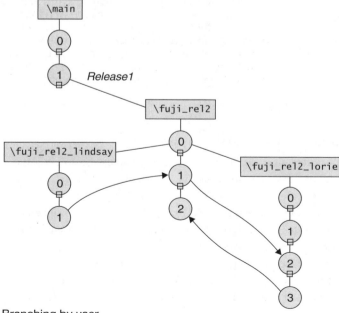

Figure 11-17   Branching by user.

A couple things to note on integration: The integrator must be able to find and merge from all the developers' branches. This is best handled by a good branch-naming convention and some tooling around the ClearCase `FindMerge` operation. Although this complicates the integration merge, it gives all developers some control over what changes they see and enables them to deliver their work at a given point and time separately.

Additionally, you need to have a way to tell the integrator that the work is ready. This can be done in a number of ways and should be set up in a way that best suits your organization. For example, it could be via e-mail. Another way would be for the developer to apply a label to the versions that are ready to be merged. Again, a good label-naming convention and scripts around `FindMerge` can automate this process for the integrator. Another approach is to use attributes on the versions to indicate status.

Another thing to note about the per-project/per-user model is that developers must integrate all the activities they are working on at the same time unless they create another branch. Say that you are working on feature A and an emergency bug fix gets assigned to you, so you fix bug X. Then, when the integrator merges from your development branch, he or she will get both bug X and feature A—that is, unless some automation has been written to support pulling these out separately, as is the case with ClearCase UCM. However, if you are not using UCM, a good approach to solving this problem in base ClearCase is to use per-activity branching.

CLEARCASE PRO TIP

If you are automating the branch-by-user process, there is one other bit of automation that you should consider. In the approach just described, the developer's branch will live on for the life of the project. The more files that users modify, the more time and complexity will be involved in the merge-out operation. This problem can be solved by renaming the branch type and creating a new branch type with the former name, after the changes have been merged into the project branch. This forces a new development branch to sprout the next time that a file changes; if the developer does not modify that file again, it will appear as if there are no changes made by the developer. The rename should be to something meaningful, to show the branch history in the version tree. So, in our example, you might rename the branch to fuji_rel2_lorie.1, fuji_rel2_lorie.2, and so on.

11.5.3   Branching by Activity

As in per-developer branching, per-activity branching creates no single remote branch for your three Boston developers. If you use a per-activity branching scheme, there will be one branch for each activity developers are working on. This leads to a very bushy version tree. For example, if remote user Lorie is working on feature A, the branch for Lorie's development would be feature_a. In this case, it is not necessary or desirable to include a project extension because this scheme gives you the flexibility to include or not include this feature in the Release 2 fuji project.

Because these branches live only for the time it takes to develop the feature or bug fix, they are usually not updated with other project changes. When developers finish their work, they inform the integrator, and the integrator merges the activity branch into the project branch (see Figure 11-18).

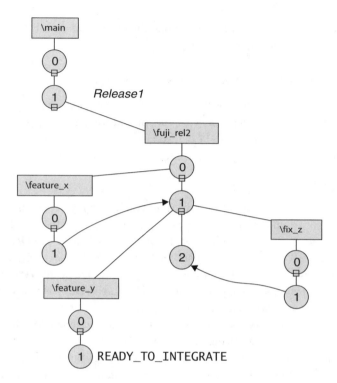

Figure 11-18   Branching by activity.

It is even more important in this branching-by-activity model than in the user branching scheme that there be a way to indicate that the branch is ready to be merged (in other words, that the activity is complete). Because no branch-naming scheme is in play here, a different approach is required. There are a couple of ways to do this. One is to attach an attribute to the branch type and then lock the branch type. This attribute can describe the status of the activity—for example, ready-to-integrate. Another approach is to attach a known label type, such as READY_TO_INTEGRATE, to the versions on each activity branch. This approach makes setting up the correct config spec in the integration view easy. Either approach requires fairly simple scripting, so developers don't need to know the implementation details.

11.5.4   Single Team: Distributed Members Summary

In some cases, the number of developers at a remote site does not warrant establishing a separate project-management structure. In these cases, the remote developers must have the technical support in the SCM tool to allow them to participate in the project remotely. ClearCase supports remote developers in four ways: by remote access, Web access, disconnected use, and local access. As a project leader, you need to determine the optimal approach for your remote team members and how best to integrate their changes.

11.6   Other Uses for ClearCase MultiSite

ClearCase MultiSite can be applied in three other ways. Although not originally designed for these purposes, it has been adopted to solve backup, product delivery, and platform interoperability problems. Because MultiSite is an add-on product to ClearCase, some of these uses may be cost-effective only if you are already using MultiSite to support distributed development.

11.6.1   MultiSite for Backup

The data you store in your SCM system is critical to your company, especially if your company's business is dependent on that software (for example, integrated software vendors, defense, e-commerce, and mission-critical IT applications). You must back up your VOB data.

To back up a VOB, a system administrator locks the VOB, backs up the files associated with it, and then unlocks it. The locking time depends on the size of the VOB but requires some downtime. One of the benefits to using MultiSite as a backup strategy is that you can back up the replica, thus leaving the primary VOB unlocked and available 24 hours a day. The cost associated with this strategy is that recovery takes longer because you need to use MultiSite in the recovery process instead of just simply recovering the original VOB files.

The frequency of VOB backups depends on your strategy but generally occurs nightly. So, another benefit of using MultiSite is that you can set up an hourly synchronization between the master and the backup replica. In a recovery scenario, you then have all but the last hour's worth of changes, without the overhead of doing hourly backups.

11.6.2   MultiSite for Delivery

MultiSite has also been employed as an automated delivery vehicle. Using MultiSite to replicate the data for and synchronize two sites that often exchange files and information means that a user can just check in a new version of a file; after the synch time, the changes automatically are available at the remote site. If the information is important, this mechanism is more secure and reliable then using `ftp` to simply copy the files from one site to the other.

11.6.3   MultiSite for Platform Interoperability

ClearCase supports interoperability between Windows and UNIX development environments. In particular, a Windows client can access UNIX VOBs and use UNIX views. Setting this up properly can require additional file system software, such as an SMB server on UNIX or an NFS client on Windows if you are using dynamic views.

MultiSite can be used to simulate a homogeneous environment by creating a replica on a UNIX platform and another on a Windows platform. In this case, each side can be better isolated from one another, and the additional steps needed to communicate between UNIX and Windows go away because the VOB exists locally on both platforms. This strategy works particularly well if you have one team developing the UNIX version of a product and one developing the Windows version against a shared source.

11.7   Summary

This chapter described the three fundamental models for distributed development and explored how ClearCase supports these models using combinations of native ClearCase client tools, the ClearCase Remote Client, the ClearCase Web client, and ClearCase MultiSite. Furthermore, you were presented with a brief description of ClearQuest MultiSite. We noted that it extends support for distributed development by replicating, controlling, and tracking change-request data. That data, in turn, can be integrated with the control and tracking of development artifacts that ClearCase and ClearCase MultiSite provide to give organizations that are engaged in distributed development a robust and complete solution.

Change Request Management and ClearQuest

This chapter provides a brief introduction to a topic that is closely related to SCM: change request management (CRM). An effective and comprehensive change-management solution can be achieved only through the application of the appropriate tools and processes in both disciplines. This chapter introduces CRM and the software product ClearQuest, and discusses how Clear-Quest extends the UCM model to support CRM. (CRM is a very important part of a complete change-management solution, and an entire book could—and should—be devoted to the topic. Regrettably, I have only scratched the surface. Refer to [Humphrey, 1989], [Whitgift, 1991], and the Rational Unified Process [RUP 5.5, 1999] for additional information.)

12.1   What Is Change Request Management?

Change request management is the recording, tracking, and reporting of requests from any stake-holder to change a software system. It includes the processes an organization uses to decide what changes to make and the resolution processes used to make them. (The acronym CRM is also used in the related but different domain of customer support. In this domain, it stands for customer relationship management. This chapter uses CRM to refer to defect and request management in the software-development domain.)

Change request management is a central part of a complete change-management solution. Without recording, change requests might be lost or might remain unknown. Without tracking, existing change requests might be forgotten or might remain unaddressed. Without reporting, project managers might have a difficult time assessing project status, determining the level of product quality, and conveying project status to upper management.

Rational Unified Process [RUP 5.5, 1999] defines change request management as a process that "addresses the organizational infrastructure required to assess the cost and schedule impact of a requested change to the existing product. Change Request Management addresses the workings of a Change Review Team or Change Control Board." Change request management is like the central nervous system of your software-development process and is integral to good software-development practice. CRM processes and tools manage data that is essential to project stakeholders and the smooth operation of a software project. Other development disciplines related to and supported by change request management are requirements management, testing, release management, customer support, and project management.

12.2   What Are Change Requests?

Rational Unified Process defines a *change request* as "a general term for any request from a stakeholder to change an artifact or process. Documented in the change request is information on the origin and impact of the current problem, the proposed solution, and its cost" [RUP 5.5, 1999]. CRM processes are often closely related to a company's internal organization, and terminology in this area is far from standard. However, change requests are often divided into two major categories: enhancement requests and defects. (The types of change requests used to manage change vary widely from company to company and even internally between projects within the same company. The types described here, defect and enhancement request, represent only the most basic kinds of change requests.)

Enhancement requests specify a new feature of the system or a change to the "as designed" behavior of a system. *Defects* are "an anomaly, or flaw, in a delivered work product. Examples include such things as omissions and imperfections found during early life cycle phases and symptoms of faults contained in software sufficiently mature for test or operation. A defect can be any kind of issue you want tracked and resolved" [RUP 5.5, 1999]. Although much of the data maintained for enhancement requests and defects is similar, these two types of change requests are often handled very differently in the CRM process.

12.3   The Change Request Management Process

When implementing CRM, you must make a number of decisions. Typically, defining a CRM process involves a number of stakeholders in a number of different functional organizations (such as project management, development, and testing). The decisions you must make revolve around what types of change requests you will track, what data you will track for these change requests, and how you will track the change requests.

The types of change requests you choose to track could be as simple as defects and enhancements requests, described previously. For large organizations, change requests can become much more complex and multilayered. For example, you might define a type of request that represents an external customer request. One or more external customer requests might spawn one or more engineering-level enhancement requests.

When you have defined the types of requests you are going to track, the next step is to define the type of information you need to record throughout the life of the request. For example, if you are tracking defects, you might want to record things such as who submitted the defect, when it was submitted, what the resolution was, whether it was a duplicate of another defect, or during what phase in the life cycle the defect was found and fixed.

The most important and often most difficult thing to define for each change request is the process used to monitor the change request. This process is typically represented in CRM tools by a state transition model. That is, you define a set of states and a set of actions to transition the change request from one state to the next.

Change request types and state transition models vary widely. However, almost all CRM processes include (or should include) the following six stages:

1. **Submission**—Requests to change a software system are recorded (submitted).

2. **Evaluation**—Change requests are evaluated, categorized, and prioritized.

3. **Decision**—Based on the evaluation, a decision is made regarding which change requests to implement and in what order.

4. **Implementation**—Changes are made to system artifacts, and new artifacts are produced, with the goal being to implement the requested change. The software system documentation is updated to reflect the change.

5. **Verification**—The change request implementation is verified as either meeting the requirements or fixing a defect.

6. **Completion**—The change request is closed, and the requestor is notified.

The following sections look at each stage of change request management, and compare and contrast the treatment of enhancement requests and defects in these stages.

12.3.1 Submission

During submission, requests to change a software system are recorded. Defects and enhancement requests usually differ in the origin of the request and the type of information collected. Enhancement requests come from a wide variety of sources. In many cases, they come from customers and arrive in engineering directly or indirectly through marketing or customer support. The key data captured for enhancement requests are the importance of the request to the customer, as much detail about the request as possible, and the identity of the original requestor (if submitted indirectly) so that engineering can ask for clarification. In some cases, enhancement requests come internally from either testing or in-house use. In these cases, make sure that product management is aware of these requests.

Defects also come from a wide variety of sources. Most are typically found, recorded, and resolved internally. The key data recorded during submission includes how the defect was discovered, how to reproduce the defect, the severity, and who discovered the defect. As with enhancement requests, defects can also be discovered by customers. Customer-reported defects usually arrive in engineering indirectly through the sales force, marketing, or customer support. The key data recorded for these defects is the same as enhancement requests, along with the identity of the customer having the problem, the perceived severity of the problem for that customer, and which version of the software system the customer is using. This is needed for the second step of the process: evaluation.

12.3.2   Evaluation

During evaluation, someone must look at all newly submitted change requests and make some determination of each request's character. Is this really a defect, or should it be an enhancement request? Is the severity assigned appropriate? Can defects be reproduced? What is its priority compared to other requests? Is this a duplicate of some other change request?

Most organizations follow different processes for evaluation, depending on whether something is a defect or an enhancement request. For example, a defect must be reproduced and confirmed. Defects are generally prioritized based on the severity and the importance of fixing the defect. Typically, defects are evaluated by engineering.

Enhancement requests do not need to be confirmed, but they do need to be prioritized in relationship to other enhancement requests and product requirements. During evaluation of enhancement requests, you are looking at things such as the number of customers who have made the same request, the relative importance of the customers who are making the request, the possible impact on market share and product revenue, and the impact on the sales force and customer support. Typically, enhancement requests are evaluated by product management.

12.3.3   Decision

In the decision stage, you choose to implement a change request, postpone its implementation, or never implement it. Defects and enhancement requests are almost always handled differently.

For enhancement requests, a product manager or analyst usually makes the decision to implement. Various factors affecting a software product come into play. How easy is it to sell? How does it stand up against competition? How easy is it to install and support? What are the existing customers demanding? What changes could be made to enter into new markets? How many development, testing, and documentation resources will be required to make this change? All the enhancement requests are weighed together, and decisions are made whether to implement each in a given release, postpone it, or never implement it, based on the information gathered during evaluation.

The decision process for defects differs depending on two factors: the development life cycle phase and the size of the development effort. Early in the development life cycle, you want to maximize change to the software while maintaining control (see Chapter 2, "Growing into Your SCM Solution"). To allow this, the defect decision-making process is often done informally early in the development life cycle. This allows more changes to be made rapidly. Typically, a defect is assigned to a developer, and the developer decides what to do. If the defect can be reproduced, he or she tries to fix it for the current release.

Near the end of the life cycle (sometimes called the end game of a software release), you want to make only necessary changes. Uncontrolled change late in the development life cycle is disruptive, introduces risk, and often causes slipped schedules and cost overruns. Later in the development life cycle, most companies institute a formal review process for all defects. For example, developers might do the evaluations, but they are no longer able to make the decision to implement or not implement. The review process can be complex or very simple, such as getting approval from the project leader or testing organization. The idea is to ensure that only critical defects are resolved during the code stabilization and final regression-testing phases.

Larger organizations usually have a formal change-review process that includes a formal review board. These review teams are commonly called change-control boards (CCBs). Very large organizations might have more than one CCB. CCBs are usually cross-functional and are concerned with making the trade-offs between product quality and project schedule during the end game.

Rational Unified Process defines a change-control (or configuration-control) board as "the board that oversees the change process consisting of representatives from all interested parties, including customers, developers, and users. In a small project, a single person, such as the project manager or software architect, may play this role" [RUP 5.5, 1999]. CCBs are typically concerned only with defects, although the occasional last-minute enhancement requests do show up.

12.3.4 Implementation

During implementation, system artifacts are modified or created as needed to satisfy a change request. In implementation, the differences between defect remediation and enhancement are more subtle. Typically, enhancement request implementation requires more design work than defect implementation because enhancements often involve a new feature or functionality. Defects, on the other hand, require setting up an environment in which the defect can be reproduced and the repair can be tested.

Some defects and enhancement requests are submitted against the documentation. In these cases, the documentation is changed during implementation. For enhancement requests, this means documenting the new features or functionality added to the system. For defects, this can mean doing nothing, changing the documentation if the fix to the defect affects user-visible behavior, or even deleting documentation (such as removing a documented workaround to a defect that has been resolved). Documentation changes might also be required when defects are not fixed at all. That is, a decision made to not fix a defect might require that a workaround be documented or that the defect be included in the release notes.

12.3.5 Verification

In verification, final testing and documentation take place. Testing of enhancement requests usually involves verifying that the changes made satisfy the requirements behind the enhancement request (as recorded by the analyst). Defect testing is simply verifying that the developer's fix does resolve the defect. This usually means trying to reproduce the defect using an official project build.

12.3.6 Completion

Completion is the final closure of the change request. This could be when the request is fulfilled or when a decision is made not to fulfill the request. The primary step during completion is to close the loop with the original stakeholder who submitted the request. This is particularly good practice if the change request originated from an external customer.

12.4   What Is ClearQuest?

ClearQuest is an IBM Rational product that provides out-of-the-box support for the change-request management process. ClearQuest is a complementary product to ClearCase. It can be integrated with other SCM tools, for projects that require more advanced change request management before they require more advanced software-configuration management.

ClearQuest has three key parts: a user interface (the client); a back-end core, which provides an interface to the data store (ClearQuest 2003.06.14 supports Oracle [on Windows or UNIX], Microsoft SQL Server, SQL Anywhere, DB2 [on Windows or Unix] and Microsoft Access databases); and a designer used to create and customize the CRM processes. The user interface has native variants that run on Windows, UNIX, a ClearQuest adapter plug-in that runs in an Eclipse IDE, and a Web client. The Windows and UNIX clients have three key panels (see Figure 12-1). On the left side is the tree view of saved queries, charts, and reports. On the right side is the results panel divided into a master/slave display. One line is shown per request in the top panel (master), with the lower panel (slave) showing the details of the request selected in the top panel.

The ClearQuest Eclipse Client provides the same information, but in a slightly different format, providing the tree view of saved queries, charts, and reports; the results panels appear in a tabbed interface. Furthermore, the ClearQuest Eclipse Client adapter allows multiple user logins in the same Eclipse session. You can now customize your Eclipse perspectives to include whatever ClearQuest data you are interested in by adding ClearQuest views. Figure 12-2 shows some of the features of the Eclipse ClearQuest adapter. Figure 12-3 shows an Eclipse Java perspective with ClearQuest views included.

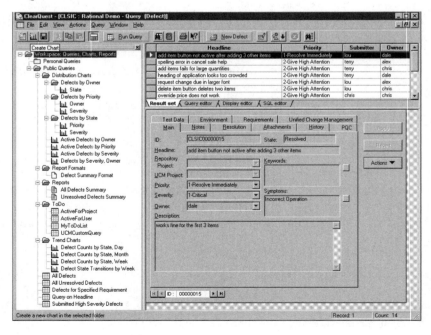

Figure 12-1   ClearQuest Windows display.

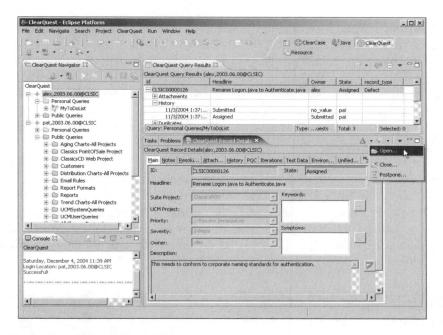

Figure 12-2   ClearQuest Eclipse Client.

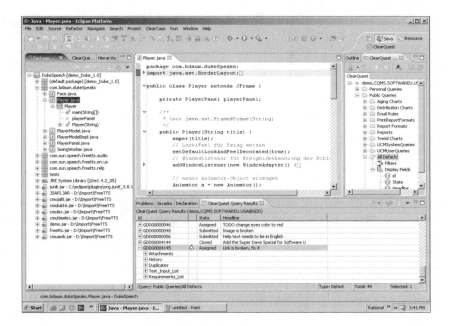

Figure 12-3   Eclipse Java Perspective.

ClearQuest provides out-of-the-box record types for defects and enhancement requests. If your change-request management processes are different from those provided, you can use the out-of-the-box types as a starting point or design your own record types from scratch. Instead of doing this definition in some proprietary language, you have available in ClearQuest a design tool called the ClearQuest Designer. It enables you to modify all aspects of the schema, creating new record types and new fields, defining a state transition model, and controlling the layout of those fields in the submission and display forms. The ClearQuest Designer also supports basic version control for the CRM schema.

Figure 12-4 shows the ClearQuest Designer. The left panel provides a way to navigate to the various pieces of the CRM process. This example shows a folder that contains all the record types in the out-of-the-box schema. You can see three types: Activity, Defect, and Enhancement Request. The Defect record type is open, and under the folder States and Actions, the state transition matrix is selected. The right panel shows the states and actions for the defect record type. This is where you define the state model for your record and the legal transitions, called actions, that get you from one state to the next.

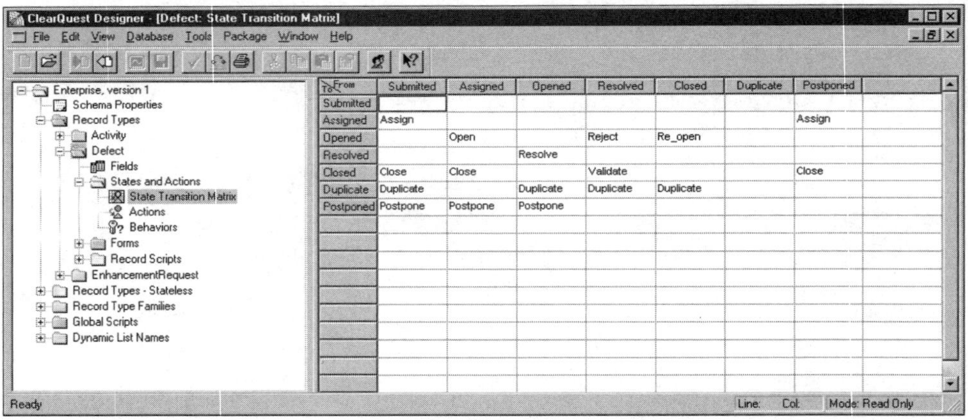

Figure 12-4   ClearQuest Designer example: record types.

In another example, as shown in Figure 12-5, you can see the forms portion of the Clear-Quest Designer. The left panel shows the defect record type. Under the forms folder, you see selected the Defect_Base_Submit form, seen in the middle panel. This is the standard form shown when someone submits a new record of type defect. This will most likely include fewer fields than the full defect form, named Defect_Base. In the right panel is the form editor interface. This interface is like Visual Basic, in that you can create buttons, fields, and labels, and so on, to lay out how the form is presented.

The ClearQuest Designer runs on Windows, but all client interfaces can use the resulting CRM schema. "Design once, deploy anywhere" is the ClearQuest marketing mantra.

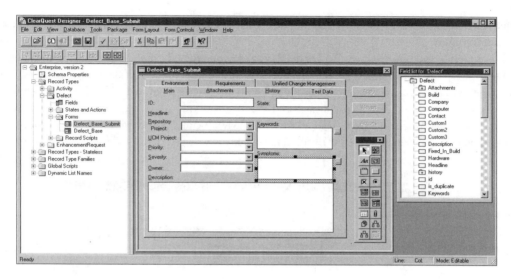

Figure 12-5   ClearQuest Designer example: form editor.

12.5   How Do I Use ClearQuest Data?

ClearQuest records a significant amount of essential project data—for example, what requests for change have been made, which ones are critical, which ones are being worked on, who is working on them, and which defects have been fixed. This is all very good and very valuable information. However, the data in a change-request management tool is useful only if there is an easy way to extract it in a form that enables you to use it. Project managers usually need this information to assess project status—determining the level of product quality—and to convey project status to upper management.

ClearQuest provides mechanisms—queries, reports, and charts—to deliver the data in a variety of forms. Queries provide a flexible means of browsing a subset of all the requests in the database (for example, "show me all the defects assigned to me"). Reports provide a means to collect data and format it in a way it can be printed, included in an Excel spreadsheet, or posted to a Web site. Charts provide online and printable graphs that offer insight into data trends, data distribution, and request aging. The following sections cover each of these areas.

12.5.1   Queries

The purpose of a ClearQuest query is to return a subset of all the records stored so that you can evaluate those records. For example, a query could be "show me the defects assigned to me," "show me all open defects on Project X," or "show me all resolved defects in Release Y." A Clear-Quest query is a set of search criteria defined by a filter that returns a list of records in a master-slave style display. That is, the top window (the master) shows the list of requests one per line, and the bottom window (the slave) shows the details of the request selected in the master window (refer to Figure 12-1).

Queries and how their results are displayed are constructed graphically by using the Clear-Quest Query Creation Wizard. This tool walks you through the process of defining the query. The first step is to decide which data fields to display in the results window and how the data should be sorted. In Figure 12-6, you can see that the `headline`, `priority`, `submitter`, and `owner` fields have been chosen from all the fields available and will be shown in the master display. You can also see that we have decided to sort this list by priority.

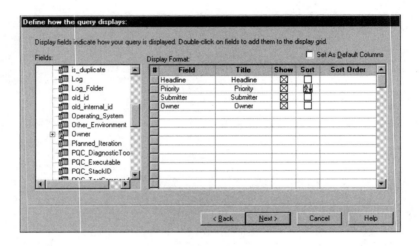

Figure 12-6   ClearQuest Query Wizard: results definition.

The second step in defining a query is to decide which records you are interested in displaying. This is done by choosing the fields and values for those fields, to filter out the requests you do not want to see. In Figure 12-7, we have chosen two filter fields: `priority` and `ucm_project`. For `priority`, we have selected the top two priority values. Records with any other priority will not be displayed. We have restricted the value of the `ucm_project` field to one or more projects.

The results of this query are displayed in Figure 12-1. Queries can be saved both as personal queries for an individual and as public queries that become available to the entire project team. Saved queries are organized on the left side (tree view) of the main ClearQuest interface (refer to Figure 12-1). ClearQuest comes with a number of predefined queries.

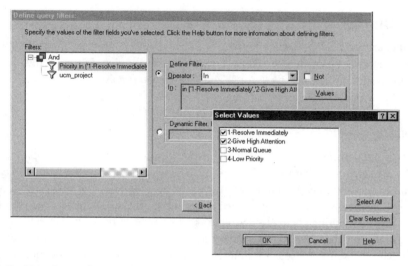

Figure 12-7   ClearQuest Query Wizard data filter.

12.5.2   Reports

ClearQuest reports provide a means of collecting a set of data and formatting it in a way that can be printed, exported, or posted to a Web site. ClearQuest includes one of the industry-standard report-generation tools, Crystal Reports, which enables you to create your own reports from scratch. Reports can be printed and exported into a number of formats, such as Excel, HTML, Microsoft Word, comma-separated text, plain text, and Lotus 1-2-3. Figure 12-8 shows a change-request summary report being exported to Microsoft Excel 5.0.

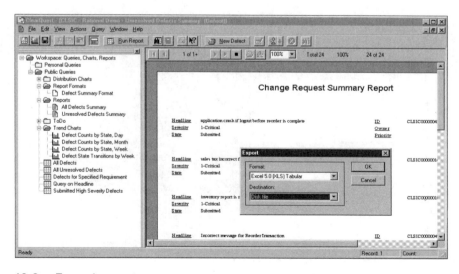

Figure 12-8   Example report.

12.5.3   Charts

ClearQuest charts graphically represent data, both online and in printable form, making it easier to analyze. ClearQuest provides three different types of charts: distribution, trend, and aging. As with ClearQuest queries, a Chart Creation Wizard walks you through the process of creating your own charts. You can then save and rerun charts as needed.

Distribution Charts

Distribution charts are used to categorize data and see how a given data sample is distributed across different categories. For example, charts can be used to balance the workload across team members and to get a look at the number of defects by category, such as priority or severity.

Figure 12-9 shows an example distribution chart. In the left panel, you see the public queries and the Distribution Charts folder. This example screen shows the Defects by Owner and State chart. In the top-right panel is the data set being used. The lower-right panel shows the chart itself. Each bar represents a developer along the x-axis. The y-axis shows the number of defects. Bars are color-coded by state. The first bar shows defects that have not been assigned or that have been closed. You can quickly see two things in this chart. First, there is a lot of unassigned work, which indicates unknown risk for the project. Second, Alex, Dana, and Devon do not have any open requests they are working on. Get to work, and assign the new requests to those three challenged individuals!

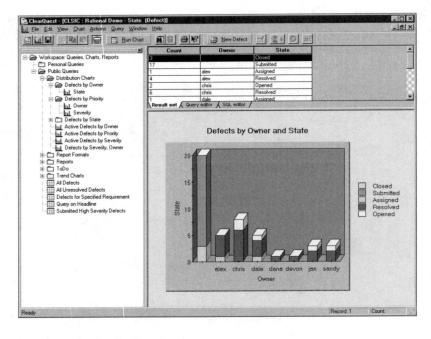

Figure 12-9   Example distribution chart.

Trend Charts

Trend charts are used to display how change requests are moving through the system over time. As defined by the ClearQuest documentation, "trend charts show how many records were transitioned into the selected states by day, week, or month." Defect tracking is quite good in and of itself. However, trend charts provide the project manager with critical information that helps him or her objectively judge the status of a project. Trend charts can provide a picture into the end game of a project by showing the rate of new defect submissions compared to the rate of defect resolution.

Figure 12-10 shows an example trend chart. Again in the left panel are the public trend chart queries. The trend chart pictured is Defect Count by State by Week. Again, the upper-right panel shows the data on which the chart is based. The lower-right one shows the chart. The x-axis is time by week. The y-axis is the number of defects. Each line presents the state of the defects. You can quickly see that as the weeks have gone by, the number of new defects submitted has risen from 20 to 40. The incoming defects have definitely leveled out, so it could be that testing has completed or is blocked. Of more concern is that the number of bugs that have been resolved per week is not going up at all. Until you see the number of submitted defects moving downward and the number of resolved defects moving upward, you are probably far away from a good-quality release.

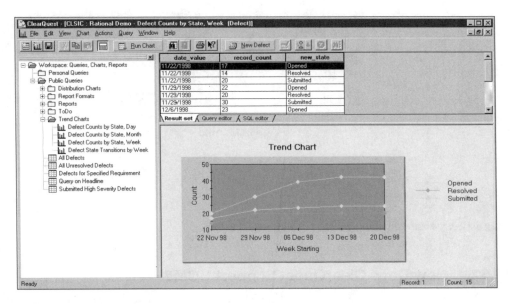

Figure 12-10   Example trend chart.

Aging Charts

Aging charts are used to see how long a change request remains in a certain state. They are useful primarily for identifying change requests that are not getting any attention. For example, if a defect has been open for three weeks, it might indicate that it is a very hard problem, that the developer has been working on other higher-priority issues, or that no one is looking at it. A change request that has been postponed for 5 years might be one that you should consider filing away as never to be implemented.

Figure 12-11 shows an example of a custom aging chart created using the Chart Creation Wizard. The x-axis represents age in months. The y-axis represents the number of defects in a given state. The bars are color-coded by state. In this chart, you can see that none of the defects has been around more than 3 months. However, you can also see that nine defects have been in the Submitted state for more than 2 months. Shouldn't someone take a look at these?

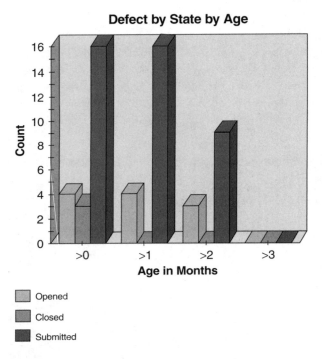

Figure 12-11 Example aging chart.

12.6   How Does ClearQuest Support UCM?

ClearQuest can be used to extend the UCM model (described in Chapter 3, "An Overview of the Unified Change Management Model") with support for change request management. The UCM process diagram (refer to Figure 3-5) shows two steps that the project manager performs: assigning and scheduling work, and monitoring project status. ClearQuest is the technology that supports these steps. With ClearCase alone, activities have only a name, a one-line description, and a change set. ClearCase maintains the essential configuration-management information, but not the change-request management information. To support change request management, additional data must be maintained—for example, state, assigned user, a long description, priority, severity, and so on. In a UCM environment, ClearQuest provides these capabilities. If you are interested in an integrated change-management solution, you need both ClearCase and ClearQuest.

With ClearCase UCM alone, activities are used as the mechanism to track a change set (see "Organize and Integrate Consistent Sets of Versions Using Activities" in Chapter 1, "What Is Software Configuration Management?"). The primary difference between using ClearCase alone and using it in combination with ClearQuest is the level of process centered on the activities.

If you are using ClearCase UCM by itself, activities are created at the point of use. That is, individual developers, working in their development stream, create activities when they check out files. These activities consist of a one-line description and so appear to the developer as kind of a metacomment for a change spanning multiple files. "Modifying Files and Directories" in Chapter 8, "Development Using the ClearCase UCM Model," goes into this in more detail. The bottom line is that ClearCase standalone with UCM does not support the process for activities you need if you want to do change request management.

With ClearQuest, activities are submitted, evaluated, decided on, implemented, validated, and completed. They can be of any record type that you define. So, they can be defects, enhancement requests, features, incidents, tasks, and so on. This is accomplished by adding UCM required fields from the ClearQuest Designer to a given record type. Many of the predefined record types come pre-UCM-enabled. Figure 12-12 shows the additional tab, called Unified Change Management, and fields added when you apply the UCM package to a record type in the ClearQuest Designer.

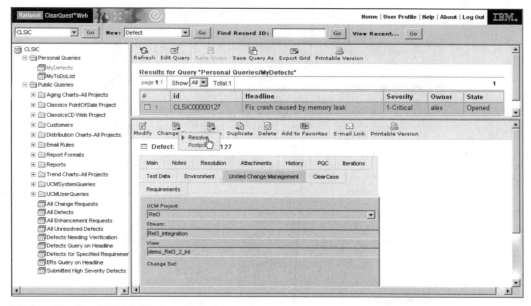

Figure 12-12   UCM fields in a ClearQuest record (Web interface shown).

An additional difference between using ClearCase by itself and using ClearQuest is that ClearQuest adds the notion of a developer's to-do list. This is a list of activities assigned to a given developer for a given project. Automation keeps this list up-to-date, adding new activities as they are assigned and removing them as they are resolved. Additionally, ClearCase knows how to retrieve this to-do list and will display it for the developer where appropriate. For example, when you check out, the drop-down activity selection list is your own personal to-do list. There is no concept of a to-do list in ClearCase by itself.

So, when do you use ClearCase alone and when do you use ClearQuest? For small projects or projects that are process-adverse, use ClearCase alone during the early phases of development when you want to encourage as much change as possible. Also use ClearCase alone if you are in an organization that already has a change-request management system that you are not able to replace.

Use ClearQuest when you are interested in change request management. I suggest that during the end game of any development project, ClearQuest should be used at least to do defect tracking. This will improve overall quality considerably. If you are uncertain, it is possible to enable and disable ClearQuest for a project at any given time simply by changing the project policy setting.

You can also use ClearQuest to track other kinds of work (although it is focused on the software-development space). ClearQuest can be customized easily to solve almost any type of tracking need.

12.7   ClearQuest MultiSite

ClearQuest MultiSite is an add-on product for ClearQuest that provides the mechanisms to replicate track and control changes to ClearQuest Schema repositories and their associated databases. ClearQuest MultiSite is discussed in more detail in Chapter 11, "Geographically Distributed Development." Figure 12-13 shows USA's ClearQuest Web client looking at a record mastered in India.

Figure 12-13   A remotely mastered record in ClearQuest.

12.8   Summary

This chapter discussed what change request management is, along with change requests and the processes that are involved in tracking and managing them. You have seen that a process that involves change requests moving from an initial Submitted state through various intermediate states until they reach some terminal state (such as Closed or Rejected) provides the capability to track the progress of a project and to use that tracking information to make informed management decisions regarding the project. ClearQuest provides out-of-the-box support for change request management with native, Eclipse, and Web clients. ClearQuest also provides highly flexible and easy-to-use means to customize not only the information to be tracked, but also the actual process, states, and transitions required for effective project management in a wide range of project types. Finally, you learned that ClearQuest and ClearCase are integrated, allowing UCM activities to be tracked and controlled through the ClearQuest change request management model. These capabilities allow projects to both control their development and see in real time the current status of the project. This status is based on nonintrusive data collection that occurs as an integral part of people working on the project.

Redoing and Undoing Change Sets with UCM

You might run into some conditions in which UCM does not supply an "out-of-the-box" solution. One condition arises when you want to "undo" or back out an activity from a stream. In most cases, this occurs as a deliver activity on the integration stream. You could always leave the activity on the stream, fix it on your development stream, and redeliver. You could also remove the activity's change set versions if it was the last activity on the stream. Or, you can utilize the `cset.pl` script to undo the activity from the stream. Another condition that might arise during UCM development is the desire to reapply an activity's change set from another stream to your current stream (a Redo operation). You can use the deliver operation to accomplish this if the desired activity has no predecessor activities on its stream that you do not want. In other cases, UCM does not allow a deliver operation to proceed, as in during interproject deliveries between projects that do not have common foundation baselines (projects that sprouted from different imported baselines off `/main`, for instance). In this case, using the `cset.pl` script to redo the activity from one stream to another can work around this issue.

A.1   Location of Script

Currently, the `cset.pl` script is maintained by David E. Bellagio. Many customers have used this at various stages when using UCM. As of the date of this publication, the script has not yet been pushed to IBM developerWorks (see *www-130.ibm.com/developerworks/*), which is where it will reside eventually. Just search developerWorks for "cset.pl." If you can't find it, send an email to `dbellagio@us.ibm.com`, and I'll send you a copy.

A.2   Limit Script Use to Integrator Role

The `cset.pl` script should be used only as needed by the integrator, not as a main development tool for the developer. If you let developers use this whenever they want, issues could arise that would have been avoided with normal UCM operations. For one, the Redo operation does not keep track of the dependencies in a way that `cleartool` diffbl will know about. So, reporting changes that were redone in other streams would have to be accomplished with other methods.

A.3   Script Interface

Here is the interface to the script (`cset.pl` version 6.0).

Usage:

```
cset.pl [-help] [-ignore] [-graphical]
        {-redo | -print | -undo | -findmerge} [activity]
```

Arguments:

`help`	Displays this message and exits.
`ignore`	Ignores check for checked-out files.
`graphical`	If specified, always uses the graphical diffmerge tool.
`redo`	Redoes the change set specified by `activity`.
`print`	Prints the change set specified by `activity`.
`undo`	Undoes the change set specified by `activity`.
`findmerge`	Merges the change set from `activity` (this is not redo).
`activity`	The specified activity-object-selector to redo, print, or undo. If not specified, you are prompted for an activity.

More details on each of these options are available from the script's `-help` interface. However, to understand the benefits of this script, you need to understand how the deliver operation works in relation to ClearCase's underlying merge utility.

A.4   Why Is This Useful?

`cset.pl` can be used to manipulate UCM activities in a different manner than what you can do using the "out-of-the-box" interfaces of UCM (such as deliver and rebase). It achieves these different behaviors by processing the UCM activity's change set with either the ClearCase additive merge or the subtractive merge. The additive merge is used when redoing an activity from another stream into your current stream (the stream from which your view is attached). It is important to know that `cset.pl` does not implement any new technology that does not exist in base ClearCase today. Thus, the redo and undo operations of `cset.pl` will suffer from the same side effects of the additive and subtractive merge operations within ClearCase.

`cset.pl` will redo an activity's change set from another stream into an activity on the current stream. A redo deals only with the activity's change set, not other changes from other activities that were predecessors of the activity to be redone. `cset.pl` can also undo an activity from the current stream into the current activity on the current stream. This essentially backs out the changes of the activity to be undone. This is most commonly used to back out deliver activities from an integration stream.

The following sections describe when and where to use this utility. As stated before, this utility should not be used in an ad hoc fashion, but should be used to facilitate the scenarios it was intended for.

A.5   Redoing an Activity on Another Stream

When using the redo operation of `cset.pl`, developers can merge changes of activities from one stream to any other stream in any order (although, for most changes, order is important).

To use the redo operation, you must be positioned in a view, attached to a stream that will accept the redo. UCM requires that all changes be done in an activity, so you need to also create an activity to accept the redo. Because there is no hyperlink support for this tool yet, users must rely on activity naming conventions to reflect the operation that was performed. So, if you have an activity named Change1 on stream1 and you are currently using a view attached to stream2, you would create an activity Redo_Change1 on stream2 (`cleartool mkact -nc Redo_Change1`), and then issue the following command:

```
ccperl c:\bin\cset.pl -redo Change1
```

This operation would move the deltas of the change of Change1 into the current activity (Redo_Change1).

Why Is This Useful?

In some cases, people on other streams might want only certain changes propagated to their stream out of a large set of changes. A deliver of the activity would attempt to merge starting at the cset version (including activity versions up to the activity's versions being delivered). `cset.pl` would simply redo that activity's cset.

Lets look at the difference between a deliver (or `findmerge -cset`) with a `cset.pl -redo`:

In Figure A-1, if you were able to deliver activities (Actp1, Actp2, Actp3) from the integration stream of Project_2 to the integration stream of Project_1, the Deliver1 activity would be comprised of the changes incorporated in activities Actp1, Actp2, and Actp3. There are a few problems with this normal sequence to be aware of:

- Currently, UCM allows deliveries of baselines only between project integration streams, so the previous example is not possible with deliver (but can be accomplished with `cset.pl`). So, pretend that Project_2 is a developer stream, and things will work with deliver. Or, make sure you have a baseline in place before attempting to deliver between projects.
- Suppose that you want to deliver only Actp3's changes? UCM requires that Actp1 and Actp2 be delivered as well, even if they don't relate to the changes in Actp3. A developer might end up having to resolve conflicts with activities he or she did not participate in.

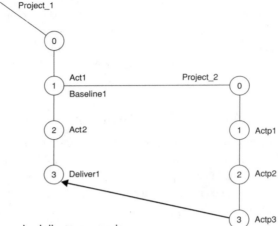

Figure A-1   A sample delivery scenario.

With only three activities here, it might not be a big deal. Suppose that you have a stream with 150 activities on it, though, and you want only 15 of those on your project stream....

Look at the picture for a `cset.pl -redo` operation, as shown in Figure A-2.

By using the `cset.pl -redo` operation, you can create a new activity called Redo_Actp3. Simply do a `ccperl cset.pl -redo` Actp3, and ClearCase will perform the merge of only Actp3's change set into your view. Note that no hyperlinks are drawn in the ClearCase version tree, nor does anything else currently stored within the activity Redo_Actp3 let you know where it came from (thus, the naming convention is important). But this solves some of the issues that arise in certain UCM environments.

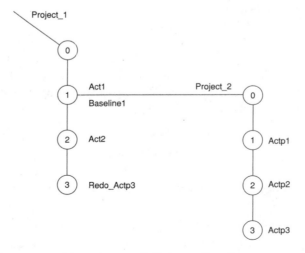

Figure A-2   Using `cset.pl` to redo an activity to another stream.

If you are doing multiple redos from stream to stream, perhaps you should be doing a deliver. We have seen this succeed at shops that have overloaded streams with mixed functionality and then want to get a small percentage of that stuff onto another stream for integration into another product.

A.6 Undoing a Delivery or Activity

Suppose that later you want to undo the activity you just redid or undo a deliver activity—or any activity, for that matter.

As with the redo option, you need to create an activity first, this time called Undo_Redo_Actp3 in your view. Then simply perform a `ccperl cset.pl –undo Redo_Actp3`. Again, make sure you use a good name for your activity because that will be an indicator in future reports of what happened. Figure A-3 shows how an undo operation will look in the ClearCase version tree.

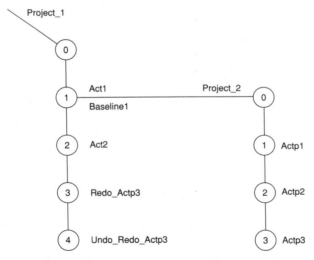

Figure A-3   Undoing the redo activity.

GLOSSARY

Most of the definitions in this glossary are taken from one of three sources: ClearCase documentation [ClearCase, 2003], Rational Software's Rational Unified Process [RUP 2003.06.13, 2004], or the IEEE's "Standard Glossary of Software Engineering Terminology" [IEEE Glossary 1990]. In some cases, these sources define a term differently. If the difference in definition aids understanding, both definitions are listed and the source is noted.

activity

1. A unit of work an individual might be asked to perform. Activities can be of different types. For example, a defect, enhancement request, and issue are all activities. This unit of work ties directly into the change-request management system and processes. An activity can also be a child of another activity that appears in the project-management system.

2. A ClearCase UCM object that tracks the work required to complete a development task. An activity includes a text headline, which describes the task, and a change set, which identifies all versions that you create or modify while working on the activity. When you work on a version, you must associate that version with an activity. If your project is configured to use the UCM-ClearQuest integration, a corresponding ClearQuest record stores additional activity information, such as the state and owner of the activity [ClearCase, 1999].

activity-based configuration management
The management of change to a software system based on higher-level activities (such as task, defect, enhancement) rather than individual file versions. This requires an SCM tool to track which file versions go to implementing a

specific activity and then to present activities as key objects. The idea is to simplify complexity and ensure that when the system says a defect is included in a specific build, it has, in fact, been included.

administration VOB

A VOB containing global type objects that are copied to client VOBs on an as-needed basis when users want to create instances of the type objects in the client VOBs. Administration VOBs are not a special type of VOB, but are defined as relationships that a VOB can have with other VOBs.

ALBD server

Atria Location Broker Daemon. This ClearCase master server runs on each ClearCase host. It starts up and dispatches messages to the various ClearCase server programs as necessary.

architecture

1. The set of significant decisions about the organization of a software system: the selection of the structural elements and their interfaces by which the system is composed, together with their behavior, as specified in the collaboration among those elements, the composition of the structural and behavioral elements into progressively larger subsystems, and the architectural style that guides this organization, these elements, their interfaces, their collaborations, and their composition. Software architecture is concerned not only with structure and behavior, but also with usage, functionality, performance, resilience, reuse, comprehensibility, economic and technology constraints and trade-offs, and aesthetic issues [Booch, 1999] [Kruchten, 2000].

2. The organizational structure of a system or component [IEEE Glossary, 1990].

3. The architecture of a software system (at a given point in time) is its organization or structure of significant components interacting through interfaces; those components are composed of successively smaller components and interfaces [RUP 5.5, 1999].

assembly integration

The software-development activity in which separate software component baselines are combined into an executable whole. See *integration*.

attribute

A metadata annotation attached to an object, in the form of a name/value pair. Names of attributes are specified by user-defined attribute types; users can set values of these attributes. For example, a project administrator might create an attribute type whose name is QAed. A user then could attach the attribute QAed with the value of yes to versions of several file elements.

attribute types

An object that defines an attribute name for use within a VOB. It constrains the attribute values that can be paired with the attribute name (for example, an integer in the range 1 to10).

backward delta

A delta storage approach that stores the latest version of the file in its entirety and stores only the delta of the previous versions.

baseline

A ClearCase UCM object that typically represents a stable configuration for one or more components. A baseline identifies activities and one version of every element visible in one or more components. You can create a development stream or rebase an existing development stream from a baseline.

branch

An object that specifies a linear sequence of element versions.

branch/LATEST development

A branching strategy in which team members work in isolated views but check out and check in on the same branch. Changes become visible to other team members at check-in time rather than file save time. Branch/LATEST development minimizes isolation and maximizes integration.

branching strategy

A strategy for isolation and integration of changes on a software project through the use of branches. A branching strategy defines the types of branches you use, how these branches relate to one another, and how you move changes between branches.

build

The process during which a build program (such as clearmake) produces one or more derived objects. This can involve actual translation of source files and construction of binary files by compilers, linkers, text formatters, and so on.

build audit

The process of recording which files and directories (and which versions of them) are read or written by the operating system during a build.

build avoidance

The capability of a ClearCase build program called clearmake to fulfill a build request using an existing derived object, instead of creating a new derived object by executing a build step.

change request

A general term for any request from a stakeholder to change an artifact or process. Documented in the change request is information on the origin and impact of the current problem, the proposed solution, and its cost. See also *enhancement request* and *defect*.

change request management

The recording, tracking, and reporting of requests from any stakeholder to change a software system. Change request management includes the decision-making processes an organization uses to decide what changes to make and the resolution processes used to make them.

change set

A list of related versions associated with a UCM activity. ClearCase records the versions that you create while you work on an activity. An activity uses a change set to record the versions of files that are delivered, integrated, and released together.

Some in the SCM industry distinguish between two terms: change package and change set. The difference is subtle and has to do with the implementation. A change set is defined as the actual delta that composes the change even if it spans files. A change package involves grouping together a set of file versions. ClearCase uses the term *change set* to denote a change package.

check-out/check-in

The two-part process that extends a branch of an element's version tree with a new version. The first part of the process, check-out, expresses your intent to create a new version at the current end of a particular branch. The second part, check-in, completes the process by creating the new version.

Performing a check-out of a branch does not necessarily guarantee you the right to perform a subsequent check-in. Many users can check out the same branch, as long as they are working in different views. At most, one of these can be a reserved check-out, which guarantees the user's right to check in a new version. An unreserved check-out affords no such guarantee. If server users have unreserved check-outs on the same branch in different views, the first user to perform a check-in wins. Other users must perform a merge if they want to save their checked-out versions.

checkpointing

The ability of developers to check in an intermediate version of a file that they have been working on without this change being made visible to other team members. The ability of developers to checkpoint their work depends on what branching strategy an organization uses. For example, a branch/LATEST strategy does not allow checkpointing.

clearmake

A make-compatible build tool that is part of the ClearCase product and that provides build audit and build avoidance features.

component

1. A physical object in the CM system containing files and directories that implement one or more logical packages. A ClearCase component is a set of files and directories contained under a common root directory. ClearCase components are versioned, shared (reused), and released as a single unit. A large system typically consists of many components. A small system might be contained in only one component.

2. A ClearCase object that groups a set of related directory and file elements within a UCM project. Typically, you develop, integrate, and release the elements that make up a component together. A project contains at least one component, and it can contain multiple components. Projects can share components [ClearCase, 1999].

3. A nontrivial, nearly independent, and replaceable part of a system that fulfills a clear function in the context of a well-defined architecture. A component conforms to and provides the physical realization of a set of interfaces. A physical, replaceable part of a system that packages implementation and conforms to and provides the realization of a set of interfaces. A component represents a physical piece of implementation of a system, including software code (source, binary, or executable) or equivalents such as scripts or command files [RUP 5.5, 1999].

component-based development

The creation and deployment of software-intensive systems assembled from components, as well as the development and harvesting of such components.

component subsystem

A stereotyped subsystem representing the logical abstraction in design of a component. It realizes one or more interfaces and can be dependent on one or more interfaces. It can enclose zero or more classes, packages, or other component subsystems, none of which is visible externally (only interfaces are visible). It can also enclose zero or more diagrams that illustrate internal behavior (such as state, sequence, or collaboration diagrams) [RUP 5.5, 1999].

composite baseline

A UCM structure that logically associates baselines together. A composite baseline can itself be a member of another composite baseline.

concurrent changes

Changes made by two or more developers to the same files at the same time. The SCM tool must also support the merging or integration of the changes, thus recombining the work that was done in parallel. Concurrent change on a large scale made by two or more teams is referred to as parallel development.

configuration

1. A labeled or baselined set of versions that form a consistent set.

2. The set of versions selected by a view.

configuration and change control

An element of configuration management that consists of the evaluation, coordination, approval or disapproval, and implementation of changes to configuration items [IEEE Glossary, 1990].

configuration control

An element of configuration management that consists of the evaluation, coordination, approval or disapproval, and implementation of changes to configuration items after formal establishment of their configuration identification [IEEE Glossary, 1990].

configuration identification

An element of configuration management that consists of selecting the configuration items for a system and recording their functional and physical characteristics in technical documentation [IEEE Glossary, 1990].

configuration management

A more general definition than software configuration management, applying to both hardware and software configuration management. See *software configuration management*.

configuration record

A bill of materials for a derived object, indicating exactly which file system objects (and which specific versions of those objects) were used by the rebuild as input data or as exe-cutable programs and which files were created as output.

configuration specification

A set of configuration rules specifying which versions of VOB elements a view selects. The config spec for a snapshot view also specifies which elements to load into the view.

configuration status accounting

An element of configuration management that consists of the recording and reporting of information needed to manage a configuration effectively [IEEE Glossary, 1990].

defect

An anomaly, or flaw, in a delivered work product. Examples include such things as omissions and imperfections found during early life cycle phases and symptoms of faults contained in software that is sufficiently mature for test or operation. A defect can be any kind of issue you want tracked and resolved. See also *change request*.

deliver

A ClearCase operation that enables developers to share their work with the rest of the project team by merging work from their own development streams to the project's integration stream. If required, the deliver operation invokes the Merge Manager to merge versions. See also *interproject deliver*.

delta

The physical change made between one version of a file and the next.

deployment

The act of moving the staged artifacts to other systems for further testing. In some cases, deployment can be the act that moves the software from the staging area to the production server to be used by the end user.

derived object

A ClearCase-specific name for the output files produced during a software build using clearmake.

development stream

A ClearCase UCM object that determines which versions of elements appear in your development view and maintains a list of your activities. The purpose of the development stream is to let you work on a set of activities and corresponding versions in isolation from the rest of the project team. The development stream configures your development view to select the versions associated with the foundation baselines, plus any activities and versions that you create after joining the project or rebasing your development stream.

development view

A view associated with a UCM development stream. A development view is used to work on a set of activities and corresponding versions isolated from the rest of the project team. You then can share changes made in a development view with the rest of the project team by delivering activities to the project's integration stream. A development view can be either a dynamic view or a snapshot view.

dynamic view

A type of view that is always current with the VOB. Dynamic views use the MVFS to create and maintain a directory tree that contains versions of VOB elements. Dynamic views are not supported on all ClearCase platforms.

element

An object that encompasses a set of versions, organized into a version tree. Elements can be either files or directories.

enhancement request

A type of stakeholder request that specifies a new feature or functionality of the system.

Enhancement requests specify a new feature of the system or a change to the "as designed" behavior of a system. See also *change request*.

entity

A record in a ClearQuest user database. Every entity is based on a specific entity type. Entities based on UCM-enabled entity types can be automatically associated with activities.

entity type

A metadata object that appears in a ClearQuest schema that describes the structure of a type of record, including its fields, states, actions, and forms.

follow-on project

A project that starts from an existing ongoing project. A follow-on project inherits the ongoing project's component baselines as its starting configuration.

forward delta

A delta storage approach that stores the first version of a file in its entirety and the other versions as deltas.

foundation baseline

A property of a stream. Foundation baselines specify the versions and activities that appear in your view. As part of a rebase operation, foundation baselines of the target stream are replaced with the set of recommended baselines from the source stream.

full baseline

A baseline created by recording all versions below a component's root directory. Generally, full baselines take longer to create than incremental baselines; however, ClearCase can look up the contents of a full baseline faster than it can look up the contents of an incremental baseline.

hyperlinks

A logical pointer between two objects. For example, a predefined hyperlink type of Merge defines merge relationships between versions on different branches. A hyperlink can have a from string as well as a to string, which are implemented as string-valued attributes on the hyperlink object.

A bidirectional hyperlink connects two objects in the same VOB or in different VOBs and can be navigated in either direction: from-object to to-object, or to-object to from-object. A unidirectional hyperlink connects two objects in different VOBs and can be navigated only in the direction of from-object to to-object.

implementation view

An architectural view that describes the organization of the static software elements (code, data, and other accompanying artifacts) of the development environment in terms of packaging, layering, and configuration management (ownership, release strategy, and so on).

incremental baseline

A baseline created by recording the last full baseline and versions of elements that have changed since the last full baseline was created. Generally, incremental baselines are faster to create than full baselines; however, ClearCase can look up the contents of a full baseline faster than it can look up the contents of an incremental baseline.

in-line delta

An approach to delta storage in which no copy of the file is stored in its entirety; only deltas are stored.

integration

1. The process of bringing together independently developed changes to form a testable piece of a software system. Integration can occur at many levels, eventually culminating in a complete software system.

2. The software-development activity in which separate software components are combined into an executable whole [RUP 5.5, 1999].

integration stream

A ClearCase UCM object that enables access to versions of the project's shared elements. A project contains only one integration stream. The integration stream maintains the project's baselines and configures integration views to select the versions associated with the foundation baselines, plus any activities and versions that have been delivered to the integration stream.

integration view

A view associated with a UCM project's integration stream. An integration view is used to build and test the latest versions of a project's shared elements. It can be either a dynamic view or a snapshot view.

interproject deliver

A deliver operation that enables developers to share their work with another project team by merging work from their own development streams to another project's integration stream (or development stream). If required, the deliver operation invokes the Merge Manager to merge versions. See also *deliver*.

iteration

A distinct set of activities with a baselined plan and valuation criteria, resulting in a release (internal or external).

label

An instance of a label type object that supplies a user-defined name for a version. A label is attached to a version of an element.

label type

A named tag that can be used to identify a consistent set of element versions. For example, you could create a label type called RELEASE1 and attach instances of the label type to all the versions of the elements that make up the first release of a software system.

license server

A host whose `albd_server` process controls access to the licenses defined in its license database file.

main branch

The starting branch of an element's version tree. The default name for this branch is main.

mainline project

A UCM project that serves as an integration and release point for multiple subprojects. It also serves as the starting point for follow-on projects.

mastership

The capability to modify an object or to create instances of a type object.

merge

The act of combining the contents of two or more files or directories into a single new file or directory. Typically, when merging files, all the files involved are versions of a single file element. When merging directories, all contributors to the merge must be versions of the same directory element.

merge integration

The resolution of parallel changes made by different team members to common files, directories, or components. In some cases, this can be automated. In others, manual decisions must be made (such as when conflicting changes have been made to the same files).

metadata

Data associated with an object, supplementing the object's file system data.

multiversion file system (MVFS)

A directory tree that, when activated (mounted as a file system of type MVFS), implements a ClearCase VOB. To standard operating system commands, a VOB appears to contain a directory hierarchy; ClearCase commands can also access the VOB's metadata. MVFS also refers to a file system extension to the operating system, which provides access to VOB data. The MVFS is not supported on all ClearCase platforms.

package

A collection of metadata (fields, actions, forms, and so on) that can be added to a schema. In the UCM model, adding the UCM package to a schema allows entities based on that schema to be automatically associated with activities and collect change sets.

parallel development

1. Concurrent changes made to individuals files or an entire software system by two or more individuals or teams. Parallel development also includes the capability to merge the changes that have been made in parallel.

2. The concurrent creation of versions on two or more branches of an element [ClearCase, 1999].

posted delivery

See *pull delivery*.

project

1. A ClearCase UCM object that contains the configuration information needed to manage a significant development effort, such as a product release. The project is used to set policies that govern how developers access and update the set of files and directories used in the development effort. A project includes one integration stream, which configures views that select

the latest versions of the project's shared elements, and typically multiple development streams, which configure views that allow developers to work in isolation from the rest of the project team. A project can be ClearQuest-enabled so that its activities will be associated with UCM-enabled ClearQuest entities [ClearCase, 1999].

2. An endeavor performed by people, constrained by limited resources, and planned, executed, and controlled. A project is a temporary endeavor undertaken to create a unique product or service. *Temporary* means that every project has a definite beginning and a definite end. *Unique* means that the product or service is different in some distinguishing way from all similar products and services. Projects are undertaken at all levels of the organization. They might involve a single person or many thousands. They might require fewer than 100 hours to complete or more than 10,000,000. Projects might involve a single unit of one organization or might cross organizational boundaries, as in joint ventures and partnering. Projects are often critical components of the performing organization's business strategy [PMI, 1996].

project VOB (PVOB)

A VOB that stores UCM objects, such as projects, streams, activities, and change sets. Every UCM project must have a PVOB. Multiple projects can share the same PVOB. See *versioned object base (VOB)*.

promotion level

A property of a UCM baseline that can be used to indicate the quality or degree of completeness of the activities and versions represented by that baseline. You can use promotion levels to define policy for a UCM project. UCM provides an ordered set of default promotion levels and also supports user-defined promotion levels. The action of changing the promotion level of a baseline is called promoting or demoting the baseline.

pull delivery

With pull delivery, developers indicate that their changes are ready for integration, but the integrator is responsible for integrating the developer's changes into the project's integration stream. See *deliver*.

push delivery

With push delivery, a developer is responsible for integrating his or her changes into the project's integration stream, where the integrator can create baselines and perform project builds. See *deliver*.

PVOB

See *project VOB (PVOB)*.

rebase

A ClearCase UCM operation that makes your development work area current with the set of versions represented by a more recent baseline in the integration stream.

recommended baseline

The set of baselines that the project team should use to rebase its development streams. In addition, when developers join a project, their development work areas are initialized with the recommended baselines. The recommended baselines represent a system configuration, or set of components, that has achieved a specified promotion level. A baseline becomes part of the set of recommended baselines when the project manager promotes it to a certain promotion level, such as TESTED.

registry server

The host on which all ClearCase data storage areas (all VOBs and views) in a local area network are centrally registered.

release

The process of putting the runtime software into its final form and making it available to its intended users.

replica

An instance of a VOB, located at a particular site. A replica consists of the VOB's database, along with all the VOB's data containers.

reserved check-out

See *check-out/check-in*.

schema

Defines the metadata for entities and other information in a ClearQuest user database.

single-stream project

A project whose UCM attributes specify that all development will occur on the integration stream for the project. No development streams or other child streams can be created in this type of UCM project.

snapshot view

A view that contains copies of ClearCase elements and other file system objects in a directory tree. You use an update tool or rebase operation to keep the view current with the VOB (as specified by the configuration specification).

software configuration management (SCM)

A software-engineering discipline that comprises the tools and techniques (processes or methodology) a company uses to manage change to its software assets.

staging

The process of putting the derived object files (executables, libraries, data files, generated header files, and so on) under version control.

stream

A ClearCase UCM object that determines which versions of elements appear in any view configured by that stream. Streams maintain a list of baselines and activities. A project contains one integration stream and typically multiple development streams.

subsystem

1. A generic name used to refer to a ClearCase component.

2. A model element that has the semantics of a package, so that it can contain other model elements, and a class, so that it has behavior. (The behavior of the subsystem is provided by classes or other subsystems it contains.) A subsystem realizes one or more interfaces, which define the behavior it can perform. A subsystem is a grouping of model elements, of which some constitute a specification of the behavior offered by the other contained model elements [RUP 5.5, 1999].

trigger

A monitor that specifies one or more standard programs or built-in actions to be executed automatically whenever a certain ClearCase operation is performed.

trivial merge

A merge between two branches in which it is possible to automatically copy the contents of one file version on one branch to another using information contained in the version tree.

un-check-out

The act of canceling a check-out operation.

Unified Change Management (UCM)

1. Rational Software's approach to managing change in software system development, from requirements to release. UCM spans the development life cycle, defining how to manage change to requirements, design models, documentation, components, test assets, and source code.

One of the key aspects of the UCM model is that it ties together or unifies the activities used to plan and track project progress and the artifacts being changed. The UCM model is realized by both process and tools. The Rational products ClearCase and ClearQuest are the foundation technologies for UCM. ClearCase manages all the artifacts produced by a software project, including both system artifacts and project-management artifacts. ClearQuest manages the project's tasks, defects, and requests for enhancements (referred to generically as activities), and provides the charting and reporting tools necessary to track project progress.

2. An out-of-the-box process, layered on base ClearCase and ClearQuest functionality, for organizing-software development teams and their work products. Members of a project team use activities and components to organize their work [ClearCase, 1999].

unreserved check-out

See *check-out/check-in*.

version

An object that implements a particular revision of an element. The versions of an element are organized into a version tree structure. *Checked-out version* can also refer to the view-private file that corresponds to the object created in a VOB database by the check-out command.

version control

A subset of software configuration management that deals with tracking version evolution of a file or directory.

version tree

The hierarchical structure in which all versions of an element are (logically) organized. When displaying a version tree, ClearCase also shows merge operations (indicated by arrows).

versioned object base (VOB)

A repository that stores versions of file elements, directory elements, derived objects, and metadata associated with these objects. With ClearCase MultiSite, a VOB can have multiple replicas at different sites.

view

A ClearCase object that provides a work area for one or more users to edit source versions, compile them into object modules, format them into documents, and so on. Users in different views can work on the same files without interfering with each other. For each element in a VOB, a view's configuration specification selects one version from the element's version tree. Each view can also store view-private files that do not appear in other views. There are two kinds of views: snapshot and dynamic.

view server

The daemon process that interprets a view's configuration specification, mapping element names into versions, and that performs workspace management for the view.

VOB

See *versioned object base (VOB)*.

VOB server

The process that provides access to the data containers that store versions' file system data.

workspace

1. A private area where developers can implement and test code in accordance with the project's adopted standards, in relative isolation from other developers [RUP 5.5, 1999].

2. A generic SCM term for a ClearCase view. Sometimes used to refer to the combination of a view and a stream in a UCM context.

workspace management

The process of creating and maintaining a workspace.

BIBLIOGRAPHY

[Appleton, 1998] Appleton, B., S. Berczuk, R. Cabrera, and R. Orenstein. "Streamed Lines: Branching Patterns for Parallel Software Development." Proceedings of the 1998 Conference on Pattern Languages of Program Design, Allerton Park, Ill., August 1998 (Technical Report #WUCS-98-25, *http://acme.bradapp.net/branching*).

[Beck, 2000] Beck, K. *Extreme Programming Explained.* Reading, Mass.: Addison-Wesley, 2000.

[Berczuk, 2002] Berczuk, S., and B. Appleton. *Software Configuration Management Patterns: Effective Teamwork, Practical Integration.* Reading, Mass.: Addison-Wesley, 2002.

[Booch, 1999] Booch, G., J. Rumbaugh, and I. Jacobson. *The Unified Modeling Language User Guide.* Reading, Mass.: Addison-Wesley, 1999.

[Brown, 2004] Brown, J., U. Wahli, M. Teinonen, and L. Trulsson. "Software Configuration Management: A ClearCase for IBM Rational ClearCase and ClearQuest UCM." IBM Redbook, December 2004. *http://www.redbooks.ibm.com/abstracts/SG246399.html?Open.*

[ClearCase, 2003] Rational Software. *Rational ClearCase Rational ClearCase LT Introduction—Version 2003.06.00 and Later.* Lexington, Mass.: IBM Corp., 2003.

[Feiler, 1991] Feiler, P. *Configuration Management Models in Commercial Environments.* Pittsburgh: Software Engineering Institute, Carnegie-Mellon University, 1991.

[Humphrey, 1989] Humphrey, H. *Managing the Software Process.* Reading, Mass.: Addison-Wesley, 1989. *http://www.sei.cmu.edu/.*

[IEEE Glossary, 1990] IEEE Standard 610.12-1990. "Standard Glossary of Software Engineering Terminology." New York: Institute of Electrical and Electronics Engineers, 1990.

[IEEE 828-1998] IEEE Standard 828-1998. "IEEE Standard for Software Configuration Management Plans." New York: Institute of Electrical and Electronics Engineers, 1998.

[IEEE 1042-1987] IEEE Standard 1042-1987. "IEEE Guide to Software Configuration Management." New York: Institute of Electrical and Electronics Engineers, 1988.

[Kruchten, 2000] Kruchten, P. *The Rational Unified Process: An Introduction, Second Edition.* Boston: Addison-Wesley, 2000.

[Kruchten, 1995] Kruchten, P. "The 4+1 View of Architecture." *IEEE Software* 12, no. 6 (November 1995): 45–50.

[Lakos, 1996] Lakos, J. *Large-Scale C++ Software Design.* Reading, Mass.: Addison-Wesley, 1996.

[Leblang, 1994] Leblang, D. "The CM Challenge: Configuration Management That Works." In *Configuration Management,* edited by W. Tichy. West Sussex, England: John Wiley and Sons, 1994.

[Milligan, 2003] Milligan, T. "Principles and Techniques for Analyzing and Improving IBM Rational ClearCase Performance: Part I." In *The Rational Edge,* July 2003. *http://www-128.ibm.com/developerworks/rational/library/content/RationalEdge/archives/jul03.html.*

[Milligan, 2003] Milligan, T. "Principles and Techniques for Analyzing and Improving IBM Rational ClearCase Performance: Part II." In *The Rational Edge,* September 2003. *http://www.128.ibm.com/developerworks/rational/library/content/RationalEdge/archives/sep03.html.*

[Oram, 1991] Oram, A., and S. Talbott. *Managing Projects with Make.* Sebastopol, Calif.: O'Reilly & Associates, 1991.

[PMI, 1996] Duncan, W., and PMI Standards Committee. *A Guide to the Project Management Body of Knowledge.* Newtown Square, Penn.: Project Management Institute, 1996.

[Royce, 1998] Royce, W. *Software Project Management—A Unified Framework.* Reading, Mass.: Addison-Wesley, 1998.

[RUP 2003.06.13, 2004] Rational Software. Rational Unified Process. Cupertino, Calif.: IBM Corp., 2004. *http://www.ibm.com/software/rational/*

[Tichy, 1994] Tichy, W. *Configuration Management.* West Sussex, England: John Wiley and Sons, 1994.

[Tykal, 2004] Tykal, J. *Best Practices for Using Composite Baselines in UCM.* IBM Developer-Works, 2004. *http://www-128.ibm.com/developerworks/rational/library/5134.html.*

[Whitgift, 1991] Whitgift, D. *Methods and Tools for Software Configuration Management.* West Sussex, England: John Wiley & Sons, 1991.

Index

THIS BOOK IS SAFARI ENABLED

INCLUDES FREE 45-DAY ACCESS TO THE ONLINE EDITION

The Safari® Enabled icon on the cover of your favorite technology book means the book is available through Safari Bookshelf. When you buy this book, you get free access to the online edition for 45 days.

Safari Bookshelf is an electronic reference library that lets you easily search thousands of technical books, find code samples, download chapters, and access technical information whenever and wherever you need it.

TO GAIN 45-DAY SAFARI ENABLED ACCESS TO THIS BOOK:

- Go to **http://www.awprofessional.com/safarienabled**

- Complete the brief registration form

- Enter the coupon code found in the front of this book on the "Copyright" page

If you have difficulty registering on Safari Bookshelf or accessing the online edition, please e-mail customer-service@safaribooksonline.com.